TRIUMPH DAYTONA
2003-2009
Road Test Portfolio

Compiled by
R M Clarke

ISBN 9781855209497

BROOKLANDS BOOKS LTD.
P.O. BOX 146, COBHAM,
SURREY, KT11 1LG. UK
sales@brooklands-books.com

www.brooklands-books.com

TD3BRP   02T2/2143

MOTOR CYCLE ROAD TEST SERIES

www.brooklands-books.com

AJS & Matchless Gold Portfolio 1945-1966
A total of 57 articles covering the Heavyweight & Lightweight Singles, 500, 600, 650, 750 & Racing Twins. Includes road tests, performance data, history, scramblers & more. 172 pages, over 300 illus. SB.
SKU: AJ45BGP ISBN: 9781855203525

Ariel Square Four 1948-1959 Limited Edition Extra
A book of contemporary road tests, specification and technical data, new model intros, development, rider's impressions, history, touring, technical articles on tuning, engine stripping & decoking. A total of 136 fully illustrated pages. SB.
SKU: A48BX2 ISBN: 9781855206236

Ariel Leader Arrow Golden Arrow Limited Edition Extra
A book of contemporary road & comparison tests, new model intros, rider reports, long term tests, development, racing & history. Technical guidance is given on maintenance, engine & fork strip-downs, supertuning & servicing. 136 pages, 350 illus. SB.
SKU: A58BX2 ISBN: 9781855206243

Benelli 750/900 Performance Portfolio 1973-1989
The story of the Benelli 750 & 900 sixes is traced through 25 articles sourced from the leading publications of the day & includes road & comparison tests, driving impressions & new model intros. Models covered: 750 Sei, Mk I, Mk 2, 900 Sei, Mk 1, Mk 2, Mk 3 & Mk 4. 120 pages. 22 in colour. SB.
SKU: BN7BPP ISBN: 9781855206687

Benelli the Fours Limited Edition Extra
The story of the Benelli fours are told through contemporary & classic articles. Including road, comparison & track tests, detailed performance data, new model intros plus many more features. Models covered: 500 Quattro, 245/4, 350 RS, 504, 504 Sport, 354, 354 Sport plus the 654. With 124 pages & 350 illus. SB.
SKU: BNFBX2 ISBN: 9781855207363

Bimota Limited Edition Extra 1978-1990
Experts from the US, Canada & Britain pass judgment on the fabulous early Bimotas. Included are road & comparison tests, model intros & ride reports. Models covered: SB2 & 2/80, SB3 & 4, KB1, A1 & 2, KB2 Laser, KB3, HB2 & 3, Tesi, DB1, F1, YB4 & EI, YB5 & 6, Bellaria & Tuatara. 128 pages with 200 illus. SB.
SKU: BT1BX2 ISBN: 9781855207080

Bimota Limited Edition Extra 1991-2000
This book traces the progress of the Bimota range of motorcycles during the 1990s. Included are road & comparison tests, new model reports & riding impressions. Models covered: Tesi 1D & ES, Dieci, DB2 & 4, 500 V-Twin, Furano, SB6 & 7, SB8R & K, YB9 & SR, BB500, Mantra, Drako 900, V-Due Trofeo & YB11. 128 pages with 200 illus. SB.
SKU: BT2BX2 ISBN: 9781855207097

BMW Motorcycles Gold Portfolio 1950-1971
50 articles covering the singles & twin bikes including road tests, engine analysis, touring, specifications, new model intros, technical features & record braking. Models covered: R27, R67/2, R69S, R50, R60/5, R75/5 & US. 172 pages, over 300 illus. SB.
SKU: BM50BGP ISBN: 9781855203778

BMW Motorcycles Gold Portfolio 1971-1976
This book on BMW bikes, deals with the twin cylinder range manufactured from 1971 on. Articles including road, comparison and long distance tests, new model intros & touring. Models covered: R50/5, R60/6, R75/6, R90/6 & R90S. 172 pages, over 200 illus. SB.
SKU: BM71BGP ISBN: 9781855203785

BMW K100 Performance Portfolio 1983-1993
This is a book of contemporary road & comparison tests, specification & technical data, long term reports & new model intros. Models include: K100, K100RS, K100RT, K100LT, K100RS ABS, K1100RT, K1100LT & K1100RS. 136 pages, 350 illus. including colour. SB.
SKU: BMKBPP ISBN: 9781855205949

BSA Singles Gold Portfolio 1945-1963
Compilation of 59 international articles covering the Starfire Scrambler, Catalina, Sports Star, Gold Star, Super Sports, 250, 350, 500 & 600. Includes road tests, touring, model introductions, sidecar reports, tuning, etc. 172 pages, over 300 illus. SB.
SKU: BS45BGP ISBN: 9781855204416

BSA Singles Gold Portfolio 1964-19745
This book is a collection of 48 articles including road, comparison & track tests, racing, performance data, engine analysis & rebuild. Models covered: Starfire, 250, 350, 441, 500, Shooting Star, Gold Star, Manx, Baja, Victor, Special & MX. 172 pages, 300 illus. SB.
SKU: BS64BGP ISBN: 9781855204423

BSA Twins A7 & A10 Gold Portfolio 1946-1962
Sixty international articles cover the Twins A7 & A10. This is a book of contemporary road, comparison & race tests, history, performance & technical data, engine analysis & rebuild. Models covered: Road Rocket, Golden Flash, Super Rocket, Gold Star, Star Twin & Shooting Star. 172 pages, 300+ illus. SB.
SKU: BS46BGP ISBN: 9781855203365

BSA Twins A50 & A65 Gold Portfolio 1962-1973
This book on the Twins covers the A50 & A65 models. Articles include road tests, touring, engine rebuild, etc. Models covered: Royal Star, Rocket, Lightning, Cyclone, Thunderbolt, Spitfire, Special, II, III & Hornet. 172 pages, over 300 illus. SB.
SKU: BS62BGP ISBN: 9781855203372

BSA & Triumph Triples Gold Portfolio 1968-1976
Forty international articles cover the British bikes with a triple engine. This is a book of contemporary road, comparison & race tests, history, performance & technical data, engine analysis & rebuild. Models covered: BSA Rocket 3, Trident, T150, T160 & Hurricane. 172 pages, over 300 illus. SB.
SKU: BT3BGP ISBN: 9781855204645

Buell Motorcycles 1985-2009 Road Test Portfolio
This portfolio reports on Buell production from 1985 up to the closing of the company in 2009. Articles, drawn from three continents, trace all models over this period. Included are road and comparison tests, riding impressions, new model intros & performance data. Reported on are the RW750A, RR1000, RR, RS, RSS1200, S2, S3T, S1, Lightning, Thunderbolt, Blast, Ulysses, Firebolt & Cyclone. A total of 272 fully illustrated pages over 300 illus. SB.
SKU: BL1BRP ISBN: 9781855208940

Bultaco Limited Edition Extra 1964-1970
A portfolio of 31 contemporary articles traces the progress of Bultaco production in the 60s. Included are road, trail & track tests, new model reports, history & racing. Models covered: Metralla, Sherpa, TSS, Mercurio, Matador, Metisse, Pursang, El Bandido, Campera, El Tigre & Lobitto. 128 pages. Over 200 illus. SB.
SKU: BU6BX2 ISBN: 9781855206915

Bultaco Limited Edition Extra 1971-1979
This book contains thirty articles, taking the story of the marque up to the end of the seventies. Included are road, track & enduro tests & driving impressions. Models covered: Lobito, El Montadero, Sherpa T, Matador, Tiron, Alpina, Pursang, Astro & Frontera. 128 pages. Over 200 illus. SB.
SKU: BU7BX2 ISBN: 9781855206922

Ducati 916 & 996 Road Test Portfolio
An aesthetic and performance revolution in its day, the Ducati 916 & 996 series has guaranteed iconic status for Bologna's blood-red bullets for time immemorial. Included are road and comparisons tests, new model introductions and full performance data. Reported on: 916, SP, SPS & Biposto, 955, SP, Corsa, 996 SPS & the Racer. Advice is given on acquiring a good pre-owned Ducati 916, 955 & 996. A total of 160 fully illustrated pages. SB.
SKU: D99BRP ISBN: 9781855209275

Ducati Gold Portfolio 1978-1982
This book on the Italian Ducati marque relates solely to the vee twins. This is a full of contemporary articles with road & track tests, new model intros, owner survey, servicing, racing & touring. Models covered: Darmah, 900, TT Replica, Pantah, 500 & 600. 172 pages, over 300 illus. SB.
SKU: D78BGP ISBN: 9781855203808

Ducati 851 & 888 Performance Portfolio 1987-1994
The 851/888 twins are undisputed classics, representing the modernisation of Ducati. This is a book of contemporary road & comparison tests, new model intros, rider's reports, track reports & special models. Models covered: 851, Strada, Sport, SP, 888, SPS & SPO. 136 pages, 250 b/w & 25 colour illus. SB.
SKU: D87BPP ISBN: 9781855205932

Harley-Davidson Sportsters Performance Portfolio 1965-1976
29 articles include road & comparison tests, touring, specifications, performance data, new model intros, owners reports. Models covered: XLH, DLCH, 833cc, 1000cc, DR-750 & XL. 140 pages, over 250 illus. SB.
SKU: HD3BPP ISBN: 9781855204041

Harley-Davidson Super Glide Performance Portfolio 1971-1981
Includes road & comparison tests, specifications, owner survey, performance and technical data. Models covered: FX, FXE, FXS 1200 Low Rider, FXS80, FXB80 Sturgis, FXWG 80 Wide Glide & FXEF Fat Bob. 140 pages, approx. 250 illus. SB.
SKU: HD1BPP ISBN: 9781855204898

Harley-Davidson FXR Series Performance Portfolio 1982-1992
It contains 29 articles giving information on road & comparison tests, touring, technical analysis, specifications, performance data. Models covered: Super Glide II, Sport Glide, FXR, FXRS, FXRT, FXRDG, FXRD, FXLR, FXDB & FXDC. With 140 pages. SB.
SKU: HD2BPP ISBN: 9781855204966

Hesketh Limited Edition Extra 1980-1991
This is a book of contemporary road & comparison tests, specification & technical data, new model intros, travel, long term reports, buying second hand & history. Models covered: V1000, V2 Vortan & Vampire. 136 pages, 350 illus. SB.
SKU: HVBX2 ISBN: 9781855205925

Honda ST1100/ST1300 Pan European 1989-2002
This portfolio of international articles, traces the progress of Honda's successful sport tourers the ST1100 & ST1300s between 1989 & 2002. Included are road & comparison tests, model intros, updates, riding impressions, touring reports, technical & performance data. Plus a detailed buyers guide advising on acquiring a good pre-owned ST1100. A total of 120 fully illustrated pages. SB.
SKU: HNSTRP ISBN: 9781855208650

Honda CB750 Gold Portfolio 1969-1978
38 articles on one of the most sought after Japanese motorcycles. Models covered: Automatic, Super Sport, K2, K3, K5, K6, K7, F1, F2 & 960. Articles include road & comparison tests, specifications, engine rebuild, overhaul, touring & tuning. 172 pages, over 300 illus. SB.
SKU: HN7BGP ISBN: 9781855204669

Honda CB500 & 550 Fours Performance Portfolio 1971-1977
The 750 Four gave Honda the machine to lead the world. 29 articles on Honda's groovy bikers dream. Articles include: road & comparison tests, new model intros, engine strip & servicing. Models covered: Super Sport, CB500, 500K2, CG550, 550F & F2, 550K & K3 & 550F-77. 140 pages, 250+ illus. SB.
SKU: HNFBPP ISBN: 9781855204959

Honda CB350 & 400 Fours Performance Portfolio 1972-1978
The CB350 & 400 bikes have always had a cult following simply because they are fun to ride. This is a book of contemporary road & comparison tests, model intros, engine rebuild & long term reports. Models covered: CB350F, CB400F, F2 & Super Sport. 140 pages, over 250 illus. SB.
SKU: HN3BPP ISBN: 9781855204157

Honda Gold Wing Gold Portfolio 1975-1995
The Gold Wing is the yard stick by which all other touring motorcycles are measured. 36 articles. Includes road, comparison & long-term tests, model changes, engine rebuild, touring & servicing. Models covered: 1000, 1100, 1200, 1500/6, Interstate & SE. 172 pages, over 250 illus. SB.
SKU: HNWBGP ISBN: 9781855204812

Honda CBX 1000 Gold Portfolio 1978-1982
It is still considered to be one of the greatest motorcycles ever produced by Honda. A collection of 29 articles covering Honda's high performance cruiser. Road & comparison tests, model intros, servicing & engine rebuild. Models covered: CBX Super Sport, Z, A, B, C & Moto Martin. 172 pages, 250 illus. SB.
SKU: HN1BGP ISBN: 9781855204805

Honda CX500 & CX650 Performance Portfolio 1978-1984
The CX500 represented a quiet revolution, low maintenance motorcycle for everyman. A collection of 28 articles cover this classic Honda. Road, track & comparison tests, model intros, history, service & a long term report. Models covered: CX500, CX650, Sport, L, TC, Custom, Turbo & Silver Wing. 136 pages, approx. 200 illus. SB.
SKU: HN5BPP ISBN: 9781855206304

Honda RC30 Performance Portfolio 1988-1992
The RC30 will surely present a new world experience to those with the will to grab it. 27 articles cover the VFR750R & Roy Gildea's RC30. Road & comparison tests, performance data, new model intros, development, specifications & engine blueprinting. 140 pages, approx. 250 illus. SB.
SKU: HNRBPP ISBN: 9781855204331

Honda CBR900RR FireBlade Limited Edition Extra
The Honda FireBlade CBR900RR from 1992-2003 is story told through 28 articles drawn from three continents. Included are road & comparison tests, model intros & buyers guides. Models covered: CBR900RR 893cc, 918cc, CBR929RR & CBR954RR. A total of 136 fully illustrated pages. SB.
SKU: HN9BX2 ISBN: 9781855207646

Kawasaki 500 & 750 Performance Portfolio 1969-1976
The H1 & H2 still turn heads and are correctly regarded as classic motorcycles. This book includes 31 articles on road tests, new model intros, performance data, inside look, racing & model guide. Models covered: H1, H1D, H1E, H1F, H1R, H2, H2R, Mach III & IV. 140 pages, 250+ illus. SB.
SKU: KT5BPP ISBN: 9781855205239

Kawasaki Z1 900 Performance Portfolio 1972-1977
The Z1 was always a show off, always a crowd-puller. 29 articles cover Kawasaki's great Z1. Road tests, new model intros, performance data, engine rebuild & long-term reports. Models covered: Z1, Z1-A, Dunstall Kawasaki, Z900 & KZ900 LTD. 140 pages, approx. 250 illus. SB.
SKU: KZ1BPP ISBN: 9781855204133

Kawasaki GPz 900R Ninja Performance Portfolio 1984-1996
The Kawasaki's GPZ 900R Ninja contribution to superbike development has been nothing short of massive. The story is told from its inception in 1984 through to the A8 model. 25 articles of road tests, model intros, comparisons, etc. Models covered: A1, A2, A3, A4, A5, A6, A7 & A8. 140 pages, 250+ illus. SB.
SKU: KGPBPP ISBN: 9781855205574

Laverda Gold Portfolio 1967-1977
37 articles on, perhaps, the ultimate in Italian motorcycle design, including 13 road test reports. Also included new model reports, track test & racer tests & engine rebuild. Models covered: 200, 250, 500, 650, 750 & 1000. 172 pages, over 300 illus. SB.
SKU: LV67BGP ISBN: 9781855203532

Laverda Jota Performance Portfolio 1976-1985
The Jota proved an immediate success on the racetrack. A total of 31 articles tell the story via contemporary articles with road & comparison tests, model intros & updates. Models covered: 1000 3cE, 120, Formula, 1200 & America, Special, RGA 1000 & 120.140 pages, 250 illus. SB.
SKU: LVJBPP ISBN: 9781855205109

Laverda 500 Twins 1977-1983 Road Test Portfolio
Laverda launched a 500cc twin cylinder 8-valve machine named the Alpina in 1977, it was renamed Alpino and Zeta in the USA. This book is a compilation of road & comparison tests, riding impressions, performance plus articles on racing. Advice is offered on acquiring a good used 500 twin. Models covered: Alpina, Alpino, S, 500T, Zeta, Montjuic, 500 Sports, Roadster & Formula 500. A total of 130 fully illustrated pages. SB.
SKU: LV5BRP ISBN: 9781855208827

Laverda Performance Portfolio 1978-1988
This book includes 31 international articles with road tests, comparisons, model intros & more. Models covered: Formula Mirage, TS, Jota 1200, America 1000/20, RGA, Motodd, RGS 1000 & Corsa, SFC 750 & 1000, 1200 & Anniversary Special. 140 pages, 250 illus. SB.
SKU: LV8BPP ISBN: 9781855205000

Moto Guzzi Gold Portfolio 1949-1973
A portfolio of contemporary articles leads us through the development of the Moto Guzzi50 articles, including 26 road test reports, plus history, record breaking & model intro & more. Models covered: Zigolo, Lodola, Single, V Twin, V7, V8, Ambassador & Eldorado. 172 pages, over 300 illus. SB.
SKU: MI49BGP ISBN: 9781855203792

Moto Guzzi Le Mans Performance Portfolio 1976-1989
The Le Mans I was a styling icon of its day. 30 articles on the sexy Le Mans series of bikes. Road & comparison tests, model intros, development & more. Models covered: 1000 Magni, Le Mans Mks. I, II, III & V850s, 1000s & CX100. 140 pages, 250 illus. SB.
SKU: MILBPP ISBN: 9781855205093

Moto Morini 31/2 & 500 Performance Portfolio 1974-1984
The Moto Morini is now one of the bikes of which the Italians are most proud. This book contains road & comparison tests, model intros & design analysis. Models covered: 31/2, Strada, Sport, K2, 500, Sport, Maestro, Sahara, Camel, SEI-V & Touring. 140 pages includes 8 pages of colour plus 250 b/w illus. SB.
SKU: MM3BPP ISBN: 9781855205680

MV Agusta F4 750 & 1000 1997-2007 Road Test Portfolio
This portfolio draws on articles from three continents & traces the development of the prestigious MV Agusta F4 superbike from 1997 to the end of 2007. Included are road and comparison tests, riding impressions plus new model reports. Models covered: 750cc Oro, Strada, S, Evo, Brutales also the 1000cc Tamburini, Mamba, the Brutale S910 & 1080 plus R & Biposto models. A total of 140 fully illustrated pages. SB.
SKU: MV97RP ISBN: 9781855208605

MV Agusta Fours Performance Portfolio 1967-1980
The MV Agusta racing & production bikes excited motorcyclists worldwide. This book of 26 articles sourced from the leading motor cycling publications of the day cover road & comparison tests & new model intros. Models covered: 600, 750, 750 Sport, 750 Sport America & 850 Monza. 120 pages. 200 b/w & colour illus. SB.
SKU: MV4BPP ISBN: 9781855206670

Norton Dominator Performance Portfolio 1949-1970
The Dominator remains as popular as ever, providing a top-notch riding experience. This book contains 42 articles on road tests, model intros & performance data. Models covered: Domiracer, Featherbed Twins, 750 Metisse, 7, 77, 88, 99, 650SS, 750 Atlas, Scrambler & Dunstall. 136 pages including 10 colour plus 250 b/w illus. SB.
SKU: N49BPP ISBN: 9781855205734

Norton Commando Ultimate Portfolio
The Commando was to become Britain's first Superbike. Included are road tests, new model intros, history, technical & performance data plus an engine rebuild & buyers guide. 208 pages including 12 in full colour with 300 b/w illus. SB.
SKU: N68BUP ISBN: 9781855205703

Norton Rotaries Limited Edition Extra
The story of Norton Rotaries is traced from its announcement in the early 80s. Included are road, comparison & prototype tests, racing & riding impressions. All models are covered including the Classic, Commander, F1 & F1 Sport. 136 pages, with 250 b/w illus. SB.
SKU: NRYBX2 ISBN: 9781855205758

Royal Enfield Big Twins Limited Edition Ex 1953-1970
This book contains 35 articles covering road & comparison tests, new model intros, racing, performance data & engine analysis. Models covered: Meteor & Super Meteor, Minor de Luxe & Standard, Constellation, Interceptor, Stage II, TT & Specials. 128 pages. 250 b/w illus. SB.
SKU: RE2BX2 ISBN: 9781855206656

Royal Enfield 250s Limited Edition Extra 1956-1967
This book features 39 articles on this popular classic British bike including new model intros, tuning, buying secondhand, classic reports, engine analysis & technical data. Models covered: Crusader, Sport, Super 5, Airflow, Turbo Twin, 246cc Grand Prix Single & Continental. 128 pages. 250 b/w illus. SB.
SKU: RE2BX2 ISBN: 9781855206663

Suzuki GT 750 Performance Portfolio 1971-1977
The GT 750 can still be seen today in Classic racing holding its own against the best. A collection of 27 articles on Suzuki's racing classic. Road & comparison tests, history, model intros, servicing & engine rebuild. Models covered: TR750, Le Mans GT 750J, GT 750K, GT 750A/M & GT 750M. 140 pages, approx. 250 illus. SB.
SKU: SZ1BPP ISBN: 9781855204904

Suzuki GS1000 Performance Portfolio 1978-1981
A portfolio of contemporary articles leads us through the development of the Suzuki GS1000. Included are road, comparison & track tests, new model intros & more. Models covered: Yoshimura, Dunstall, CS, XT, GS1000, HC, E, S, L, GT & E7. 140 pages, 250+ illus. SB.
SKU: SZ2BPP ISBN: 9781855205031

Suzuki GSX-R750 Performance Portfolio 1985-1996
The Suzuki GSX-R750 - it's still a world-beater today. This is a book of contemporary road & comparison tests, technical data, riders impressions, long term reports & new model intros. Models covered: GSX-R750, XG, F, G, H, J, K, L, M, WN, WP, WR & T. 136 pages, 350 illus. SB.
SKU: SZ3BPP ISBN: 9781855205956

Suzuki GSX1300R Hayabusa Limited Edition Ex 1999-2007
When in 1999 Suzuki introduced the GSX1300R Hayabusa it was the fastest production motorcycle in the world, this book tell the story up to 2007. Its progress is traced through road & comparison test, new model introdutions and a full owners guide. All models are reported. A total of 128 fully illustrated pages. SB.
SKU: SZ4BX2 ISBN: 9781855208315

Triumph Bonneville 2001-2009 Road Test Portfolio
The new Triumph Bonneville, started in 2001, carried on the twin tradition with all its virtues: relative simplicity and lightweight plus an instantly recognisable style. Models reported on include the T100, Speedmaster, America, Thruxton and the Scrambler. Included are international road tests, performance data, full specifications and a comprehensive buying guide. With a total of 134 pages & 350 illus. SB.
SKU: TB1BRP ISBN: 9781855208964

Triumph Daytona 1991-2006 Road Test Portfolio
SKU: TD1BRP ISBN: 9781855209480

Triumph Daytona 2003-2009 Road Test Portfolio
SKU: TB3BRP ISBN: 9781855209497

Vincent Gold Portfolio 1945-1980
The Vincent legacy is one which continues to attract enthusiasts. A total of 60 articles covering road tests, new model intros, history & touring. Models covered: Firefly, Egli-Vincent, NorVin, Comet, Meteor, Rapide, Grey Flash, Black Shadow, Black Prince & Black Lightning. 172 pages, over 300 illus. SB.
SKU: VINBGP ISBN: 9781855203860

Yamaha XS-650 Performance Portfolio 1969-1985
The Yamaha XS-650 is a true motorcycling classic that looks good too. 31 articles includes road & comparison tests, history, new model intros, owner survey & engine rebuild. Models covered: XS-1, XS-1B, XS-2, XS-650, B, C, D, E SE, F, SF & Special. 136 pages including 7 full colour. Approx. 250 b/w illus. SB.
SKU: YX6BPP ISBN: 9781855205741

Yamaha RD350 & 400 Performance Portfolio 1972-1979
This portfolio traces the development of the Yamaha's air-cooled RD models through thirty articles. Included are road, comparison & long term tests, model intros & updates, performance data & engine rebuild Models covered: RD350, B, RD400, C, D, E, F & Daytona Special. 140 pages, approx. 250 illus. SB.
SKU: Y34BPP ISBN: 9781855204140

Yamaha RD250/350LCs Performance Portfolio 1980-1996
The Cult of Elsie is still going strong. A portfolio of contemporary articles leads us through the development of the RD250/350LCs. Included are road & comparison tests, new model intros, long term tests, racing, buyer's guide & history. 136 pages, 350 illus. SB.
SKU: YRDBPP ISBN: 9781855206250

Yamaha FZR 1000 Road Test Portfolio
The FZR 1000 was a superbike right from the start, in 1987. By 1989 it had a top speed of 167 mph, it had pulling power from low revs, seamlessly, up to the red line at 11,500 rpm. Production ran through till 1995. Included are road & comparison tests plus full performance data. Models reported on: Genesis, EXUP, OWO1, FXUP, RU, AC and the Vance & Hines specials. A total of 140 fully illustrated pages.
SKU: YFR7RP ISBN: 9781855209138

Yamaha YZF R1 Limited Edition Extra 1998-2006
Articles from three continents trace the progress of the prestigious one litre class Yamaha YZF R1 from its intro in 1998 through to 2006. Included are road & comparison tests, new model reports, riding impressions, a historical account of year by year changes & advice on acquiring a good pre-owned R1. A total of 136 illustrated pages. SB.
SKU: YZFBX2 ISBN: 9781855208278

CARS
To see our full range of over 800 titles visit www.brooklands-books.com

Contents

Acknowledgements

Regular readers of Brooklands portfolios will know that books like this are an attempt to create a living archive and to make available to owners and enthusiasts material about their bikes which have become difficult to find.

We are indebted to the writers, photographers and managements of the leading motorcycle magazines for generously allowing us to include their copyright road tests and other articles. As always these anthologies could never come to fruition without the co-operation of the original magazine publishers and authors who for over 50 years have allowed us to include their copyright stories. Our thanks in this instance go to the managements of *Bike, Cycle World, Fast Bikes, Kiwi Rider, Performance Bike, Ride* and *Superbike*. Our thanks also go to Rowena Hoseason Editor of RealClassic magazine for penning the informative introduction to the marque below.

R.M. Clarke

When I tested an early Daytona 600 in 2003, it appeared that Triumph had gone a long way towards curing the reported problems of the Daytona's predecessor, the ill-fated TT600. Where the TT was stuttery and hesitant, the Daytona was smooth and precise. The TT's curved bodywork seemed to suit an earlier decade: the Daytona bristled with angular aggression. The TT tried to cater for two-up travel: the Daytona was a bike built for a single purpose, steered by a lone pilot in search of high performance entertainment. The Daytona delivered where the TT had not.

Yet even so, the four-cylinder machine wasn't quite up to the challenge of the mass market 600 supersports sector. It could match the prowess of its rivals in one or two aspects, but it couldn't provide the same mix of performance and price as its Japanese competitors. That's no great surprise – the Big Four manufacturers have been slugging it out in this territory a decade or more and had mastered the art of getting the most from a 600cc four.

So wisely Triumph opted out of a struggle they couldn't win and took the fight to home ground. Development of a three-cylinder 675cc supersports machine began in 2000, alongside the 955i Daytona triple. The first 675 engine was tested on the dyno in 2003 (around the same time that I was riding the 600/4), and the first pre-production prototype 675 took to the streets in 2004. The new triple boasted a 10bhp power boost over the 650 four-cylinder machine with no weight penalty – Triumph had finally found the right formula for their world class middleweight.

Such was the buzz about the three-cylinder 675 when it was launched in 2006 that demand outstripped supply; waiting lists weren't uncommon and some UK customers had to wait six months for their bikes to arrive. The 675 has been hailed as 'the best British sportsbike ever' and 'possibly one of the greatest sportsbikes of all time'.

Thanks to the efforts of the team at Brooklands Books, you can now re-live how the middleweight Daytona made its mark in motorcycling.

Rowena Hoseason, RealClassic magazine

A DESIGN TRIUMPH

WHERE DOES A BIKE ACTUALLY COME FROM? DOES A STORK FLY DOWN WITH A BLOODY GREAT BASKET OR IS IT CHISELED FROM A HULKING PIECE OF METAL? SIMON ROOTS BLUSHES AS HE ASKS TRIUMPH HOW THE DAYTONA 600 WAS CONCEIVED

Bikes aren't magically created. The Great Suprendo doesn't perform his piff-paaf-poof trickery in an exotic pit garage before a world launch. Sorcery is at work, but only in the guise of hard work and inspiration.

Triumph's first foray into the middleweight class, the TT600, wasn't wholeheartedly received. Bruno Tagliaferri, Triumph's marketing chief, outlined the TT's fundamental problem. *"The design was signed off three years before the launch in 1999. All-rounders like Yamaha's Thundercat were dominating the category then and the TT was designed accordingly."* The market had moved on and 1999 saw hard-edged competitors piss on Triumph's chips.

Triumph pencils in strategies over five year periods and always knew that early 2000 would see work begin on the new 600. Tagliaferri outlined his targets, *"Weight and power figures had to be better than the Japanese bikes, we just had to make the new bike lighter and faster."* Ross Clifford, Triumph's commercial manager, explained that designing isn't done on a blank canvas. *"We knew what we needed engine wise and because the TT was a great handling machine we just needed to fine-tune the handling package."*

Styling is something that needs that initial spark of imagination so Triumph sent the brief to styling houses to produce sketches. These were reviewed and taken to 'styling clinics' where worldwide focus groups give their opinions to the designs on offer.

When the styling is agreed the engineering team commences work. Most of the initial engine testing is completed on test rigs, so Triumph used the TT engine in the new chassis to develop the bike's handling. The chassis and suspension work was kept in-house, they took what they knew and made it better: for example, the brake pads weren't using the last 2mm of the front discs, so they were made smaller. The frame design used Finite Element Analysis (FEA) where computer programs examine stresses upon parts allowing engineers to either skim weight or bolster components.

Engine development has been brought in-house but many suppliers furnish the new bike with parts. Each component is developed on an individual basis. Some features require a close relationship between the two parties; Clifford noted the fuel injection, *"Keihin produce the best systems and we worked together on the fuelling. We've learned from this relationship and now all mapping work is done in-house."*

Engines are tested extensively on the rigs to simulate real world conditions. Structured cycles are completed to ensure power and reliability are within brief. The 'abuse test' redlines the bike from cold and the engine will spend well over a day on the limiter. If it pops then they start over again.

The only way to discover a new bike's response on the road is to run it on the road. Everything is tested to ensure optimum performance, even in non-optimum conditions. Testers travel up to 600 miles a day on roads, both in the UK and abroad, and tracks are also used for faster work. Each rider is vastly experienced; some are ex-racers with masses of set-up experience while others spend their life on the road, analysing everything from the brakes to the mirrors. The testers know the performance of the competition and record their feedback accordingly. The bike is now being constantly refined. Human input is backed by engineering tests before any part gets signed off.

The bike's final form is now close, so the team has to ensure that it can be sold worldwide. Legislation in certain countries means that a single generic bike isn't possible. The Frenchies insist on a power limit, but we Brits wouldn't accept this compromise and get a full-fat bike. Choices such as tyres need to be made at this point, *"We decided on Pirellis because they work best with the bike – price was never an issue,"* said Clifford.

When the bike gets signed off, the factory gears up for production. Engineers constantly check the design team to ensure manufacture is feasible. Some retooling is required but trial builds and extensive training mean that the staff know how to build the bike before it comes down the production line – with a decade of experience they've seen it all before anyway.

The marketing phase now becomes vital. New bikes are normally launched at an international bike show and the new 600 graced the NEC show in November. The bike is named, which in itself is an important decision (focus groups felt Daytona was a classic name, highlighting Triumph's sporting heritage), colour choices are finalized, pricing is settled and the advertising campaigns are created. The next big date is the press launch, which is about the same time as the bikes are available in the shops. So Dave gets sent out to test the Daytona in Spain, he reports back, and you go to a dealer with your cash. This bike making lark's a cinch, isn't it? **SB**

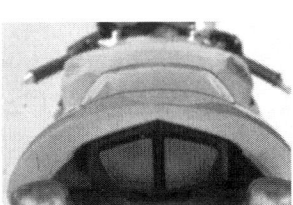

mean, how would you feel? You put a motorcycle out there and it repeatedly gets the smack-down from journalists worldwide. The three year old TT600 simply didn't have what it takes to stand up to the big four Japanese manufacturers, but only because of a collection of small problems.

Triumph has recognised the fact that the TT600 was struggling in the ultra-competitive middleweight class, and its answer comes in the shape of the new Daytona 600. A sharper edged supersports bike has been created to take the place of the soft and rather dull TT600. Instead of a decent chassis held back by a lacklustre engine and terrible fuelling, the Daytona is going in the opposite direction of the TT600, attempting to become the ultimate sportsbike package through correcting the old ailments and improving on the TT600's strong points.

Having recognised the fuelling and overall engine performance problems of the TT600, Triumph went back to the drawing board. What it came out the other side with is an entirely new bike from the ground up. From the frame and engine to the forks and brakes, the new Daytona has had a complete overhaul. In fact, the only similarity it has with the old TT600 is the yellow colour of the shapely new bodywork. Quite obviously the idea was to reduce weight while improving power, but considering that this is the focus of nearly every engineer and designer worldwide, Triumph needed to produce something special.

The Hinckley firm had a new fangled computer program to assist it in this quest. The Finite Element Analysis (FEA) computer aided design program was heavily used in every aspect of design on the Daytona. This examines what sort of stress any given part will be subject to, then applies strength where needed and saves mass (therefore weight) elsewhere.

Sure, Triumph isn't the only one to use such computer assistance, but it is starting from scratch instead of improving on an older model.

In terms of competition, British racing fans will now have some home-grown machinery to root for. V&M Racing has teamed up with Triumph and is competing in the British Supersport class with Isle of Man legend Jim Moodie and young boy Craig Jones on board. They both came along to the launch (albeit under the watchful eye of team owner Jack Valentine) to show us wank journalists how the new Daytona could really perform.

Triumph's venue of choice for any track-orientated bike is the demanding Cartagena circuit in Spain. The front straight leads into the first of four double right-handers, any of which can catch you out if you're not careful. These seemed to suit the nimble Daytona quite well because line adjustment and even a touch more brake trailing into those bends wasn't a chore at all. Bigger bikes might not have been quite so cooperative though. The rest of the circuit was busy, but not too demanding mentally. Elevation changes and a blind crest keep you on your toes though and the first session evolved into more of an extended sighting lap than an evaluation of the new bike.

By the end of the second session the track was less of an issue than the surprising performance of the Daytona. It was beginning to provoke giggles occasionally, because as confidence increased, so did lean angles, yet the hero blobs only skimmed lightly at best. Granted, Jim Moodie was scratching the exhaust, but TT rider extraordinaire I am not.

The first aspect that, er, doesn't stick out like a hangnail is the improved fuelling. As with all fuel-injected bikes, they shouldn't receive praise for getting it right, yet boy howdy how they take a shellacking when it goes like shit. The Daytona does, however, deserve praise for correcting the horrendous fuelling of the TT600. The new bike doesn't take any getting used to in the matter of throttle control, thanks to the new 32-bit processor and the four Keihin twin-butterfly throttle bodies.

Unlike the TT600's Sagem injection system of standard single throttle body and injector, the Keihin's twin butterflies are fed information from seven different sensors including a barometric pressure sensor. It measures the ambient air pressure while also determining if it'll be raining or picnic time tomorrow, which can come in handy for those weekend rides. A wheel speed sensor matches the ignition and fuelling to the throttle and crankshaft position, each of which also have their own sensors. The airbox and water temperatures are also monitored to keep fuelling correct. It sounds like a lot of hassle, but the end result is what we like.

Usually a poorly fuelled bike will make itself known during the transitional period during turn in. Coming off the brakes and back onto the power can sometimes turn into a head lunging and bike lurching ◗

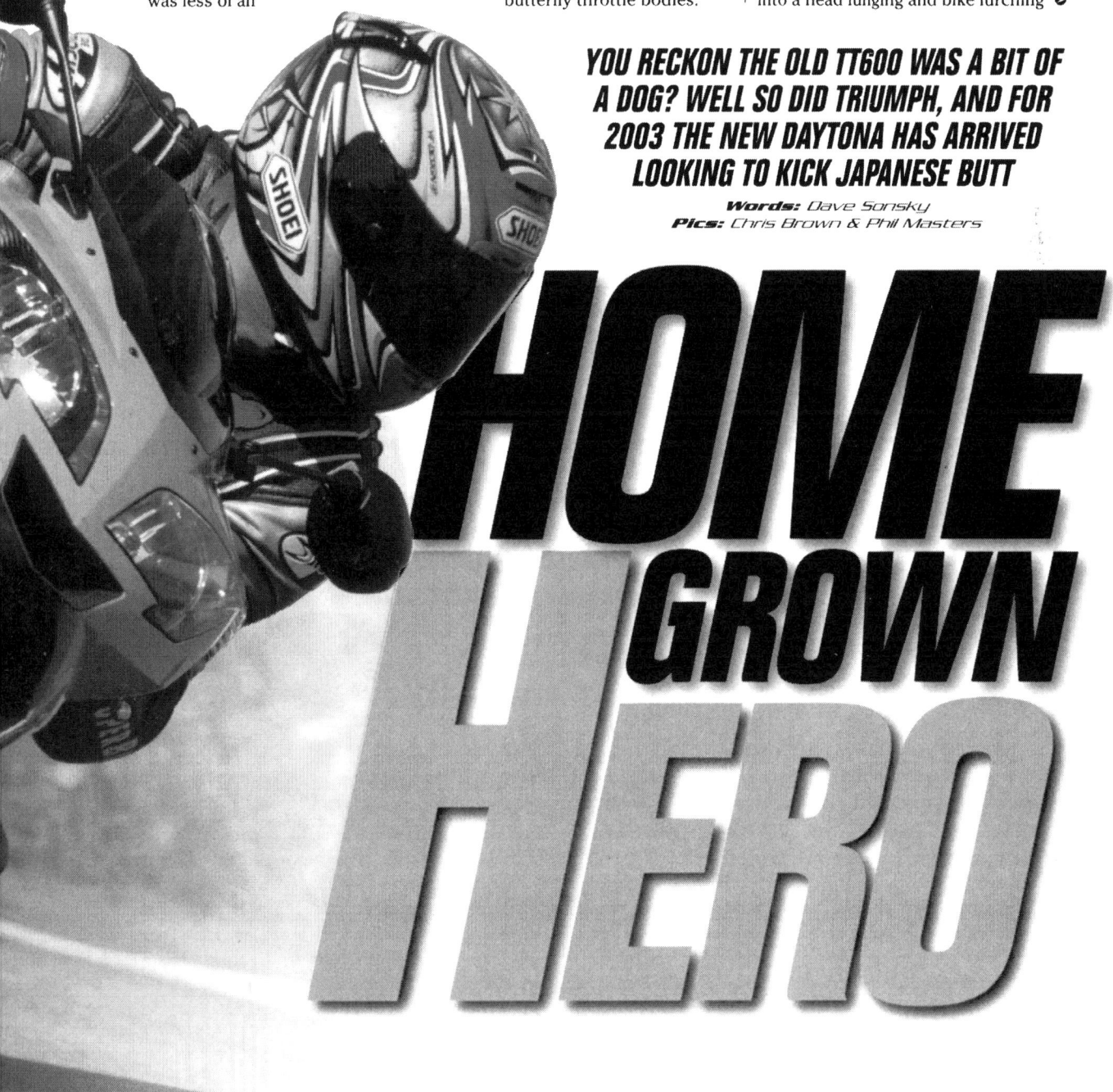

YOU RECKON THE OLD TT600 WAS A BIT OF A DOG? WELL SO DID TRIUMPH, AND FOR 2003 THE NEW DAYTONA HAS ARRIVED LOOKING TO KICK JAPANESE BUTT

Words: Dave Sonsky
Pics: Chris Brown & Phil Masters

HOME GROWN HERO

dance, something we obviously don't need. Smooth and linear power delivery is the aim, and the Daytona manages this quite admirably. Slow trawling through congested city streets may see otherwise, because during a lunchtime wheelie session, the extreme bottom end of the rev range felt a bit unsteady under the rear brake. It's something that certainly irons itself out by the middle of the rev range, but a test ride should include some experimentation with the low down revs.

Along with the fuelling, the Daytona's engine internals have received serious attention from the labcoat-clad clipboard boys. As power begins with the intake process we'll start with the sucking. The stylish, angular intake duct under the headlights feeds 15 per cent more air into the eight and a half litre air box. Moving on to the engine internals we see that the inlet and exhaust ports have sat their time on the flow bench. The inlet flows two per cent extra while the exhaust flows 11 per cent more. The combustion chamber and ports are now CNC machined allowing for more accuracy and consistent performance, which

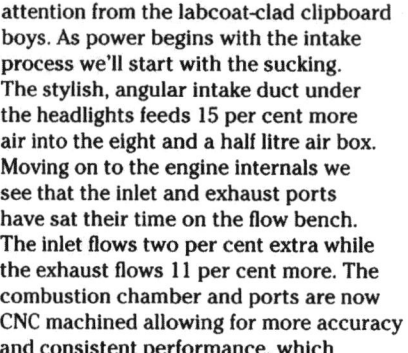

Tech Spec	> Triumph Daytona 600
Price	£6,999
NU Ins group	14 (tbc)

Engine

Type	I/c 16-valve in-line four
Displacement	599cc
Bore x Stroke	68 x 41.3mm
Compression	12.5:1
Carburation	Keihin EFI, twin-butterfly throttle bodies
Gearbox	six-speed
Max Power	110bhp@12,750rpm (claimed)
Max Torque	50ft/lbs@11,000rpm (claimed)

Cycle Parts

Chassis	Aluminium beam perimeter
Suspension	Front: 43mm cartridge forks, fully adjustable Rear: monoshock, fully adjustable
Brakes	Front: twin 308mm discs, 4-piston Triumph calipers Rear: single 220mm disc, single piston caliper
Wheels/Tyres	Front: 120/70-ZR17 Pirelli Diablo Rear: 180/55ZR17 Pirelli Diablo
Rake / Trail	24.6°/89.1mm
Wheelbase	1,390mm (54.7in)
Capacity	18 litres (3.96 gal)
Weight	165kg (363lb)
Contact	Triumph UK 01455 261954

equates to a new exhaust system as well. The header lengths have been adjusted and also see a linked header system to suit the new intake system, head porting and combustion chamber.

It all sounds very good on paper, but that doesn't always mean much on the road. What it comes down to is smooth power all the way through to the limiter at 13,000rpm. There isn't the familiar old Suzuki-esque top end rush, but that's a good thing because you can drive from the middle of the range and not worry about high side city while cranked over. This lets the Daytona's engine suit most riding styles. Keeping the Triumph screaming didn't provoke any moments in the tighter hairpins, and as the day went on and laziness set in, it was equally agreeable to drive out from one gear higher.

After such praise there must be a hang-up somewhere, and unfortunately it comes in a rather crucial area. A smooth gearbox is a subject much like fuel injection because it either goes quite well or needs some attention. As with all the Triumphs I've tested, there's a bit left to be desired in the tranny department. Neither slick nor quick quite fit because the gears hang up a bit unless given a taste

› Engine

Japanese firm Keihin worked with Triumph to develop the twin butterfly 38mm diameter throttle bodies specifically for the 599cc engine. For improved airflow, the first butterfly is controlled by the throttle cable, while the injector itself has been repositioned in the throttle body to inject fuel directly at the back of the first butterfly. The second butterfly is controlled by the Keihin Electronic Control Module which improves drivability. All four intake trumpet lengths have been optimised for intake pulse tuning and new transition pieces employed for the throttle bodies which are controlled by a 32-bit processor. The engine internals have also been changed by flowing the ports, and are now CNC machined for more accuracy and consistent performance.

› Chassis

Using a three-cell system as opposed to the four-cell on the TT600 has lightened the aluminium twin spar frame. Rigidity remains the same while weight is reduced by 685 grams. The bolt-on subframe is also lighter than the previous, yet still has a degree of 'flex' that aids shock absorption.

› Styling

The dated and rather silly looking TT600 is forgotten. An angular front end with coordinated air intake looks primo, and the general theme is aggressive all the way to the split tail lights.

› Clocks

Last year's clocks are actually better because they're easier to read. The silly font used on the tachometer and the fact that it counts by twos doesn't make much sense.

› Suspension

The front 43mm forks have had a complete overhaul. All of the internals (rods, cartridges and fixings) are made of aluminium, which saves a kilo of unsprung weight. They're fully adjustable, as is the rear shock that has been re-valved for a tauter feel.

› Brakes

The optimisation of the brake pad/disc interface allows for a reduction of the disc diameter from 310mm to 308mm without losing any power. With this 170g of unsprung weight has been lost. Four piston calipers grab the front discs that refuse to fade on hard track use. The rear 220mm disc has a single piston caliper.

› Exhaust

The previous exhaust needed an update because of the engine adjustments. The 1.2mm thick steel tube is of a 4-2-1 design with headers 1-2 and 3-4 linked for optimum power. The header lengths have also been tuned to suit the new motor.

TRIUMPH DAYTONA 600: TECHNICAL

of the clutch. For delicate road riders who abide by the textbook gear change system this shouldn't be a problem, but on track days you may come away with a sore toe and ground down teeth. The front straight had me grinding my molars several times when I found either false neutrals or it took several attempts to kick in the next cog. A quick listen could pick up the other riders struggling as well. To be fair, two of the three bikes I rode were better and it could be that they may need a little more breaking in to smooth it out.

The chassis had always been a strong point (if not the only one) on the TT600, and through more employment of the FEA the designers managed to improve it even more. The aluminium twin spar frame looks much like the older version, but in fact it incorporates a three-cell construction as opposed to the four-cell on the TT600, thus making it lighter while retaining the same rigidity. The

rake and trail haven't changed, but the wheelbase has shrunk by five millimetres. For a quick-steering motorcycle the front end keeps its composure surprisingly well and simply will not flap about. On the exit of several second gear corners I gave a hearty nudge left and right

under acceleration to see if it would go into a headshake, but there was simply nothing. One crest saw the front wheel landing on its left edge repeatedly, and again it refused to flap. In this day and age of quick steering, lightweight and powerful motorcycles that's quite an ➔

Moodie and Jones underline the importance of a good start in supersport racing

"... The new Daytona provides some real competition for the other manufacturers..." 🔗

accomplishment. Upon corner entrance there were two perfect situations to get the rear a little loose, not for benefit of speed as much as for pleasure. What would have had many other sportsbikes hanging the rear out saw the Daytona remaining quite composed. It takes a lot to upset this motorcycle, and this should make for a good result at the Isle of Man TT races.

Although the brakes are relatively unchanged they have had some minor tweakage. The discs are down from 310mm to 308mm, reducing weight and increasing pad to disc interface. Again, that's all well and good, but the true test came when all 27 stone of Jim Moodie and I did a couple of brisk laps. The man brakes late and hard, yet even with all of that weight on board the brakes stayed true and didn't fade at all. During one my own sessions they seemed to, but it turned out that the lever adjustment was between positions and slipped in to the closer setting. It was my mistake, not the brakes. They may even outdo the Kawasaki ZX-636R's radial jobbies, because they're more progressive and manageable as opposed to manic and awkward.

Styling is a crucial element, and the new Daytona looks light years ahead of the goofy TT600. The angular and flowing lines are attractive at the least, and from behind it looks better than J Lo wearing Daisy Dukes. The sharp front end produces a whistle that Mother Clanger herself would be proud of, and it will make it easily identifiable coming down any straight stretch because of the high pitched wind-splitting sound it makes. An

optional double bubble screen isn't really necessary because wind protection is about as good as it gets in the 600 class.

New bike launches can be a little misleading because of 'launch syndrome', or the lack of having a comparison bike to ride. The Daytona exceeded my expectations and didn't seem to disappoint anybody else on the test either. The racer boys were well pleased with it as a track tool, but as far as a road bike goes it still needs to prove itself. A few days around dear old Blighty should do it, but until we get our hands on one, a definitive

verdict shouldn't really be made. As it stands, Triumph has spawned a definite competitor in the middleweight class. Had it come out a year ago it would easily be at the top of the ladder, but in this year's tough crowd it will need a back to back comparo to really give it the test it deserves. It's fast and stable, looks ace, and it's from the motherland. Give it a shot, because this is a serious motorcycle. Triumph's dedication has produced a faster, smoother, and better handling machine than the old TT600, and some real competition for the other manufacturers.

DAYTONA 600

Does Triumph's late middleweight have what it takes?

BY MARK HOYER

TRIUMPH IS COMPLETELY off its nut, 100 percent whacked. Non-Japanese factories just don't take on the Big Four head-to-head. Ducati doesn't do it, Aprilia doesn't do it, BMW doesn't do it, nobody does it. And yet, here is Triumph, the restarted upstart that's been rebuilding the British brand since John Bloor put the marque back on the market in 1991, lining up and squaring off against the giants in segment after segment. It's one thing to build niche bikes with alternative engine layouts such as inline-Triples, or to retread traditional British territory with a parallel-Twin, but to build a 600cc super-sport bike, and to choose to make it an inline-Four, is absolutely crazy for a smaller-volume manufacturer.

But here Triumph is, stepping up to the plate with its new $8699 Daytona 600, a bike based upon the old TT600, but with top-to-bottom tweaks centered on making it competitive in what is a quickly changing, always evolving class.

They picked a tough year to

Lighter, faster, stronger: Triumph knows the recipe for success in the supersport class and the Daytona 600 shows it. Grams were shaved from almost everywhere. Brake discs are slightly smaller in diameter, while aluminum internals dropped more than 2 pounds from the fork. Tires are Pirelli Diablo T models, wherein the "T" stands for Triumph, as the construction is specifically suited to the Daytona chassis.

DAYTONA 600

go super-supersporty, with everybody save Suzuki introducing new bikes, all of which are more track-focused than ever. But not only is Triumph hanging tough, it's making progress.

How so? This Daytona works. After a half-day on the tight-and-technical Cartagena track in southern Spain with the other half spent on the road, it's clear that Triumph has exorcised many of the demons that haunted the old TT.

One thing that didn't haunt the old TT was handling. In fact, it was one sweet-turning package. The Daytona carries this tradition forward, but with a frame redone to be lighter. Chassis geometry–24.6-degrees rake/3.5-inches trail–is identical to that of the TT, although the wheelbase has been shortened by .2 inch to 54.7 inches. The fork now features all-aluminum internals, for a weight loss of more than 2 pounds. Further, the bodywork is molded at Triumph so that they can control the thinness of the panels, and weight-reduction has taken place here, as well. Triumph puts the claimed weight at 363 pounds dry, 11 less than the TT.

Some of this also came from the engine. The crankshaft has shed weight, the starter is lighter, a magnesium cam cover is fitted and the exhaust exhausts the same way but with fewer pounds.

First item of note when saddling up is that the riding position is more aggressive. Next is the fact that the engine

is greatly improved. The cylinder head is new, with CNC-machined combustion chambers and ports for improved airflow and combustion. Dual-butterfly Keihin fuel-injection is used, which through the use of secondary, computer-controlled butterflies, helps maintain optimal intake-air velocity. This system is similar to those used by the Big Four. The ol' butt dyno suspects around 95 horses at the rear wheel, and Triumph's claim of 110 horses at the crank (up 2 bhp from the TT) suggests this is a good guess. It definitely feels spicier than the Honda CBR600F4i we had in our recent 600cc comparison, but not as sizzling as the Yamaha YZF-R6 or CBR600RR, and certainly nowhere near the big-bluey Kawasaki 636 in terms of torque.

The best thing about the Daytona engine, though, is that the great cave in the midrange the early TT600s exhibited, and even the later "fixed" versions still displayed somewhat, has been nicely filled in. Delivery wasn't without its problems, however. Both the bikes we used on the track–fitted with louder accessory slip-on cans–and the stockers we rode on the street, were hard to start when warm. Also, throttle response was soft off the bottom. This, combined with somewhat abrupt clutch engagement at the end of lever travel, put the motor flat on its face frequently during leisurely getaways. That's the only real delivery problem other than occasional hiccups from trailing throttle

Clean styling and kitsch-free paint–silver or yellow–make the Daytona a tasteful choice. Warranty is a full two years, with unlimited mileage. Under-headlight "mouth" is ram-air inlet feeding new dual butterfly fuel-injection system.

DAYTONA 600

to on the gas. Shift quality was a little notchy, but about on par with our last Ducati 749.

As it is with middleweights, there isn't much happening below 8000 rpm anyway, but the Daytona pulls cleanly and deliberately from 6K until the power comes in, which is especially nice in street riding. It pulls hard to the 14K-plus redline–so well, in fact, that during early laps the soft rev-limiter was frequently visited.

Out on our brief street ride, suspension compliance was excellent. Stability and feedback were pretty much faultless at a brisk street pace. This on some seriously bumpy roads, fraught with hazards: Renaults in our lane on blind corners, mule-drawn wagons, herds of sheep and little girls riding pink bicycles toward traffic. There is little resistance to turning while braking, and trailing it in deep while on the track didn't induce fear of the lowside. I'd also like to add that the damping through the gravely whoop section outside of Turn 1 was quite adequate,

with excellent resistance to bottoming...

It is difficult to take a supersport bike such as the Triumph Daytona 600 entirely seriously without an attendant race effort. Which is one reason Triumph took the Daytona 600 launch as an opportunity to introduce the press to the two riders–Isle of Man TT legend Jim Moodie and British up-and-comer Craig Jones–who are spearheading Triumph's official return to racing. Established Brit squad ValMoto is handling the bike mods for the 600cc British Championship with the Triumph factory lending support. Early results have been good, with both riders finishing in the top 10 at the second round. Triumph America is mum about a possible stateside racing effort, but you can't help but think they're going to take the plunge soon.

Of course, they'd be insane to do it, but there is a certain beauty to the madness that has bred this Daytona 600. It's more of an alternative than ever, although it still isn't truly all the way there. But fettle the fuel-injection, squeeze out a few more bhp, and one day we might be referring to the Big Five. Nuts, ain't it? ◘

Part ant, part alien –
the waspish face of the
new Daytona 600

WHAT'S THE STORY?
■ Capable Brit entry in the ultra competitive 600 market
■ Radical new look
■ Superb chassis and steering

PATRIOT MISSILE

Triumph are ready to upset the established order with a real contender in the supersports 600 class

Triumph aren't pissing about. Their new supersport 600 is sharp, focused, and quicker on track than Kawasaki's attitude-packed ZX-6R, while retaining the usability of the previous TT600. At last Triumph offer a very real alternative to buying Japanese. And about time too.

Finding out the new bike is being launched at the twisty, undulating Cartagena circuit in south-east Spain is astounding luck – it's where we carried out our 600s group test for the March issue, so each rival for the Triumph has already been ridden on the same track and the same roads. It also means we know how fast the other bikes went, and we're happy to report the yellow bike is more than on the case.

Triumph openly stated they'd tweaked rebound and compression damping on the forks and shock for the track, which is fair enough as we did exactly the same during our test. After two full days the Kawasaki's on-board lap timer showed my best as 1m 52.7s, but after only three 20-minute sessions the Daytona is almost two seconds faster, with a 1m 50.8s best. That's only three tenths slower than the fastest bike round the circuit in our test, the GSX-R, and all our bikes were using full-on Michelin Pilot Race tyres. Blimey.

The reason the Triumph is right up there in the hunt for top track honours is the same one that allowed the Suzuki to clean up: the chassis. Sorry to be blunt but Christ does this thing turn. Direct sight roughly at the exit of a corner and the Daytona tips in and carves a tight line with barely a weighted peg or nudge to the clip-ons. It rattles round at serious speed without feeling like it's trying. More on this later...

Steering is R6-fast but without the flighty feel of the diminutive Yamaha, the Daytona getting right on its side with no fuss or drama. It just goes wherever the rider wants with perfect manners. Tighter line? No problem, sir, and feel free to change gear or abuse the throttle if you so desire.

Feel from the fully adjustable forks is superb, at least equalling the barrage of information thrown back from the ZX-6R's chunky usd arrangement. Although the 4-pot calipers lack the initial grab and brick wall power of the Kawasaki's radials, they're easily as good as the *'normal'* brakes on the other competition. There's also a direct relation between lever movement and pads, which combines with the instructive front end to allow the brake to be trailed later and later.

Applying front brake up to the apex with knee skimming the surface is against

■ The TT's yawn-a-rama looks are a fading memory...

St George kneesliders find their spiritual home

every instinct and usually the reserve of sickeningly talented racers, yet feels totally secure on the Daytona.

It works on the road, too. Triumph test rider and local boy David Lopez is on hand to guide a road thrash on every imaginable surface to show the bike works. Bumps and poor surfaces that would have an R6 slapping away merrily produce no more than a mild twitch from the bars, it goes where intended as easily as it does on track.

Stock suspension settings are, well, fine, but maybe lacking the ultimate refinement of Honda's sublime CBR. And on occasion the suspension feels 'loose'. It's difficult to explain this exactly, as it isn't too soft and moving about, but it's not overly firm and losing grip. It's as if the wheels are rapidly flying up and down over bumps, the suspension not resisting the movement, but at the same time not transmitting anything to the rest of the bike. Which is no bad thing.

It's obvious to see why Triumph selected Cartagena circuit and the surrounding twisty roads. The track really only has one straight, the rest of the circuit being a series of second and third gear bends strung together with various sweeps that perfectly displaying the agility of the bike's chassis. Using somewhere with more straights would have highlighted the fact the engine isn't quite as strong as the class leaders.

The 599cc lump uses a shorter stroke than the Japanese opponents – usually the sign of a rev-happy engine. And sure enough it howls to the 14,000rpm redline, but stops dead a few hundred revs later. By comparison, the CBR, ZX and R6 make peak power at around 13,000rpm but will rev to past 15k, meaning less gear shifts as one cog can be held through flowing sections of track.

It's also a little lacking in the midrange. Long, constant radius turns which could be driven out of cleanly in third on the ZX and R6 need second on the Triumph, as it takes time to build revs if there's less than 8000rpm showing on the analogue tacho. It's the same away from the track; when negotiating unknown winding roads it's all too easy to open the gas with 6000rpm showing and have to wait for the engine to catch up.

But at the end of the day it's a supersport bike, and keeping the Daytona above 10,000rpm isn't really problem. Injection is no longer the troublesome system found on the TT. Triumph have accepted it wasn't exactly the smoothest in the world and have replaced it with a new set-up developed with Jap bods Keihin. The 38mm throttle bodies (same as R6, GSX-R and ZX) have twin butterflies like a GSX-R, with one controlled by the hamfisted rider and one by the much more intelligent 32-bit ECM.

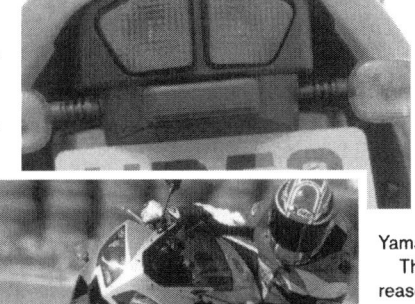
■ Silver ones go round corners too

There's none of the farting, popping and stalling of the old TT, and starting the bike with a hot engine no longer sees the choke coming on for the first few seconds until the electronic brain susses what's going on. Quite a few of the launch bikes were difficult to start when hot though, needing a long prod of starter and a handful of gas to fire.

There's still a small amount of jerkiness when getting back onto a small throttle at lower revs, otherwise it's a smooth and stepless delivery. Triumph are claiming 110bhp at the crank which, given the assumed average transmission loss of 10%, equates to some 99bhp. And they're probably not too far off the mark – it'll definitely be well up the nineties.

And speaking of transmissions, the Daytona isn't blessed with the slickest 'box in the world. But at least gears stay in once selected and, by contrast, the clutch is remarkably light.

Having such a smooth delivery could mean the

["Triumph have come a long way with the new Daytona"]

Daytona is faster than it seems. Triumph are claiming very linear power and a flat spread of torque, and gaffer of the ValMoto Triumph race team Jack Valentine says the same: *"It's a lovely linear curve with no dips or surprises, and a flat torque curve across the rev range. It's deceptive, as there are no sudden kicks in the delivery, in the same way Ducati's don't feel very fast until you look at the speedo or get to a corner."* And he could be right.

All this results in an un-intimidating engine to use, and the way it makes power means there's no worries getting on the gas out of turns. Blending this with a very capable chassis and brake package makes one usable bike, inspiring you to go harder and harder.

Things are helped by the riding position, which is sporty enough for the track without being crippling on the road. Where the new ZX-6R is harsh with tiny dimensions, and the CBR is equally dwarf-like, the Daytona has clip-ons above the top yoke and is a little more accommodating. It's a high, sloping seat with a fairly easy to reach bars, giving a nice, sat-on position not unlike Yamaha's R6.

There's also a reasonable distance between the seat and pegs making it comfortable for lanky types, but not at the expense of poor ground clearance. Pegs touch down on track but are unlikely to be creating sparks on the road.

The styling will, though, as it's striking to say the least, especially in yellow. The angular design is at least 300% better than the old TT, and the fairing looks far better in the plastic than it does in pictures. The tank and seat are causing more debate, though, and for my personal tastes the seat has too much bulk to suit the sleek front. The analogue tacho also carries numbers which look like they come off a grandfather clock and are at odds with the up-to-date lines of the rest of the bike. Down to taste, obviously.

One area not open to debate is build quality. Shabby it isn't. As with previous Hinckley offerings the paint is about an inch thick, and panel fit is spot on. The only things letting the side down are cheap-looking castings for some of the smaller components, for example the rear footrest hangers.

Triumph have come a hell of a long way with the new Daytona. Their first sports 600, the TT, was several metres off the mark – yes, the chassis potential was there, but the motor was a big disappointment and the styling was dated even before release. Triumph know this, and have tried as hard as they know how on the Daytona. If the original TT had been this good it would have been a revelation, but with Honda and Kawasaki moving the game on, it could have been all too easy for Triumph to miss the boat again.

Thankfully they haven't. While the engine may not offer the experience of a ZX-6R and the suspension doesn't have the quality action of the Honda, my money would go on the Daytona matching the GSX-R in a straight line, while having the turning ability to top the class. Triumph's engineers have come up with a superb chassis in a near-complete, rounded package, and anyone seriously contemplating a hot new 600 now has another test ride to arrange before they sign any dotted lines. It really is good.

Good points: stunning chassis package, ease of use, built in Blighty
Bad points: motor doesn't feel fast, may lack midrange go

Verdict: very real alternative to Jap 600s

■ Clip-ons are an easy reach; tacho numbers are an easy retch

BRAKES

One area Triumph have never skimped on is stopping, although it's tended to be defined by immense initial bite but a slight lack of feel. The Daytona's 4-piston calipers are typical Triumph, but grip discs reduced in diameter by 2mm, after it was realised there was a section of disc untouched by the pads. Which are now a slightly different compound, by the way.

Taking discs down to 308mm diameter has no effect on brake performance but saves 170g on unsprung mass, reducing gyroscopic inertia and helping the bike turn. And although there are no other changes, these brakes have a much better action than before, with sensitivity, progressive power and feel by the container load. How's that work, then?

FRONT END

Triumph are sticking with rwu Kayaba forks on the Daytona. But there's a host of changes over the TT aimed at reducing unsprung weight and improving steering.

All internal gubbins including cartridges, rods and fixings are now aluminium, saving 1kg on unsprung mass. Springs are single rate, too – the TT had *'progressive'* dual rate affairs which become harder the more they compress. Single rate, as favoured by racers the world over, give a consistent and predictable action across their stroke.

Fully adjustable for rebound, compression and preload.

ENGINE

Based on the TT600 lump but heavily revised, the Daytona's 599cc engine gets new injection, different electrickery, a new cylinder head and has been on a diet.

Combustion first. Air comes in via an intake on the front of the nose, which is in a positive pressure area and supplies 15% more to the airbox than the TT's twin scoops. Intake stack lengths are revised, too. Fuel gets squirted in by a Keihin set up, developed as a joint effort with Triumph and using 38mm throttle bodies with twin butterflies, just like those GSX-R things. The first butterfly is controlled by the throttle, with the injector nozzle positioned to blast fuel straight on the back at full throttle to improve atomisation; the second is in the hands of the new 32-bit ECM, to improve driveability.

While we're on the subject, the ECM gets information from seven sensors – manifold air pressure, ambient air pressure, wheel speed, throttle and crank position, and airbox and water temperatures.

Extra gasses get in and out of the new head thanks to inlets flowing 2% more charge and outlets passing 11% more waste. Combustion occurs chambers that have been in CNC machined to ensure accuracy and consistent performance, removing the possibility of casting irregularities, and cams get tweaked timing and duration. A new 4-2-1 stainless exhaust system with *'tuned'* headers gives an escape route for the various poisons.

Triumph claim they've slashed 2.29kg from the motor with a lighter crank, starter, magnesium covers and other trinkets. Power is claimed at 110 crankshaft ponies at 12,750rpm – which should equate to around 99bhp at the rear wheel.

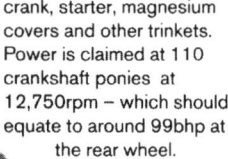

■ Let's just hope they never put that engine in a naked bike...

CHASSIS

Looks like the TT, right? Yep, indeed it does, but it's a new design. Extruded main beams (formed by pushing the material to shape, like ketchup out a squeezy bottle) now use three internal cells over the TT's four to decrease weight by 685g, the design being done with big, clever 'pooters to ensure rigidity remains intact.

The subframe bolts on and is fabricated from 2mm box section aluminium, and saves another 200g. Triumph claim it also has a precise amount of flex designed in, to absorb energy from the rider being buffeted by high speed windblast instead of passing it to the chassis.

Geometry is tweaked from that of the TT, with rake and trail going to 24.6° and 89.1mm from the previous 24° and 82mm. There's a 5mm reduction in wheelbase to 1390mm as well.

REAR END

Triumph are not saying anything about the swingarm, so we can only assume it's the same as the one which graced the previous 600. Any movement of the wheel is controlled through said swingarm by a fully adjustable, remote-reservoir shock as found on the TT, but with a dose of re-valving to suit its new role. And, er, that's it at this end...

SPECIFICATION

Model	Triumph Daytona 600
Price	£6999
Warranty	2 years, unlimited mileage
Available	now
Contact	01455 251700
Colours	yellow, silver

ENGINE

Type	4-stroke, liquid-cooled, dohc 16v inline four
Bore x stroke, cc	68x41.3, 599cc
Comp ratio	12.5:1
Fuel system	Keihin fuel injection, 38mm throttle bodies
Claimed power	110bhp@12,750rpm
Claimed torque	50.5ft-lb@11,000rpm
Transmission	6-speed

CHASSIS

Frame	aluminium beam perimeter
Front end	43mm rwu forks, fully adj.
Rear end	monoshock, fully adj.
Front brake	4-pot calipers, 308mm discs
Rear brake	single pot, 220mm disc
Front tyre	120/70ZR17 Pirelli Diablo
Rear tyre	180/55ZR17 Pirelli Diablo

DIMENSIONS

Rake/trail	24.6°/89.1mm
Wheelbase	1390mm
Seat height	815mm
Dry weight (claim)	165kg
Fuel capacity	18 litres

TRIUMPH BLOKE

This handsome chap is Ross Clifford, product manager for Triumph. Tell us some things, Ross: *"As soon as the TT was launched we started styling sketches on this new bike.*

■ TT was "too soft and a little bland".

"The TT was designed as an all-rounder but before it was launched the R6 moved the game on. But we were already committed.

"So the new bike needed more focus, and we accept the TT was too soft, a little bland and suffered with its injection. Once we had a new look we developed a brief for the chassis and engine, and development got started. 600s are a never ending evolution, so we needed to push on."

So have you started on a Daytona replacement already?

"Most models have a two year life cycle, depending on the bike. We have ideas for a new model, but nothing has started yet. We see the Daytona as being here for two or three years, although obviously it may receive tweaks. And of course we need to wait for a response to the bike before planning what to do next."

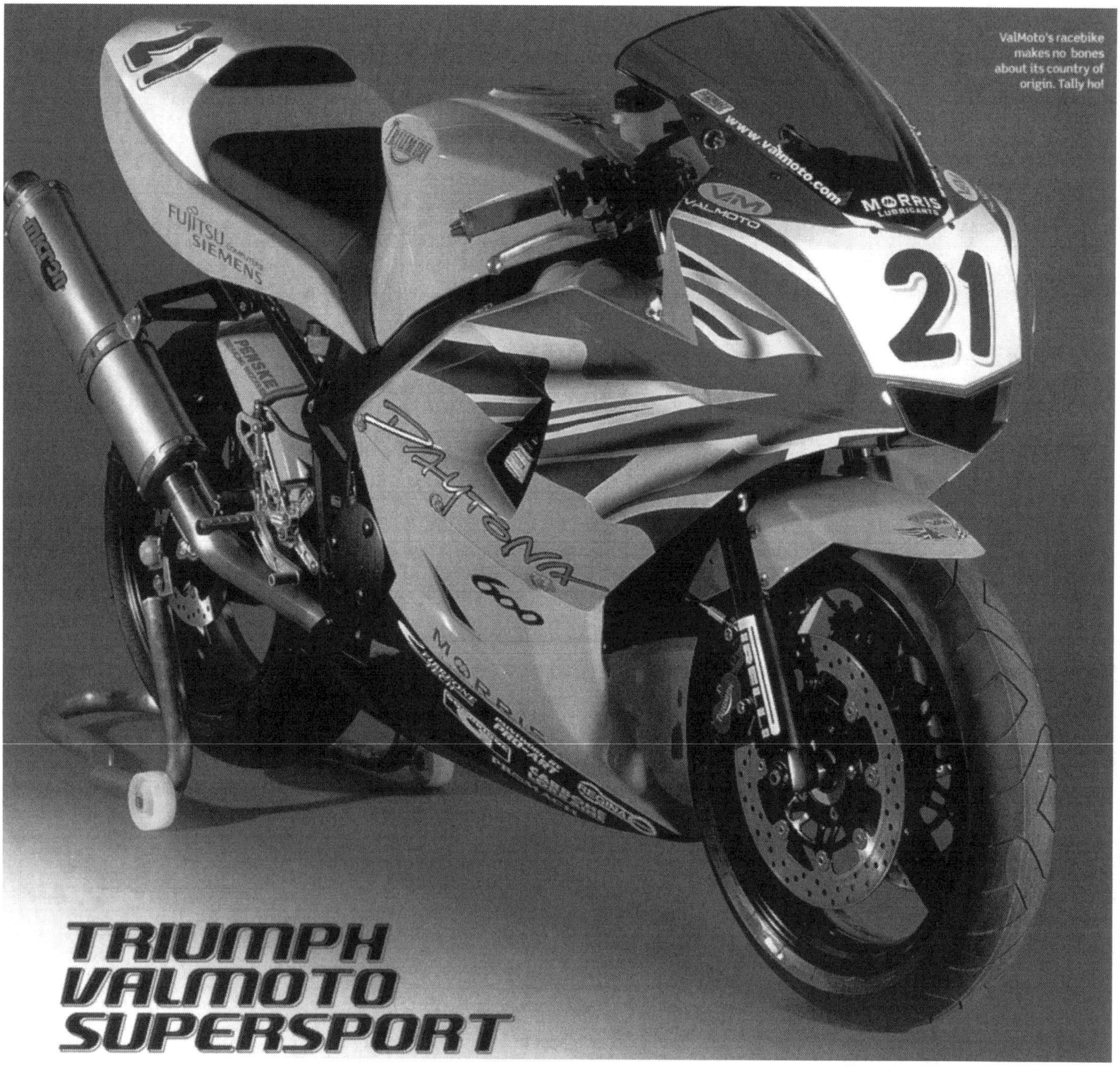

ValMoto's racebike makes no bones about its country of origin. Tally ho!

TRIUMPH VALMOTO SUPERSPORT

WHO?

For the first time since nobody can remember there's a factory supported Triumph race team. The team is ValMoto and run by ex-V&M gaffer Jack Valentine, with old partner Steve Mellor filling the role of chief engineer. Between them the pair racked up seven British titles and 15 TT wins, so they should know what they're doing. The team will be competing in this year's Supersport championship and there's every indication they'll be hunting a British victory at the TT as well. Get the Union Jack boxers at the ready...

RACE PACE

ValMoto's engines are spannered up by Steve Mellor to comply with strict Supersport regulations. Obviously he's not giving a lot away, and there's not a great deal that can be changed, but expect some serious blueprinting and fettling.

By the time exhaust gasses find their way out of the Micron system, ValMoto reckon it will be producing an impressive 138bhp at the crank. This is transmitted to the rear wheel via a Regina chain running on Renthal sprockets, and should allow a top speed something in the region of 185mph. From a road based 600. So not slow, then.

CHASSIS

As with the motor, the rest of the bike is restricted by the tight Supersport regs. ValMoto re-valve the Kayaba forks to suit the preferences and style of the two riders, but out back the stock shock is junked in favour of a swanky remote-adjustment Penske unit. And an Öhlins steering damper hangs about waiting to catch any unwanted shaking from the front end.

Brakes are obviously the stock units but gain additional grip on the discs from Carbone Lorraine race compound pads, with fluids guided by Goodridge braided lines. Sticky Pirelli Supercorsa tyres replace the standard issue Diablo rubber.

AND THIS...

ProMach rearsets let riders put their feet exactly where they want while providing even more ground clearance. An SPA digital dash nestles beneath a Skidmarx screen mounted on a Fibreone Tech race fairing, with Pro-Art paint finishing the whole shebang off with a healthy dose of patriotism. ★

HI, I'M JIM

■ Moodie: expects to be on the pace

This is one Jim Moodie, eight-time TT winner and double British Supersport champ. He's piloting the ValMoto bikes along with Junior Superstock champ Craig Jones. He says: *"Even on my first ride it felt familiar, and reminded me of my R6 race bike. It's a similar riding position, with even quicker steering but stability too.*

"I'm making no predictions, but I'll be disappointed if we don't get a podium before the TT."

Jim and Craig tried some two-up antics at the launch. The pair got faster and faster until they were both dragging knees and did a 1m 51.8s best. Respect and then some.

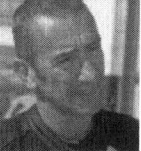

Triumph Daytona 600

Fresh British challenge to the might of the Japanese sportsbike makers

+ 599cc + 16v DOHC IN-LINE FOUR + NU15 + 155MPH (EST) + £6999

IT'S THE FINAL track session of the day and it seems like the right time to push as hard as possible. On some bikes this would be the moment to take a deep breath and calm things down a bit, but there's something reassuring about the Daytona that makes it feel okay to keep going hard to the last wave of the flag. So we do. One more lap.

Halfway round, the Daytona dives into the long, fast third-gear right-hander – the fastest corner on the track. It's the quickest I've gone into the corner all day and there's a pang of tension as I wonder if, finally, I've overcooked it. The Daytona's quick steering rips into the early apex with my toe slider grinding hard. It feels so good. Then it's a matter of holding it steady as the bike drifts out to the left, suspension working to mop up the bumps, tyres grappling with grippy Spanish tarmac. Tension gives way to euphoria as the Daytona carves a perfect, arcing exit and zings across the circuit ready for the next sweeping left.

This is one hell of a track bike – and a great road bike. Full stop. It lets you push as hard as you want and somehow manages to keep you from going over the edge. There may be other issues, but right now that's all that matters.

I'm grateful for the moment of clarity because until then I'd spent the day wrestling with questions and doubts about Triumph's new Daytona 600. Is it up to the fearsome competition posed by the Japanese quartet of

CBR600RR, R6, ZX-6R and GSX-R600? Is the fuel injection sorted? Will it stay sorted? Is there enough power? Enough midrange? Is the handling really as good as it feels, or is it flattered on these lovely roads and this track? Does it seem so stable because the engine couldn't pull the skin off old custard? Am I being blinded by the marketing splurge, perfect weather and sumptuous hospitality?

The reason for all this soul searching? Well, we've been here before. Three years ago, Triumph announced a bike that would take on the Japanese in the hardest sector of all: the 600cc sportsbike class. At the first test it was all roses. Sure, the TT600 had funny tubes sticking out of the fairing and a headlight shaped like a pair of Y-fronts, but it handled like a dream and the engine seemed revvy and smooth, with a pretty feeble midrange and a screaming top end. Much like any Japanese sports 600. Initial reports glowed.

Then the TT let us down. After a few hundred miles the well-behaved, if slightly gutless, engine started coughing, spluttering and lurching like a sickly kangaroo. In a matter of weeks the TT's reputation plummeted and those of us who rode the bikes at the launch were bewildered that we'd got it so wrong. Which is why now, riding the TT's replacement, I have so many doubts.

The TT's problems mean the Daytona's fuel injection is under close scrutiny. It doesn't ➤

New angular wrapping encases Triumph's most focused sportsbike. The gap is closing on the opposition

The exhaust sounds good and there's a factory carbon can
Top right **Lights are on as standard**
Right **Single air intake increases flow and power**

behave badly when chugging along, but there's still a bit of jerkiness if you're on and off the throttle at low revs in low gears. The system's not as refined as Suzuki's, but it's not bad. The jerkiness wasn't noticeable on the track, but on twisty back roads – where you spend a lot of time hovering at that doubtful moment before opening the throttle fully – there was a tiny but definite pause between wrist twist and the power coming in, as the electronic brain does all its calculations.

The engine is an updated version of the TT600 lump, with new cylinder head, reshaped combustion chambers and revised cam lift and timing. Instead of the two dodgy looking intake ducts on the TT600, there's one scoop in the middle of the fairing where there's more aerodynamic pressure to help charge the airbox. That, along with the revised fuel injection and reshaped exhaust header pipes, gives a claimed power output of 110bhp at the crank. That's likely to translate to just under 100bhp at the back wheel, which will make the Daytona almost as powerful as the Japanese opposition – but not quite. Which is how it feels. Having ridden a 2003 Yamaha R6 in the week before this test, the Daytona's power delivery felt pretty close, but a shade less potent and it needed more revs.

The need for top-end power has inevitably resulted in a midrange that's not going to scare anyone. Crack the throttle at 3000rpm

The all-new fuel injection system, with double butterfly valves, was developed with Japanese fuelling experts Keihin. It works well, so far

and you get a slow build to around 8000rpm, when the engine begins to wake up, the exhaust note changes and you can get going.

On the road this means you have to get all Michael Flatley on the gear pedal if you want to make decent progress through traffic. Several times I pulled out from behind lorries and had to tread down a few gears while alongside to bring the engine to life. Once acclimatised to the necessary box-stirring it's not an issue and as soon as the engine hits the sweet zone above 9000rpm it seems Triumph's top-end fiddling has been worthwhile.

On the track, the blank midrange is more

obvious. As you always want maximum drive, trying to power out of a corner at anything less than that magic 9000rpm feels like a no-man's land. You've just got to be on the ball and be in the right gear, but that's really no different to the other supersport 600s.

Perhaps it's the Daytona's stunning cornering ability that accentuates this. As it makes going fast round corners so easy, you subconsciously expect everything else to be equally effortless. Once you get used to thrashing the living daylights out of it, though, the Daytona flies.

Witness the performance of the Daytona in the British Supersport championship where tuning guru Jack Valentine's ValMoto team has already scored top ten finishes in the first two rounds. The team has, of course, done as much with the engines as the rules will allow – but they haven't changed the brakes because they're happy with the performance of the standard fittings. That's because they are as powerful and subtle as you like. Not grabby when applied gently, but the power soon kicks in with a bit more squeeze and can be feathered off accurately as you ease into a corner.

The front suspension behaves well in these conditions too, seeming comfortable with as much into-corner braking as you dare to try. Triumph has reduced the weight of the fork internals from the TT600 set-up and fitted

FIRST RIDE
DAYTONA 600

**Ride fast or admire the view, you decide
Top right Handling is superb: quick steering and stable
Right Neat and easy-to-read clocks**

BIKE'S TEN POINT CHECKLIST

Styling ★★★
Distinctive and angular, but the front air scoop makes it look like a tropical fish, or a tweety bird.

Comfort ★★★
Standard fare for this class: a pretty sporty position but not uncomfortable.

Clocks ★★★★
Nothing stunning, but everything's where it should be, clear and easy to read.

Engine ★★★
Revvy and feels powerful enough once you get it spinning. Not blessed with a huge midrange, though.

Gearbox ★★★
At the clunky end of the slick scale, but works well as long as you use a positive boot.

Handling ★★★★★
Su-bloody-perb. Quick steering, stable, intuitive. Fantastic fun on track or road.

Suspension ★★★★
Nice. Not harsh, yet firm enough to cope with hard riding.

Brakes ★★★★
Plenty good enough. Initial bite is gentle, power comes in on demand.

Practicality ★★★
Not bad for this type of bike. Big, protective fairing, bungee hooks, pillion seat but no grab rail.

Finish ★★★
Doesn't have the slickness of the competition from the Honda, Yamaha or Kawasaki. But catching up with Suzuki.

Shock and ore. Well, aluminium. The rear shock has been revalved since it was on the TT. At the front, the fully adjustable forks have new, lighter internals

single-rate springs, while at the back the monoshock has been revalved.

The TT's handling was the one area where that bike excelled and all Triumph had to do for the Daytona was not cock it up. They've redesigned the frame, making it lighter, and tweaked the suspension, but the Daytona retains that precious mix of quick-steering yet stable handling that makes exploring its limits (or more realistically, yours) an addictive joy.

Accelerating along the bumpy roads around Cartagena, I try to provoke the

Daytona into shaking its bars – but it's having none of it, staying composed and reassuring. Then I come to the next set of bends and it takes the merest of nudges on the bars or just a shift of body weight and the Daytona's there, keen to lean and snapping at apexes. It's a really clever mix.

Apart from having to keep the engine revving, it's a bike you can ride fast with the minimum of stress and effort. The riding position is pleasant enough, without too much weight on the wrists. There's a slightly taller seat that extends the distance between bum and footpegs, making the bike more comfortable for lanky riders who found the TT600 a bit cramped. There's decent protection from the fairing and a taller screen is available as an optional extra.

The styling strikes most people as a massive improvement on the TT600, but the jury's still out on the angular lines. The bike looks physically bigger than the slender Japanese opposition, except perhaps for the Suzuki GSX-R600, but that might not be a bad thing if you're none too slender yourself.

This is a good evolution, an improvement over the TT600 and a definite step forward, provided the fuel injection keeps working. And just sometimes, when you're in the mood and in the right groove, it feels like the best bike in the world. ■

'The Daytona is a bike you can ride fast with a minimum of stress and effort'

THE BIG QUESTIONS

So have Triumph caught up?
When they unveiled the TT600, Triumph found that the opposition had moved the goalposts and they were lagging behind in terms of performance and styling. You could say the same has also happened this time. It's unlikely the Daytona is going to be able to quite match the new Honda CBR600RR or Kawasaki ZX-6R in a straight fight. But it's getting closer – and the handling is just superb.

Will the Daytona win a British Supersport race this year?
Triumph are really excited about going racing again, so you can be sure that if they don't, it won't be for lack of trying. Something like 120 staff from the Hinckley factory turned up at Silverstone for the first BSB round to watch Craig Jones and Jim Moodie come ninth and 11th first time out. By the next round, they were up to seventh and eighth. Team boss Jack Valentine is convinced the Daytona has potential. A few podiums this year and they'll be happy.

Will the fuel injection work this time?
Only time will tell, but Triumph won't want a repeat of the TT600, where the fuel injection worked for a bit and then began to deteriorate. They've developed the new system with Keihin.

INTERVIEW
David Lopez Cordoba **is Triumph's test rider. Cartagena is his home circuit**

Why do you do so much testing here? Cartagena has got many qualities. You have many tight corners but also fast corners where you have to keep the throttle open quite a lot, and in some areas it's quite bumpy. On this bike I've ridden about 1000 laps of the track. And of course you get perfect weather for eight months of the year.

So do you test the bikes in Britain too?
In Britain we do a lot of mileage and stability work, as well as work on injection settings, at various test facilities and on the road.

How do you go about testing?
Triumph say the bike must be so much orientated for the track and so much for the road. This is a sportsbike so it's very important that it performs well on the track. It's probably the most radical sportsbike we've done.

What's the best part of your job?
My background is racing and for me the most satisfying part is working with sportsbikes – on the chassis and suspension.

This bike is very quick-steering and yet stable too. How do you do that?
That's a secret.

UNDER THE SKIN

Engine
It's the same basic unit as the TT600, but with a revised top end. Bore and stroke are the same but compression is up. Repositioning the air intake duct into the high-pressure area at the centre of the fairing has resulted in a 15 per cent increase of airflow into the 8.5-litre airbox. Cam timing and lift has been adjusted to give 2 per cent more inlet gas flow and 11 per cent more exhaust. Power is up to 110bhp at the crank according to the Triumph dyno.

Fuel injection
Triumph developed the new system with Keihin. Its twin-butterfly system aims to control the induction air speed, smoothing out power delivery – especially at slow engine speeds.

Chassis
The frame looks similar to the TT's, but it's a new design with less internal bracing. New aluminium fork internals save weight and the rear shock's damping has been adjusted to suit the altered geometry. Wheelbase is down 5mm, but rake and trail are increased slightly.

Brakes
Optimisation of the pad/disc interface allows a 2mm reduction in disc diameter. As usual on Triumphs, braided hoses come as standard.

Equipment
The Daytona comes with a colour-coded hugger, digital speedo and analogue tacho.

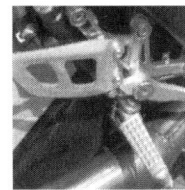

Top For British riders, that logo's as familiar and reassuring as the Union Jack
Centre Superb ground clearance with nice, high footpegs
Bottom You can take a pillion if you want – or fit the cowl that comes as standard

DAYTONA 600
Great Brit hope for supersport glory
- Handling, easy to ride fast
- Slightly lacking in midrange

Price	£6999 otr
Top speed	155mph (est)
Power	110bhp@12,750rpm (claimed)
Torque	50lb.ft@11,000 (claimed)
Engine	599cc, 16v, dohc, in-line four
Bore x stroke	68x41.3mm
Compression ratio	12.5:1
Fuel system	fuel injection
Transmission	6-speed, chain
Frame	aluminium twin spar
Front suspension	43mm fork
Adjustment	preload, compression, rebound
Rear suspension	rising-rate monoshock
Adjustment	preload, compression, rebound
Brakes front; rear	2x308mm discs/4-piston calipers; 220mm disc/single-piston caliper
Tyres front; rear	Pirelli Diablo 120/70 ZR17; 180/55 ZR17
Dry weight	165kg (claimed)
Wheelbase	1390mm
Seat height	815mm
Rake/trail	24.6°/89.1mm
Fuel capacity	18 litres
Fuel consumption	37mpg (est)
Insurance group	NU15
Colours	yellow, silver
Available from	Triumph UK 01455 251700

TRIUMPH
DAYTONA LAUNCH

Words: Chad - Pics: Gold & Goose

Triumph's first foray into the 600 class was such a disaster that they simply had to get the Daytona 600 right.

★ BRITISH BUILT 4-CYL 600 SPORTSBIKE
★ FUEL INJECTED
★ LIGHT WEIGHT AND COMPACT
★ FANTASTIC HANDLING
★ POWERFUL & BALANCED BRAKES
★ VERSATILE SPORTSBIKE

£6,999

After the disaster of the TT600, there was some doubt as to whether Triumph would be able to produce a competitive 600, particularly as the standards have improved so much for 2003. I was kind of hoping that Triumph would come up with something special though. After all, it is a small British manufacturer fighting the might of the Japanese, and I do like to support the underdog. Determined to give the Daytona a fair and thorough work out, I didn't even take full advantage of Triumph's hospitality the night before, although the free porn did keep me up slightly longer than I'd originally intended.

The Daytona looked striking in the early morning Spanish sunlight. The angular lines made it look more like a concept bike than a production model. From the front it looked friendly, yet also aggressive, with its angular mouth placed dead centre for optimum air supply to the air box. On looks alone it can stand proud with the rest of the 600s (especially with a union jack Valmoto paint job), something the old TT could never do.

The tank is both distinctive and functional. It's relatively wide at the seat and those rectangular shape box sections on its sides help keep your legs in place, and give something to lock your leg under when hanging off the bike mid corner. The Daytona feels larger than the new CBR, ZX-R and R6, but it's also very comfortable. The seat's soft and supporting, the bars relatively wide, and the pegs aren't wedged up your arse. It gives the impression of being the largest and heaviest of the 600s, although the statistics paint a different picture. It has the equal shortest wheelbase with the R6 and CBR, but it's lighter than either of them (or at least claims to be) by quite a few kilos.

Triumph had fitted a carbon race can to the launch bikes – not to effect power

output, they reckoned, but rather just to sound and look good. As Jack Valentine (team manager of Valmoto) put it:

"You can't have a standard sounding bike on the track, it just sounds shit."

I couldn't agree more.

After a few blips of the throttle, for no reason other than it sounded good, I followed Craig Jones, Junior British Superstock Champion and Triumph works rider, onto the track. Craig had previously agreed to show me a few lines around Cartagena and, desperate to impress him I wheelied onto the track from pit lane – lofting it in first with surprising ease before hooking second and playing with the

"...On the track with the ENGINE PINNED, it was a JOY TO THRASH..."

balance point up to the first corner. Considering I'd only ridden the bike about 20 feet I was astonished how easily it wheelied and how natural it felt. Arguably not the best way to rate a bike, but reaching the balance point so quickly gave instant confidence in the Daytona. It usually takes at least a few attempts to get that comfortable on a new bike.

After a few laps, Craig pulled into the pits and I had the whole of the Cartagena racetrack to myself. For a second I thought about taking it steady. I say for a second, 'cos as soon as I saw the main straight unfold from the last corner I nailed it. Fuck the foreplay, let's get it on.

The engine pulls hard, especially past 8,000rpm and right up to the 14,000rpm redline. Below 8K on the track it doesn't feel particularly strong, and on the road the soft bottom end is even more obvious.

Specifications

Engine	Liquid-cooled, DOHC in-line 4-cylinder
Capacity	599cc
Bore x Stoke	68x41.3mm
Compression	12.5:1
Fuelling	Fuel injection
Claimed Power	110bhp @ 12,700rpm
Claimed Torque	68.5nm @ 11,000rpm
Frame	Aluminum twin spar
Front Suspension	43mm conventional forks, fully adj
Rear Suspension	Monoshock fully adj
Front Brakes	Twin 308mm floating discs, 4 piston caliper
Rear Brakes	Single 220mm disc, single piston caliper
Wheelbase	1390mm
Seat Height	815mm
Dry Weight	165kg
Fuel Capacity	18litres
Price	£6,999
Manufacturer	Triumph 01455 251700

Technical Highlights

Triumph may have been the first to use fuel injection on a mass-produced 600, but their first attempt on the TT was a disaster. With the Daytona they worked closely with Japanese specialists Keihin to develop new, 38mm diameter, twin butterfly throttle bodies, similar to Suzuki's set-up.

Both inlet and exhaust ports as well as the combustion chamber have been reshaped and CNC cut to improve flow.

The length of the headers on the exhaust has also been re-tuned to suit the new intake arrangement, head porting and combustion chamber. The end result is a quoted 110bhp at 12,750rpm with peak torque at 11,000rpm.

The aluminium frame is brand new, incorporating a three-cell construction as opposed to the four cell of the original TT. The fully adjustable, 43mm cartridge forks benefit from a complete redesign, saving 1kg in the process.

Brake discs are down 2mm to 308mm, saving 170g on unsprung weight. The front discs are gripped by four piston calipers while the rear brake is a single 220mm disc.

The fuelling – the old TT600's Achilles heel – was faultless and the power progressive, it just seemed to lack thrust in the midrange. As a result I was using second more often than third for passing slower moving traffic.

On the track, with the engine pinned and never dropping below eight grand, it was a joy to thrash. The engine revs freely but, as I started to get into the groove, I noticed the Daytona's weak point – the gearbox. It isn't overly heavy, in a leaving-blisters-on-yer-foot kind of way like last year's R6, but it's clunky and requires a solid and distinctive kick on the selector. Hopefully this is just a prototype glitch.

The handling is excellent and the front end so, so confidence inspiring. Brakes have always been a Triumph strong point and these four-potters carry on that tradition. With so much feedback from the front-end, the brakes could be carried deep into the turn, right up to the apex. The Triumph technicians had set-up the bike slightly stiffer for the track than the road bike we rode in the afternoon, and it seems they'd definitely done their homework. The rebound as the brakes were released towards the apex was

"...mid corner the LEAN ANGLES were so ACUTE they were verging on BEING STUPID..."

spot-on and incredibly well controlled.

Even hard on the brakes, viciously letting out the clutch at high revs, firing down the gearbox aggressively couldn't get the back moving. I can't remember on any occasion all day where I felt the rear lift or move on the brakes. The rear is equally composed mid-corner, delivering

instant feedback from the new Pirelli Diablos, which is just as well because the Cartagena track is seriously demanding, combining fast chicanes and blind crests with long sweepers and hairpins. Determined to really push the bike I increased the pace for my third session. Braking later, leaning over further and

TRIUMPH RACING

JACK VALENTINE

How did the Triumph partnership come about?

I approached Triumph towards the end of last year.

What is it like working with Triumph compared to Honda and Yamaha?

It's far easier. If I need a part, or to ask some questions, I just pop down the road rather than dealing with Japan. Things get done quickly.

What were your first impressions of the bike?

We looked at parts all through development, so we already had a good idea what to expect before the bike arrived in mid-December. It's as good as any bike we've had before.

How's it going so far?

Amazingly well. This is the first part of a two-year plan and next year we're planning to be in World Supersport. We were pleased with Silverstone, but the bike is still very new and we tried a bit too hard, changing set up at the last minute, which affected our results.

Any problems with the bike?

No, you just have to remember we have to make all the parts, there isn't a kit you can buy from Japan. We have the engine producing nearly the same power as the R6 was pushing out last year, and that took us two years of development, we've only had the engine just four months, so there's plenty to come.

What are your ambitions this year?

We are out to win – the front row soon then the rostrum and wins.

What about road racing?

We're 90 per cent sure we'll be at the Isle of Man. Jim is confident the bike will do the job. We're planning a three-man team for the North West as practice, Jim Moodie, Bruce Anstey, and John McGuinness.

No Craig?

Craig has no ambition to road race, and I would never force anyone.

Any chance I could have a go round Oliver's Mount?

(Laughs) You must be joking, I've seen you ride.

JIM MOODIE

What were your first impressions of the bike?

I was so used to the R6 that the Daytona felt wide at the tank. The race bike felt excellent from the off, I knew straight away it had potential.

If you were a privateer rider, what would you change first?

Erm (pause), I suppose maybe the suspension, although the stock suspension is actually very good; we sometimes fit the standard shock if we are trying to eliminate a problem. For example we were having problems at Snet' so the other day at Croft we fitted the standard shock and went quicker.

How do you think it will run at the Isle of Man?

It's a good road bike out of the crate, which is what you need for the TT. It's probably a better road-racing bike than track bike at the moment.

Did you mind Craig beating you at Silverstone?

No because each race is like a test at the moment, we just want the bike on the front row so I wasn't that bothered. Sure if it was for first place I would be. Craig is a top lad, hugely talented and he fits in well with the team.

CRAIG JONES

What were your impressions when you first rode the bike?

From the start I could see the bike had huge potential.

What is it like riding for Jack and having Jim as a teammate?

Jim is like my mentor, I really look up to him. Jack's great also, anything I want changing is done instantly.

Who do you see as the main competition this year?

There are so many. Harris, Haslam, Crockford, Coates, Frosty if he gets the bike to handle – and obviously Jim.

What are the Triumph's strengths?

I can't really think of a weak point.

What are your hopes for this year?

I'm aiming to win – what else? Silverstone was a bad indication, we have a top class team, we'll be winning races soon.

"What the fuck have you done to your hair?"

getting on the power sooner, the Triumph remained rock steady. Mid-corner the lean angles were verging on the stupid side, the pegs brushing the ground on the odd occasion, but with still more ground clearance than

"...though I'm NOT THE TALLEST, the fairing did a good job..."

you'll ever need on the road. Later in the session I was firing through the fast chicane in third rather than second, still with effortless input through the pegs – nothing seemed to unsettle the bike or move it off line.

Away from the smooth racetrack I was slightly concerned that the quick steering might affect the handling and stability. I needn't have been. No matter how hard I tried to make it slap, even putting down the front slightly crossed up caused little to no reaction from the front. I later asked Craig if he ran a steering damper

on the race bike:

"Yeah it's fitted but I have it turned off – there's just no need to have it really."

The road section was a combination of a bit of hooligan riding – wheelying over third and fourth gear crests, flying up mountain passes – and steady touring. On the road the Triumph's usability really shone through, as I could appreciate the smaller details without concentrating on the racing line. The fairing does a reasonable job of keeping off the windblast, although I'm not the tallest member of staff. The seat is comfy, mirrors work well, and it's an easy bike to ride around town.

Triumph may be the last to enter the most competitive category of 2003 but being British and retailing at under £7,000 should help in the sales charts. The chassis and handling are excellent on the track, and the bike retains a high level of real world usability. Apart form the clunky gearbox, (which hopefully is only a problem on the early prototype models) it's a struggle to find any serious negatives.

So have Triumph won the fight with Japanese 600s, and the Italian 749? On first impressions they've got a serious contender, but only a back to back test will tell. ⚡

Welcome to
FIGHT CLUB

Triumph get their finger out and produce a sorted supersport 600. But can it go toe-to-toe with Honda's reigning CBR? Only one way to find out, let's get it on...

Triumph have a lot riding on the Daytona. Or rather, they need to get a lot riding on the Daytona to make up for a dearth of people riding the previous TT600. Despite all the claims and marketing razzle-dazzle they could muster, there was no denying the TT was a little, well, lame. Not much wrong with the chassis or brakes, admittedly, but the engine suffered with awful fuel injection, not to mention a lack of power, and the poor bugger was as exciting to look at as a Nissan Sunny. A success it was not.

Thankfully the Daytona seems to have addressed all the problems. Well, most of them. We came away from the launch seriously impressed with the handling and suspension quality, happier with the engine, unsure about the looks, and ranting how the new bike is a serious option over buying Japanese.

So it's time to prove it. Or disprove, of course.

Back in the March issue our 600s group test crowned the new, RCV-inspired Honda CBR600RR as top dog, so it's a head-to-head battle. We know the Suzuki GSX-R is still a devastating track weapon, and equally that Kawasaki's ZX-6R has the strongest engine and brakes, but we've not included them – as a complete package the CBR had them beat, so it's the benchmark for the bright yellow Hinckley flier. Points will be awarded on the basis of one for a win, and nothing for second place.

Donington Park has a heady combination of high-speed sweeps, flat stick straights and tight hairpins, so it's off to the Midlands first. Then several hundred miles on our favourite twisting B-roads around Lincolnshire and Cambridgeshire, with the odd dual carriageway thrown in, before measuring performance at Bruntingthorpe Proving Ground and a spell on BSD's overworked dyno.

This is what happens...

THE TESTERS

Bruce Dunn
In the blue corner. 37 year old welterweight Brucie. FB tester and 250 racer, he's fast and skilful, and punches above his weight.

Mike Armitage
In the food court. 28 year old heavyweight Mike. FB tester and 250 pounder, he's vast and rarely full, and launches above his weight.

TRIUMPH DAYTONA 600
Price: £6999
Top speed: 156.49mph
Power: 93.7bhp

ON THE TRACK

HANDLING

First impressions are, according to my mother, extremely important. And with supersport 600s, razor handling and pant-wetting corner speed not only win races but sell bikes too. Triumph obviously agree with Mrs A and understand their market, as both Bruce and I return from early track sessions babbling about the way the Daytona handles.

"On the day, out the crate, the Triumph is the bike to be on round here," says Bruce, almost with an air of disbelief. *"It's outstanding – it brakes, turns and holds a tight line everywhere, be they tight corners, left-right flicks or high speed sweeps."*

Never one to mince his words, Bruce has summed it up precisely. Get off the brakes (or trail to the apex if testicle size allows) and the Daytona flicks over to full lean with no effort. Steering is light and quick, and once on its ear only requires a nudge of bar or shift of ample (and increasing) body mass to revise a line or nip past slower riders.

By comparison the Honda feels as though it needs substantially more effort to change direction. It seems to have slow steering and missing agility, traits that weren't apparent during our group test. This is because it isn't slow steering and doesn't have stodgy handling. It's more than capable enough – the Triumph simply needs a lighter touch and responds to more nimble actions. The Daytona also nudges ahead of the CBR by offering more lean angle before the pegs meet the surface.

Neither bike suffers with instability on track, although the Honda has a more secure feel when tramping on. It's a very safe motorcycle at full lean, failing to misbehave even to my ham-fisted input. Darting from right to left while barrelling down Donington's glorious Craner Curves has the Triumph moving around very slightly, with a trivial motion about the headstock. It's nothing even nearing a problem, and actually a nice reminder it's a sharp handling sportsbike being ridden fast.

Both bikes have lovely suspension as well. Standard settings on each are good enough for hooning on track, but obviously could be slightly improved with tweaks. We don't feel the need on either, but as a chassis package for track use the yellow bike's finer.
Triumph 1, Honda 0

ENGINE AND GEARBOX

Of course even the twistiest tracks have sections devoid of turns, Donington being no different. Starkey's Straight under the Dunlop bridge, the Wheatcroft Straight over the start line, and the drive to and from the Melbourne Loop are all areas where it's nice to have a portion of go. Yes, we buy 600s for stunning handling balanced with usable performance, but it's nice if not too many R1s come past between corners – there's less to pass on the brakes then.

Both engines are 599cc, the Triumph having 1.2mm less stroke and slightly wider bore in the chase for revs. Despite this, a limiter ends play at 14,500rpm (on the clocks; 13,000rpm in real money), some 500rpm past the redline but short of

Big by modern 600 standards, the Daytona could wear 955i badges and still look right. If only the 955 actually handled like this...

■ Reaching for the stars - or the tarmac, whichever comes first...

■ The Daytona may respond easier, but the CBR feels ultra stable at full lean

["The Daytona flicks over to full lean with no effort. Steering is light and quick"]

the howling 15,000rpm of the Honda. Both bikes are past peak power by this point but the CBR's ability to over-rev is a handy tool, allowing gears to be held through corners where the Daytona needs an extra cog.

Gearing is causing debate. The CBR is on noticeably taller ratios, needing first (which is good for an indicated 78mph) for the Esses, Melbourne Loop and Goddards. It's screaming on the way in and out the turns, which is unsettling; the Daytona gets away with second without sacrificing drive, which suits numpties like me. It feels safer.

Proper racer-types like our very own Bruce may favour the Honda's ratios, though: *"The engine is brill, and revving it to 15,000rpm through the gears is deliriously addictive, helped by a gearbox that's slick and precise with well-spaced ratios. And the tall first gear is good for track work. By comparison the Triumph box is crap."*

It is as well. Too much lever travel and a notchy action aren't good, and neither is finding a false neutral heading into the Old Hairpin.

The lower gearing helps the engine on track,

though, as the Triumph is down on straight-line go. Once in its stride the CBR sneaks away, and with a smoother, more refined feel. It's a little uninspiring, with a linear delivery and no real top-end rush, but it *is* faster. Luckily, having gears closer together as well as lower ratios helps the Triumph disguise this. Gear selection is less critical – try and get drive in a gear too high and the CBR seems to take an age before getting going, where the Triumph spins up more readily. Keep the CBR on the boil in the right gear, however, and it'll show an underseat exhaust to the British contender.

Fuelling was a major flaw with the TT, and thankfully the new Keihin system adorning the Daytona is a giant leap forward. With the motor living above 10,000rpm on track, the only noticeable glitch is a small lurch when rolling the throttle back on going into the Old Hairpin. The Honda does it too, but you have to concentrate to notice it – it's more apparent on the Trumpet.

There's no denying the Daytona's engine is a vast improvement for Triumph, but it can't yet match the performance and elegant nature of the CBR's lump.

And its gearbox is nasty. Bruce: *"I know the bike is one of the first in the UK and was rushed to us, and we're extremely grateful. But for the gearbox of a new bike to be like this is pretty poor."*
Triumph 1, Honda 1

BRAKING
Both bikes have four-pot calipers on the forks, and both systems are good enough to lift the rear or sway the headstock about when used in anger.

Triumph have never skimped on stoppers and the Daytona maintains their high standards, but does so deceptively. There's a lot of lever travel, only requiring a small tug to bring the lever back. Initially it gives the impression the brakes aren't very good, until the bemused rider realises they've lost too much speed already. It's probably down to lever ratios – we had a Gas Gas supermoto last year with a big, fat four-pot caliper operated by the standard lever and master cylinder, and this exhibited the same properties (only to a higher degree) due to the ratio being different to the one the caliper was

designed for. Or something. Strangely Triumph's launch bikes weren't like this.

There's certainly enough power and feel from the Daytona's set-up, and once used to the lever action the thing can be slung in on a handful of brake without fear. The Honda offers a little more bite from less lever travel, giving the impression of better brakes. It's supported by a progressive increase in retardation and a little more power than the Triumph when it comes to oh-heck-I'm-going-to-taste-gravel braking situations. Back brakes? Yes, they both have them.

For my tastes, I can't decide whether I prefer the feel and light action of the Triumph, or the outright power and bite of the Honda. Bruce is more decisive, declaring the CBR to be better and swaying the point in Honda's direction.
Triumph 1, Honda 2

OVERALL LAP TIMES
It's nearly impossible to ride on track without someone asking which is better, by which of course they mean fastest.

We're at Donington on a trackday, so there's virtually no chance of a clear track for datalogging lap times. But it doesn't really matter, the Daytona's great chassis and agility (plus lower gears) make it the easier bike for both Bruce and I to go noticeably faster on. So in this duel, handling conquers performance. As an indication of what this means, I can almost hang with Bruce when he's on the CBR, but swap bikes and the Daytona whisks him away into the middle distance.

There is another limiting factor as well. Triumph kindly supply their bike on Pirelli Diablos, a capable road and track tyre, but the CBR turned up on Japanese-made Dunlop D208s – okay on the road, but not a match for the Pirellis on a track. Both Bruce and I experience enough out-the-seat moments to knock our confidence, and feeling the rear drift on a neutral throttle – like on the way into Redgate – isn't right.

"There's no excuse for a supersport bike being supplied on such low-performance tyres," says Bruce. Tell it like it is, boy. *"I can't believe how much it's moving around. On matching rubber the Honda would substantially close the gap, but the Triumph's great chassis and tyres gives it a strong advantage over the CBR."*
Triumph 2, Honda 2

ON THE ROAD
LOOKS
Away from the track, a scary number of people buy a bike for how it looks. Or because it matches the leathers they bought cheap at last year's NEC jumble sale. If a bike's a minger or uninspiring, there's more than a good chance it isn't going to sell very many. Did somebody say TT600?

Parked up at Donington, there's the expected interest in the two new bikes. Most point at the CBR, grin, crouch and look at the pipe, and make *"ooooh"* noises. They then turn to the Daytona, frown, run fingers over the bulges on the tank and make *"hmmm"* noises. Hmmm...

Being compact, slim and looking like that Rossi bloke's RCV are sure-fire selling points for the CBR. Triumph don't have a race bike to base their road bike on, so the look is completely new. Headlights and fairing are very tidy, but the sharp edges, bulbous tank and big seat unit seem to be leaving most folk cold. Better than the TT, yes, but as Bruce puts it: *"Triumph are wide of the mark. The CBR dates it already."* Good, but sadly, not quite good enough.
Triumph 2, Honda 3

BUILD AND FINISH
Hop aboard and the Triumph is bigger to sit on as well as look at. The CBR has a flat seat reminiscent of an SP-2, but the Daytona cossets buttocks with a degree of plushness, although it's higher than the Honda. Bars feel close and quite high, in an R6-stylee, but it's nearer in size to a GSX-R after jumping off the diminutive CBR. In fact the Honda is positively tiny – my 6ft 2in frame giving a view over the screen to the tip of the nose. Bruce is shorter and lighter, and favours the Honda's more focused seating position: *"It feels more compact than the Triumph, with a lower seat height and narrower tank, and comfort is good despite minimal seat padding."* Being taller and fatter, my carcass is happier slumped on the Triumph. So this one's a dead heat, and neither bike scores.

But flicking levers, pressing switches and wobbling plastics shows the Honda is better finished. All switchgear has a nice feel, where the

[**"The Daytona's engine can't match the performance and elegance of the CBR's"**]

■ The Triumph has the widest mirrors known to man. This is good, but makes the 600 look like a wasp...

Radial calipers-schmalipers. The Honda's brakes have loads of bite, without sacrificing feel, evidently...

Daytona seems a little flimsy and, I hate to say it, cheap. It also gets a trademark fragile-feeling Triumph ignition and the top fairing plastics are thin and lack the CBR's well-finished substance.

Turn the key and the Daytona tacho whips round while the digital display flashes into life, but the bike won't even turn over until it's done this, then sat for a couple of seconds and thought about what's for tea. A small but frustrating point. Turn the Honda's key and it'll fire straight away, and the display is nicer, too. Plus the CBR's brake lever has six positions over the Triumph's four.

Another point for the CBR, and it's starting to pull away...
Triumph 2, Honda 4

ENGINE AND GEARBOX
As we transfer to the road, it becomes more obvious the Honda's mill is the fitter of the pair. And it doesn't need its top two ratios – for example, an indicated 110mph in second gear almost matches my Kawasaki ZX-6R long termer in third.

Scooting round a track it's easy to keep the engines spinning; throw in some hedges, cars and horse muck, and the gap between the CBR and Daytona becomes wider. The Honda gets away time after time, and side-by-side in second the RR pulls away regardless of which rider is on it.

The Triumph claws back ground out of slower bends, where those lower ratios and a surprisingly decent midrange allow it to get the jump. Which is

nice. Unfortunately, it's a bit harsh next to the silky Honda, as well as being slower. Which isn't. The clunky gearbox still isn't too hot, either.

Both are terrible on fuel: over the course of a full day's heavy thrashing on the road, the Triumph only manages 28.2mpg, the fuel light coming on at 77 miles, while the Honda gulps away at 26.5 to the gallon. Anyone who wants to explain exactly how injection is cleaner and more efficient than carbs should write in immediately. In the meantime, the CBR gains another point for a nicer engine and gearbox, although the ballistic ZX-6R would waste both bikes.
Triumph 2, Honda 5

HANDLING
It's not party time for Honda yet, though. For charging down unknown backroads the sweet steering and turning ability of the Triumph make it easier to avoid ditches on than the Honda.

The CBR feels better on the road than it did on track, the chassis coming across as more sprightly. This could be down to Honda aiming the bike at road riders who will do the odd trackday, and not the other way round. It'll pick a line through stray spuds at the apex without a conscious effort from the rider, but the Daytona does it more easily still, down partly to those clip-ons being above the yoke.

If wasting hours on a roundabout constitutes your weekend fun then place your wedge with a Triumph dealer tomorrow. The Daytona pulls one back...
Triumph 3, Honda 5

CHASSIS
Racetracks don't have bumps. Well, no really big ones. The B660 is riddled with the things though, along with crests, surface changes and all manner of corners. After the launch we knew the Triumph's suspension was good, but suspected the high quality forks and Unit Pro-Link on the CBR would hold their own.

However Bruce is frothing after swapping the Honda for the Daytona: *"It's like riding round on £10,000's*

["The Daytona's outstanding – it brakes, turns and holds a tight line everywhere"]

worth of fancy suspension. The damping quality is stunning throughout the stroke, from full extension to fully compressed – it's got great control."

Praise indeed. Triumph have made a lot of noise about the single-rate springs, revised damping and lighter, aluminium internals in the forks, not to mention the reworked rear shock – and it seems they're completely justified. Despite steep geometry and quick steering the bike is stable too, remaining composed when common sense is warning a huge slapper or trip to A&E is on the cards.

The CBR stood out for its ride quality in our group test, and we stand by our comments – it is well sprung and damped. But it's a little harder than the Triumph on the road, which can perhaps get

away with mildly softer springs thanks to superb damping. Maybe. Whatever, the Honda lacks a bit of the Hinckley bike's plushness, and now the Daytona is reeling in the CBR...
Triumph 4, Honda 5

BRAKES
Which brings us to braking again. On the track Bruce swung for the CBR while I scratched my head; on the road we're both doing Stan Laurel impressions and sucking air past teeth. Outright power or feel? Bite or light action? We simply can't decide. Honours even, and the points stay the same:
Triumph 4, Honda 5

Triumph Daytona 600

Engine

■ Based on the TT600 mill but lighter and with proper injection, different electrics, revised cylinder head, new exhaust... the list goes on. Injection is Keihin using 38mm throttle bodies with twin butterflies like a GSX-R, with a 32-bit ECM watching over things. There's good attention to detail – the new head flows 2% more inlet charge and 11% more waste gas (they say), and combustion chambers are CNC-machined for accuracy. It feels a lot better, but the last TT we dyno'd made the same torque and 0.7bhp more. Ride the two back-to-back, though, and the Daytona would win

Chassis

■ The frame looks familiar but it's a new design, using extruded main beams with three internal cells over the TT's four. They claim this reduces weight but retains rigidity, and that there's a precise amount of flex designed in. Steeper rake, less trail and a shorter wheelbase help it slice through turns. Front end is rwu Kayaba with lighter internals, single-rate springs and revised damping. Out back there's a fully adjustable, remote-reservoir shock as found on the TT, but revalved. The Triumph brakes use smaller discs to reduce unsprung mass and gyroscopic inertia

■ Poor old Triumph. Having been slated for the boring TT600's looks, they pen this daring, angular design - and seem to be off the pace again. Lots will love it though

■ If only that redline was a few clicks higher...

■ Like other details - functional but uninspiring

PERFORMANCE

STRAIGHT LINE

Bruntingthorpe at the end of April and it's wet, cold and a touch windy. Not ideal for speed testing but still a direct comparison of the two bikes in identical conditions. Into a crosswind, through standing water, the Daytona hits 144.6mph and the CBR reaches 149.4mph. Pretty close. (While we're at Brunters, so is Kenny Roberts Snr testing his new V5 Proton KR MotoGP bike. We find out the largest Allen key in the Triumph's tool kit is the exact size for the rear sprocket bolts on the GP machine – Kenny and the boys are out for a spot of testing, and short on tools...)

We return when the sun comes out to try for actual flat-out speeds. And the Honda wins again, with 162.9mph to 156.5mph. Not so close. As far as standing quarters and top gear roll-ons are concerned, the Honda cleans up in both. And it pulls away on the points total again...
Triumph 4, Honda 6

POWER AND TORQUE

So to the dyno at Fenland's finest fettlers, BSD. Up to 10,500rpm the Triumph has the edge on power and torque. Yes, really. However the CBR holds on to its torque past 12,000rpm, allowing a crest to the power peak the Daytona can't match, with 101.3bhp to the Triumph's lowest-in-class 93.7bhp. The Honda also gets the edge on torque, although the Triumph has by far the nicer curve up to its peak – if the Triumph engineers could find another 1500rpm and maintain the shape, they'd have a class-leading lump.

But as it is, they haven't.
Triumph 4, Honda 7

▲ TOP SPEEDS & ACCELERATION

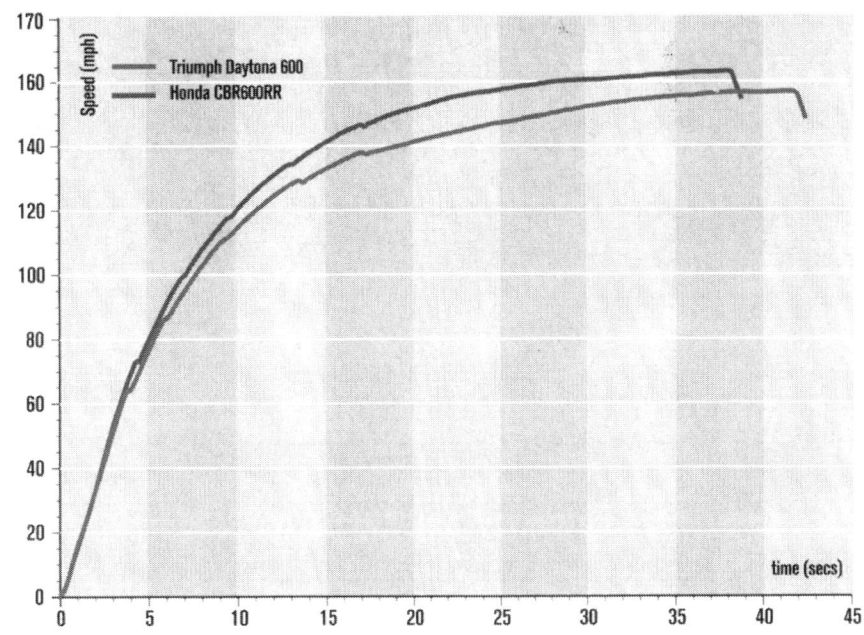

Triumph Daytona 600
Honda CBR600RR

	Honda CBR600RR	Triumph Daytona 600
Top speed	162.89mph	156.49mph
0-60mph	3.42s	3.53s
¼ mile	11.45s @ 128.34mph	11.75s @ 123.27mph
40-90mph roll-on	10.69s	13.39s
70-0mph braking	52.86metres	50.21metres

There's no arguing here – the CBR walks away with it. Honda's class-leading engine output lets the RR hit 140mph some five seconds before the Triumph does, by which time the CBR is well past 150mph. Giving both a fistful in top gear at 40mph may not mean a lot in the real world, but it shows the Honda's thrust advantage in the high gears as it hits 90mph nearly three seconds sooner. And it's quicker off the line, too. Oh well

Honda CBR600RR

Engine

■ Lightened, strengthened and seriously developed over the years, the latest, silky smooth incarnation of the CBR lump pushes things ever onward with over 100bhp, 15,000rpm and a lovely ability to rev on past peak power. Injection uses 40mm throttle bodies and separate injectors for high and low engine speed, with a virtually faultless delivery. Engine dimensions are compact and nick Yamaha's tried and tested stacked gearbox design, the ratios themselves being significantly taller than all the opposition. Good job it's got the most power, then

Chassis

■ Honda have jumped on the trendy bus, using a die-cast alloy frame and subframe instead of boring old extrusions. Design is remarkably similar to an R6 at a glance, and looks tiny. Forks offer nothing out of the ordinary, but check out the swingarm - it looks like it's been robbed straight from HRC. The top of the shock is fixed to the swingarm, the bouncy bit only being tied to the frame by the linkage. It must work, as it's appearing on more and more MotoGP tools. Damping and ride quality are superb, but more than matched by the new Triumph. Brakes borrowed from the FireBlade complete a sorted package

■ Years of refinement and the hunched-up, squat poise of Honda's RCV-like mass centralisation efforts are plain to see. One step ahead again, it would seem

■ That 15,000rpm redline is a useful tool on track

■ Swinger shames Triumph on looks, not on function

POWER & TORQUE

Triumph Daytona 600 93.7bhp @ 12,250rpm
Honda CBR600RR 101.3bhp @ 13,500rpm
Triumph Daytona 600 41.8ft-lb @ 10,750rpm
Honda CBR600RR 42.5ft-lb @ 11,000rpm

Ignore the fact the Honda has more power and more torque, and compare the shape of the curves. Up to 10,000rpm the Daytona has more of both, delivered in the smooth and linear manner Triumph boasted about at the launch. It's impressive, but the way the Honda holds on to its torque past 14,000rpm ultimately gives it a higher power peak. The CBR will also merrily rev past peak power, which is useful on track as it allows gears to be held through turns. The Triumph drops off more abruptly and hits a wall some 2000rpm earlier than the Honda, meaning more gearshifts or more considered ratio selection on track. Chasing the Honda on the road, it's also too easy to find the limiter as the Daytona needs to be used hard to keep touch. Maybe between them Triumph and ValMoto can find another 1500rpm for next year

THRUST CURVES

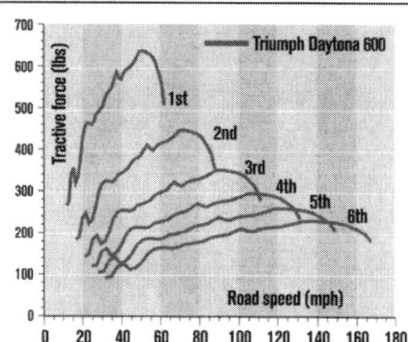

Think of these curves as a measure of how hard the bike boots you up the arse in each gear. These are nice, smooth curves, showing good driveability for the Triumph. Slightly higher peaks at lower speeds in the bottom gears show why the Daytona feels more lively...

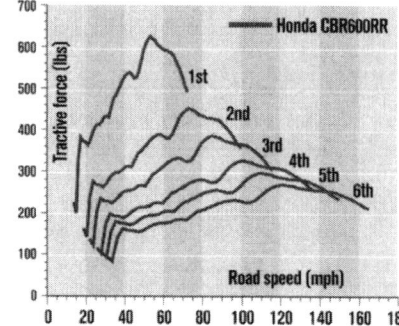

...but look at how the Honda makes substantially more thrust from third gear onwards. Dips in the curve correspond to the drop in torque at around 8750rpm, and the peaky nature of the thrust in first makes it seem a bit flat unless caned. From 80mph onwards it kicks arse, though

◄ After the heat of battle, the bikes lick their wounds amid bucolic splendour...

So the Honda CBR600RR wins over the Triumph Daytona 600. Seven points to four is a fairly substantial margin, but it's not the whole story – these two are closer than it appears. Let's do a quick comparison with another rival to these bikes, Suzuki's much-loved GSX-R600. We know from our group test and hundreds of datalogger traces that it loses out to the CBR on the track as far as engine and brakes go, but wins on the chassis and lap time front – two points each. On the road, it again loses on engine and brakes as well as looks and gizmos/finish and also on ride quality, only gaining a point back for the chassis agility again. Three to Suzuki, seven to Honda. And seeing as the Suzuki went faster, the Honda made more power and they had virtually identical quarter mile times, we'll leave the points tally at that. It's an even more convincing win for the Honda than over the Daytona, but the GSX-R is a great bike. It's just not as complete as the CBR. And it's the same case with the Triumph.

The Daytona is blessed with an extremely capable and easy-to-use chassis, and frankly stunning suspension. Brakes are good, but the engine is unfortunately off the pace. It's not the wheezing mill of the TT, but it's still not quite there. And the gearbox is too agricultural. If it looked as good as Natalie Imbruglia we could forgive it, but the angular and sizeable design already looks dated next to the CBR.

By contrast the Honda doesn't really have a flaw. The suspension is superb, just not quite as well damped as the Triumph's, it's got a smooth, powerful engine, equally strong brakes and looks bang on the money. It won't hold the Daytona on track, but it does stay in gear when it's expected to.

So the CBR keeps the top spot. But while the Daytona may not have won, it's still a blinding bike – if the CBR isn't for you, don't buy Japanese until you've tried one. ★

TELL YOU WHAT I THINK...

■ **Bruce Dunn:** *"I'd choose the CBR600. It looks tricker, makes more power and with better tyres should be as quick on track. It's more compact, the engine's great, brakes have power and feel, and I can't really fault the handling.*

"For track work the Daytona is stunning. It pissed all over the CBR at Donington, the standard tyre and the chassis gave a strong advantage, despite being less powerful. Suspension is posh - forks have a smooth, creamy feel with lovely damping throughout the travel and the rear shock works well too. Brakes are strong, but the gearbox can need effort to swap cogs, and the motor requires a good flogging to get the most out of it. At the end of the day a serious supersport contender shouldn't be 8% down on power. Add the not-quite-right looks, and the CBR edges ahead."

■ **Mike Armitage:** *"It's difficult to call. On paper, test strip and dyno the CBR has it, and after riding them on road and track I accept the CBR is the better bike.*

"But... given the choice I'll take handling over power any day, and on track the Daytona turns and inspires in a way the Honda can't. It's the same on the road, where suspension action is superb. There's no hiding the fact the slower engine needs abusing to keep up, but it feels raw and has a bit of character where the CBR is a little too sanitised - I can't help but find it a bit uninspiring. The bigger Triumph also suits my build, and everyone will have a CBR, won't they?"

THANKS

■ Triumph for getting a Daytona to us before everyone else
■ Honda for producing a CBR after only 10 minutes notice
■ Hottrax for places on their lovely trackday (www.hottrax.co.uk or 01908 330445)

SPECIFICATIONS

	Honda CBR600RR	Triumph Daytona 600
Price	£6799	£6999
Contact	Honda UK 01753 590500	Triumph 01455 251700
Engine		
Type	liquid-cooled, four-stroke, dohc, 16v, inline four	liquid-cooled, four-stroke, dohc, 16v, inline four
Bore x stroke	67 x 42.5mm, 599cc	68 x 41.3mm, 599cc
Compression ratio	12.0:1	12.5:1
Fuel system	PGM electronic injection, 40mm throttle bodies	Keihin injection, 38mm throttle bodies
Transmission	6-speed	6-speed
Chassis		
Frame type	cast aluminium alloy twin spar	aluminium beam perimeter
Front end	45mm rwu fork, fully adj.	43mm rwu fork, fully adj.
Rear end	Unit Pro-Link monoshock, fully adj.	monoshock, fully adj.
Front brake	4-pot calipers, 310mm discs	4-pot calipers, 308mm discs
Rear brake	2-pot caliper, 220mm disc	1-pot caliper, 220mm disc
Tyres	120/70-ZR17 Dunlop D208 180/55-ZR17 Dunlop D208	120/70-ZR17 Pirelli Diablo 180/55-ZR17 Pirelli Diablo
Dimensions		
Wheelbase	1390mm	1390mm
Rake/trail	24°/95mm	24.6°/89.1mm
Measured wet weight	203.5kg	200.5kg
Seat height	820mm	815mm
Fuel capacity	18 litres	18 litres

FACE OFF

The theory is that a capacity hike should put Triumph's new Daytona 650 on the pace – but does it? Suzuki's impressive GSX-R600 asks the hard questions

WORDS BY DAMON FANSON • PHOTOGRAPHY BY CHIPPY WOOD

Triumph Daytona 650
£6499, 646cc, 101bhp, 165kg
Triumph take on the Japanese in
the most tightly contested class.
Does big-cube cheating win out?

Suzuki GSX-R600
£6849, 599cc, 97bhp, 161kg
The class leader of 2004 and
the latest of a long dynasty
of hard-core track 600s.

SUZUKI'S GSX-R600 is our favourite 600, currently leader of the track-rep middleweight field and one hell of a benchmark against which to measure the latest Brit kit. Unchanged for 2005, it will certainly remain very competitive against next year's crop of revised sports 600s, so if the Daytona 650 can live with the Suzuki, then it can live with any of them.

Only tiny degrees of difference separate the bikes in this most competitive of classes, but the GSX-R just edged ahead of the 2004 pack, mainly thanks to its beautiful balance of midrange power, fleetness of tyre and, well, beautiful balance.

Balance was also what the Triumph Daytona 600 was all about. It had a well-deserved reputation for fine handling, was spacious and comfortable for such an agile machine and the only major gripe levelled against it was a weak-ish engine, 5bhp down on the Japanese bikes at the top end, with a big flat-spot in the lower midrange. All it needed to mix it with the big boys was more oomph and cleaner fuelling.

The easiest way of getting on peak power and midrange terms, while providing the extra torque to carry it through the fuelling glitch, was to make the engine bigger. Cheating? Maybe, but they're not the first and the 636cc Kawasaki ZX-6R has certainly gained acceptance, despite its capacity hike, so let us also allow the Daytona the same honorary 600 status. Unless we're taking our bikes racing at weekends the Triumph's extra 47 cubes mean very little to the road rider.

Whereas Kawasaki bored-out their ZX-6R to go 636cc, Triumph have altered the crankshaft's throw to increase the stroke, increasing capacity to 646cc. Both approaches will raise power and torque, but a longer stroke will tend to deliver the goods further down the rev-range. And in the Daytona's case, the fattening of the lower midrange should be just the thing to overcome the biggest criticism of the 600cc version, that midrange hole, while helping the powerplant to meet the 600-class standard 97bhp.

So what's new in the Daytona's chassis department? Nowt, bar a new black exhaust finish and a direct gear shift. Components look dated: conventional starving-whippet forks; skinny spindles; and an unbraced swingarm. The brakes, Brembo-alike four-pot calipers, were the cutting edge just a couple of years back, but can't match the spangle factor of anodised upside-downies tricked-up with radially mounted stoppers. But then, none of this can be seen from the saddle and in action the Daytona 600's chassis was already a match for any sporting road bike out there.

What can be seen from the seat is hardly art. The clocks have the usual functions, are clear ➤

to read, but look very bland and stale. Beyond them the fairing's cockpit lacks inners, which would be of no practical purpose, but this cheapens the view.

The Triumph has its own identity, a very distinctive, blunt outline and it looks big sat next to the GSX-R600. Its very angular looks mark it out as something of an odd fish, but this and the generous dimensions don't necessarily translate to a bad thing. The Daytona stands out from the pack and size means space, means comfort.

Start your engines

The dyno says Triumph's tactics have worked and the way it rides backs up the squiggly lines. The Daytona 650 has shuffled its way from bottom to top of the horsepower pack, level with the ZX-6R (2004-model) at 101bhp. The Triumph, though, makes its power at lower revs and wins the torque war hands down. On the road the 650 feels faster and more frantic than the old 600, yet at the same time it manages to be smoother and more tractable. The extra ccs win from all angles.

There is still fluffing through a low-to-middle-rev power transition, especially at part throttle, but it's nowhere near so noticeable as it was on last year's bike and the big hole around 5500rpm has, to a large extent, been filled. There remains a dip, though – enough that the Daytona 650, like the previous 600 version, still clears its throat and picks up power suddenly at around 6000rpm, whacking the front wheel into the air like a wildly tuned Yamaha RD350LC with Pavarotti riding pillion. It's great fun – but also goes some way to demonstrate the lack of refinement in the bike's fuel injection system. As does the comparatively rough and grumbly running below 5000rpm.

The Suzuki, with its two throttle valves, is outstanding in silkiness right across its wide rev-range and, for a 600, is mega chunky through the middle. Though it will pick up cleanly whatever the revs, there's little going on grunt-wise below 4000rpm, from where the midrange kicks in with incredible gusto and more motive urge than 600ccs have any right to produce.

There's no dramatic power step as the revs rush on, no wheel-hoisting lunacy. The overriding sensation rises from under the GSX-R's tank – somebody is torturing howler monkeys in the airbox. The roar emitted by this road legal bike is nothing short of incredible, intoxicating. Whether by accident or design, it does not require a fruity end-can to make it sing.

Though the Triumph has a less evocative soundtrack, a fractionally slower throttle response and fluffs a bit at the foot of the rev-scale, its new

Yellow doubles: even the fairing cut-outs are very similar

This is easier on the GSX-R, thanks to lovely low-speed fuelling

Without even Swifty to listen to his tales, Damon got the hump

cubes are working hard for it, backing up the bike's credentials as a superb all-round middleweight road bike in a sharply focused race-rep world. The Daytona can run around in the midrange, pulling more strongly past traffic than it did as a 600. Or let it off the leash and spin it up to five figures. Only in town does the Daytona's more primitive fuelling irritate and it takes a few revs to get it off the line and clear the rough running zone.

But more annoying still, if you do a lot of stop/start riding, is the injection's insistence on reverting to cold start mode when you fire it up, regardless of the engine temperature. It's several minutes after every restart until the revs drop back to tickover. This might burn a tad more fuel, but it doesn't go all the way to explain why the Triumph, at 35mpg, got five miles less from a gallon than the Suzuki did in damp conditions. This all but eliminated any advantage the Triumph may have got by carrying an extra litre of fuel, both bikes' fuel lights coming on at around 120 miles.

Technically the Triumph's engine performance is inferior to the Suzuki's,

SECOND OPINION

I may be accused of bias, being a GSX-R owner, but the Suzuki is a better bike. Everything about it feels tighter, sharper, from the brilliant front brakes to the smoother, snappier engine. The Triumph makes more power, but the Suzuki's engine still manages to feel better. It's less coarse, doesn't feel as stressed and the low-speed fuelling is superior. The Daytona's chassis is one of the best. It's so light to turn in, yet remains utterly stable. The supersport 600s are all great bikes, including the Daytona 650.

Paul Swift, Staff writer

being neither so smooth nor, in terms of power delivery, as linear. But it feels stronger in the top half of the revs and goes like a chuffing rocket. It's plain old exciting. More exciting than the flawless Suzuki. Much like a Kawasaki ZX-6R, you can really feel the extra cubes and the Triumph pulls like a 750 of just a few years past – except with less mass to push and on a shorter wheelbase. And, just like a ZX-6R, it wheelies right through to third gear if you've got the throttle to the stop and push up through the gearbox.

Overall the Triumph's transmission, while no slouch, is less precise than the Suzuki's and requires a more concerted shift, especially first-to second. Like the rest of the engine unit it's not perfect, but it's plenty good enough to keep it in the hunt.

Show us your chassis

The old Daytona 600 had a deserved reputation for being a fantastic handler. While running one as a long-term test bike last year I spent a summer marvelling at its huge reserves of lean and turn. With nothing meaningful changed on this model, >

Above **See that corner? He's on one of the best tools there is to go round it**
Below **The standard-setting Suzuki won't leave the Triumph into or out of bends**

'I can't think of a comparable blend of comfort and agility'

we should be able to expect more of the same – except that now the chassis has to handle more than ten per cent more power. But I wasn't disappointed. It brushes off the extra go with ease.

The new bike still has an inherent rightness, incredible balance and a standard set-up that combines compliance with feel. The chassis deals effortlessly with the motor's output and the level of feedback – combined with the way weight is transferred front to rear, and vice versa – gives the confidence to play at the edges of tyre adhesion. Accuracy, stability and predictability are at the top of the play list. The spring rates and damping are so in tune with the chassis I'd almost believe this bike had been for a specialist re-valve. It is a joy to chuck around and a delight midcorner.

Of course, so is Suzuki's pocket missile. It turns a touch faster, but the trade-off for this is a hint of 'nervousness' and for road riding the Triumph inspires a degree more confidence. In pure pace terms, corner-through-corner on real roads, there's nothing to split these two. But the Triumph, for me, does sneak an advantage, simply by being higher and wider while feeling no heavier.

The relatively lofty saddle and bars make the Daytona's riding position more VFR than CBR and the consequent advantage – besides comfort – is a better view of the road and more relaxation. Wider bars also give plenty of leverage, further enhancing the bike's flickability. By no means is the Suzuki particularly uncomfortable or a poor distance bike, but the extra size makes the Triumph a clear winner on motorways and when you just want to knock the pace off a bit. Unless you want to knock the pace off in a real hurry…

The brakes on this Daytona 650 don't feel quite so immediately responsive as the brakes on the 600 I ran last year – especially in the wet. They get better with heat and, indeed, familiarity. Or perhaps it's just that the braking game has moved on this year. With the latest radial-mount kit, the Suzuki has a superb directness and immediacy at a digit's brush of the lever and, good as they are, the Triumph brakes just don't have this feel.

Can the Daytona 650 cut it?
Yes it can. But the latest GSX-R600 is still technically the best middleweight sportsbike out there right now. It's more compact, solidly assembled and drips trick bits. And that fuelling. Compared with the Triumph, almost everything about the Suzuki looks more modern and feels that two per cent crisper: controls, gearbox, brakes and fuelling. Some of these factors could be down to each bike's individual preparation (and Suzuki generally prepare their press bikes immaculately), but I fear the difference lies a little deeper than that. A company the size of Triumph simply does not have the resources to stay on the pace and match the Japanese firms' rate of change.

Nevertheless I, personally, would still prefer to own the Daytona because in this most competitive and refined of classes the criticisms are at the level of minor detail. It's just as quick as the Japanese bikes, with unrivalled road manners, pulls the most ludicrous twist-and-shout wheelies and I'll suck my Sidis if it's not within two per cent of 600-class all-comers on the racetrack.

I also like the British offering because it's got some character. Most of all, though, I like the Triumph because it fits me and the kind of

Both bikes love this sort of thing. The Triumph excels here

The giveaway. Black silencer and stickers differentiate the new 650

Extra 50cc leads to 101 lovely bhp. He's looking at porn

riding I most like to do – long, fast road rides and track work. Hopefully in conjunction.

There are times when I might like to jockey something the size of a 250 race bike – like in a 250 race, if I dared – but most of the time I want a level of comfort that allows me to enjoy those long, fast rides. Even for a sleek and gorgeous 5ft 8in, the GSX-R feels small. Swifty, six very odd foot of butcher's pencil, rode with me for a portion of the test period. He is a dyed-in-the-gusset GSX-R600 fan – he owns one, loves it, thrives on his racy Telefonica self-image and is unshakeable in his Gixxer love. He remarked on the Daytona's throttle response, commented on the cold start issue, didn't much like the way it looked, but he was amazed at the Triumph's composure in the twisties.

If it fits you, and if you like things a bit different, then the Daytona is as good and as quick, as any 600. If you want the sports tourer angle then it's the best. Perhaps not on a detail-by-detail countback, but it all comes together very well. I can't think of a comparable blend of comfort and agility.

The Daytona also has the keenest list price of the sports 600s, but Triumphs tend to see less discounting than the market-flooding Japanese models, so prices tend to level out mid-summer. If you're looking for a damn quick and fine-handling new sports 600-ish, it would be foolish to overlook the Daytona 650. Roll-on the Bike Test Route and the big test of 2005's 600s. ∎

SUZUKI GSX-R600

Price	£6849
Top speed	148mph
Power	97bhp @ 13,200rpm
Torque	43lb.ft @ 10,900rpm
Engine	599cc, 16v, dohc, in-line four
Bore x stroke	67 x 42.5mm
Compression ratio	12.5:1
Fuel system	fuel injection
Transmission	6-speed, chain
Frame	aluminium twin spar
Front suspension	43mm usd telescopic fork
Adjustment	preload, compression, rebound
Rear suspension	monoshock
Adjustment	preload, compression, rebound
Brakes front; rear	2 x 300mm discs/four-piston calipers; 220mm disc/two-piston caliper
Tyres front; rear	Dunlop D208 120/70 ZR17; 180/55 ZR17
Dry weight	161kg (claimed)
Wheelbase	1400mm
Seat height	825mm
Fuel capacity	17 litres
Fuel consumption	40mpg
Insurance	NU14
Colours	black, blue, yellow
Available from	Suzuki UK 01293 518000

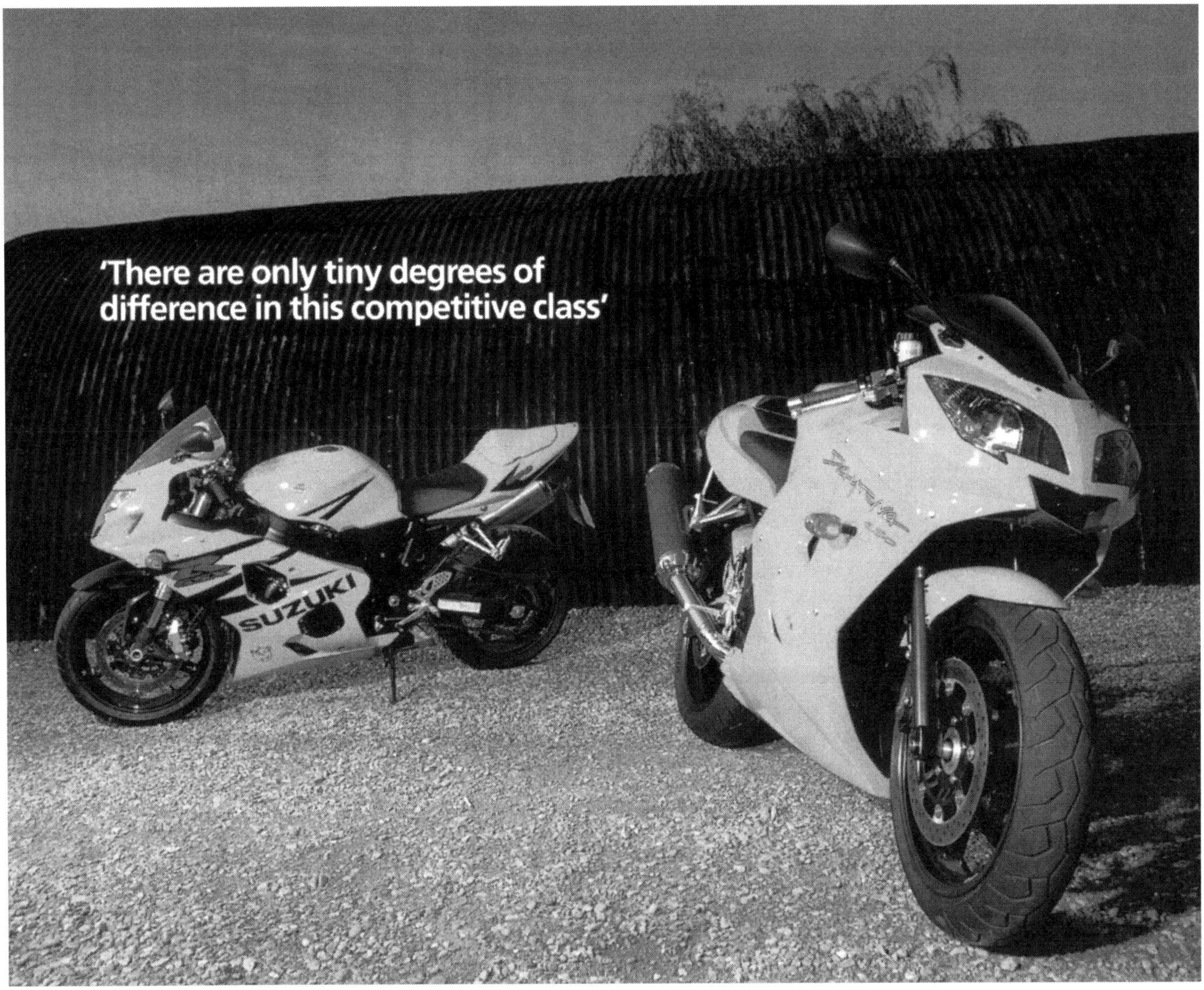

'There are only tiny degrees of difference in this competitive class'

TRIUMPH DAYTONA 650

Price	£6499
Top speed	156mph (est)
Power	101bhp @ 12,300rpm
Torque	46lb.ft @ 10,600rpm
Engine	646cc, 16v, dohc, in-line four
Bore x stroke	68 x 44.5mm
Compression ratio	12.8:1
Fuel system	fuel injection
Transmission	6-speed, chain
Frame	aluminium beam perimeter
Front suspension	43mm telescopic forks
Adjustment	preload, compression, rebound
Rear suspension	monoshock
Adjustment	preload, compression, rebound
Brakes front; rear	2x308mm discs/four-piston calipers; 220mm disc/single-piston caliper
Tyres front; rear	Pirelli Diablo 120/70 ZR17; 180/55 ZR17
Dry weight	165kg (claimed)
Wheelbase	1390mm
Seat height	815mm
Fuel capacity	18 litres
Fuel consumption	35mpg
Insurance group	NU15
Colours	red/yellow
Available from	Triumph 01455 453188

DYNO TEST

Dyno graphs explained

As well as the Daytona 650 and GSX-R600, we've included the Kawasaki ZX-636R and the old Daytona 600 for comparison. Immediately, Triumph's improvements are apparent: the lowest line on both graphs is the old 600; the highest line on both graphs is the new 650. But the still-poor fuelling shows up too. Look at the torque lines, they're near identical in shape, with the same dips. In particular, the huge dive at 3000rpm makes pulling away difficult. The GSX-R looks to be weaker on the dyno, but feels less so on the road.

120
100
80
60
40
20
0
0 2 4 6 8 10 12 14 16

50
45
40
35
30
25
20
15
10
5
0
0 2 4 6 8 10 12 14 16

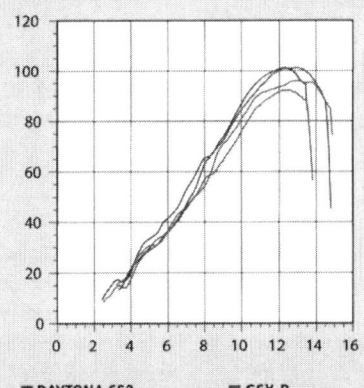

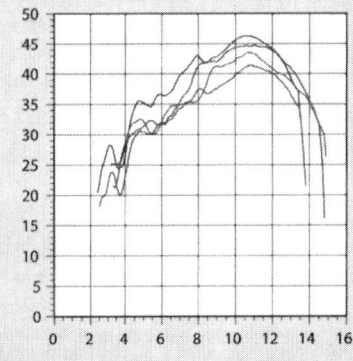

■ DAYTONA 650
101.4bhp @ 12,300rpm
46.3lb.ft @ 10,600rpm

■ GSX-R
97bhp @ 13,000rpm
43.6lb.ft @ 10,700rpm

■ ZX-6R
101.4bhp @ 12,900rpm
44.8lb.ft @ 11,000rpm

■ DAYTONA 600
92.2bhp @ 12,500rpm
41.5lb.ft @ 10,800rpm

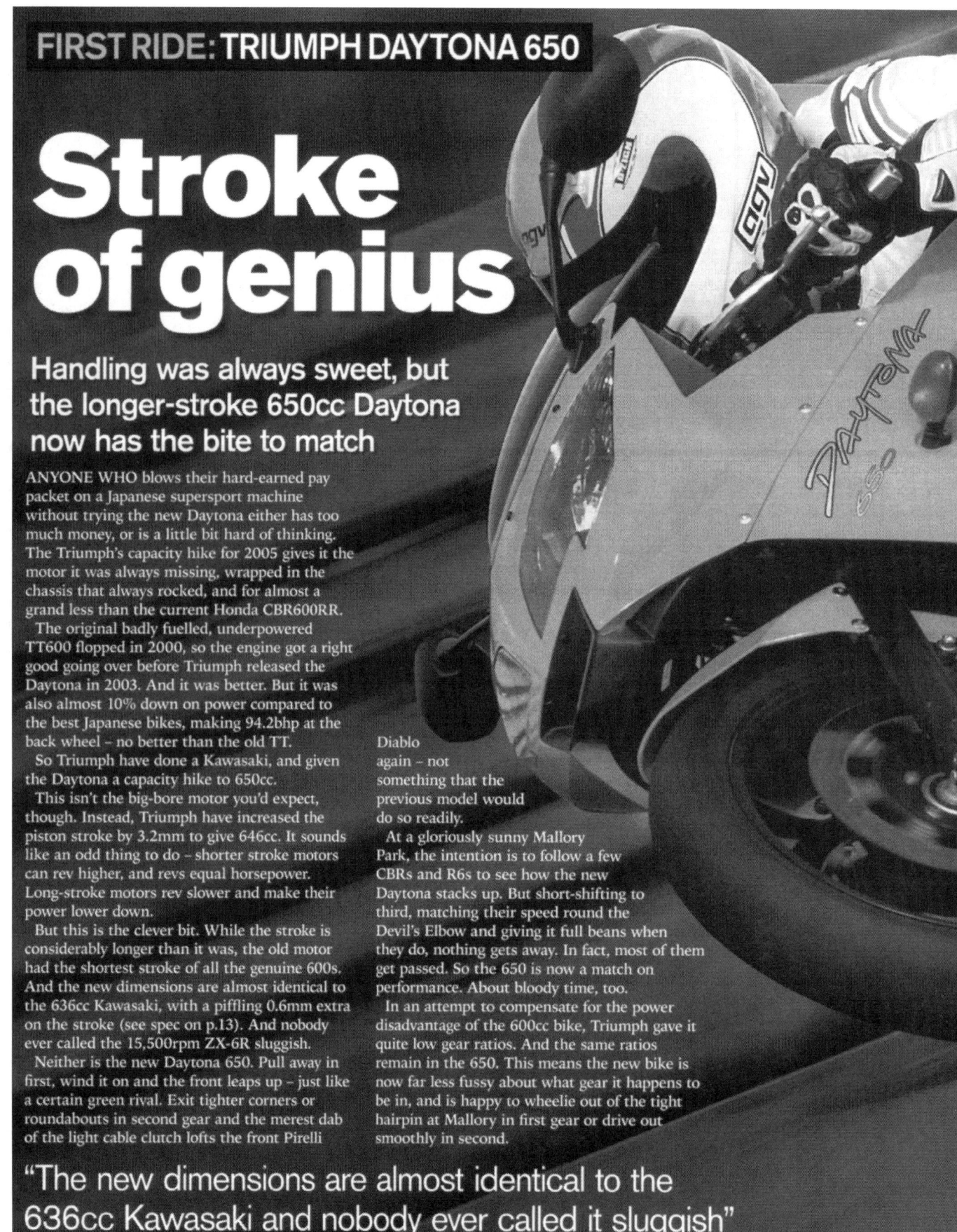

FIRST RIDE: TRIUMPH DAYTONA 650

Stroke of genius

Handling was always sweet, but the longer-stroke 650cc Daytona now has the bite to match

ANYONE WHO blows their hard-earned pay packet on a Japanese supersport machine without trying the new Daytona either has too much money, or is a little bit hard of thinking. The Triumph's capacity hike for 2005 gives it the motor it was always missing, wrapped in the chassis that always rocked, and for almost a grand less than the current Honda CBR600RR.

The original badly fuelled, underpowered TT600 flopped in 2000, so the engine got a right good going over before Triumph released the Daytona in 2003. And it was better. But it was also almost 10% down on power compared to the best Japanese bikes, making 94.2bhp at the back wheel – no better than the old TT.

So Triumph have done a Kawasaki, and given the Daytona a capacity hike to 650cc.

This isn't the big-bore motor you'd expect, though. Instead, Triumph have increased the piston stroke by 3.2mm to give 646cc. It sounds like an odd thing to do – shorter stroke motors can rev higher, and revs equal horsepower. Long-stroke motors rev slower and make their power lower down.

But this is the clever bit. While the stroke is considerably longer than it was, the old motor had the shortest stroke of all the genuine 600s. And the new dimensions are almost identical to the 636cc Kawasaki, with a piffling 0.6mm extra on the stroke (see spec on p.13). And nobody ever called the 15,500rpm ZX-6R sluggish.

Neither is the new Daytona 650. Pull away in first, wind it on and the front leaps up – just like a certain green rival. Exit tighter corners or roundabouts in second gear and the merest dab of the light cable clutch lofts the front Pirelli Diablo again – not something that the previous model would do so readily.

At a gloriously sunny Mallory Park, the intention is to follow a few CBRs and R6s to see how the new Daytona stacks up. But short-shifting to third, matching their speed round the Devil's Elbow and giving it full beans when they do, nothing gets away. In fact, most of them get passed. So the 650 is now a match on performance. About bloody time, too.

In an attempt to compensate for the power disadvantage of the 600cc bike, Triumph gave it quite low gear ratios. And the same ratios remain in the 650. This means the new bike is now far less fussy about what gear it happens to be in, and is happy to wheelie out of the tight hairpin at Mallory in first gear or drive out smoothly in second.

"The new dimensions are almost identical to the 636cc Kawasaki and nobody ever called it sluggish"

Using a bigger engine isn't cheating, it's sensible. Okay, it's cheating, but who cares when it's this good

Looks the same, goes round corners the same, but fires out the other side faster

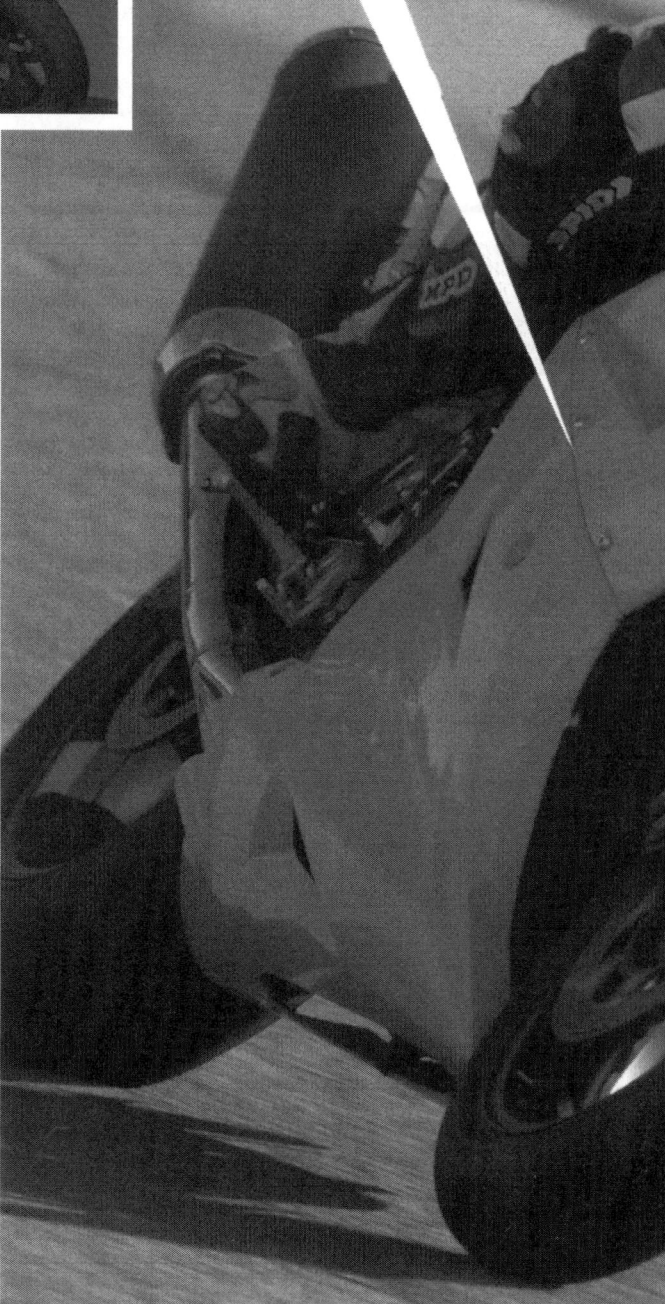

ENGINE

The old Daytona had a bore and stroke of 68 x 41.3mm, compared to 67 x 42.5mm for the CBR and GSX-R, and 65.5 x 44.5mm for the R6. A short stroke means the piston's average speed is lower at any given revs, as it has less distance to cover, so maximum engine speed can be increased. The Triumph's stroke was easily the stubbiest in the supersport class so, by increasing the stroke by 3.2mm to give 68 x 44.5mm and enlarging capacity to 646cc, Triumph haven't ended up with a slow-revving, long stroke motor at all. In fact, the stroke is identical to that of Yamaha's howling R6, while compression increases to match the ZX-6R at a heady 12.8:1. Claimed output is 112bhp at the crank, but we measured 101.3bhp at the back wheel on the dyno.

Other modifications include a gear linkage that acts directly on the shift drum, making for lighter gear changes, revisions to the injection and engine management to give a much needed ability to over-rev right up to an indicated 15,000rpm, and a completely new slipper clutch.

The old bike had a gearshift with all the finesse of a pissed-up Chris Moyles, but the linkage now acts directly on the shift drum, and the action is light and smooth.

There's also a slipper clutch to stop the rear locking up on downshifts or chattering when hard on the front brakes. Pretty irrelevant on the road (although going down two gears too many and leaving black lines is a lot of fun). But the Daytona isn't as smooth as it should be banging down three gears for the hairpin.

Triumph have also tweaked the electrics and injection gubbins. Where the old bike eventually wheezed to peak output then stopped dead just past 13,500rpm, the 650 merrily whips past its peak, nodding politely to the 14K redline as it flies by to meet the limiter at an indicated 15,000rpm (we stress indicated – peak power of 101.33bhp is at 12,300rpm and it's all over by 13,500rpm).

At the track, this ability to over-rev lets you hold a gear for longer than you otherwise would. On the road it just makes things more fun – giving you the option of sticking another gear in around 12,000rpm or wringing its neck.

The chassis has always been a peach. At a previous test at Donington the Daytona's handling and steering were spot on. In fact, it felt like it had some expensive aftermarket suspension fittted. And nothing's changed on the new bike.

However, the brakes may be getting left behind a bit. We've always liked Triumph's stoppers, but doing back-to-back sessions at Mallory is enough to cook the Daytona's set up. What were strong enough to only need two fingers at the start of day need all four, a dab of rear and frantic down shifts by lunch. Away from the track, there shouldn't be any problems, but will we see the radial-mounted calipers from the new Speed Triple next year?

Despite a sharp, aggressive nose, the bikes's blend of curves and edges doesn't work from certain angles. And it looks big compared to some rivals. The clocks look a bit dull and plasticky, as well.

But the riding experience is brilliant. If you just want a bike to gawp at get an MV Agusta.

But if you fancy a sports bike that steers like a 250, devours corners, is substantial enough to be comfy over long distances and can hang with the best in its class on the straights, the Daytona has to be on your shortlist.

Had the new bike been included in our last 600s group test, its 152.9mph top speed (in wet and windy conditions, just like the group test) would have beaten them all except the 154mph ZX-6R, with a top gear roll-on time midway between the ZX-6R and CBR600RR.

The main difference between the new Daytona and its Japanese rivals is that it's significantly cheaper, and there's nothing like some new leathers and a lid to go with your new bike.

Mike Armitage

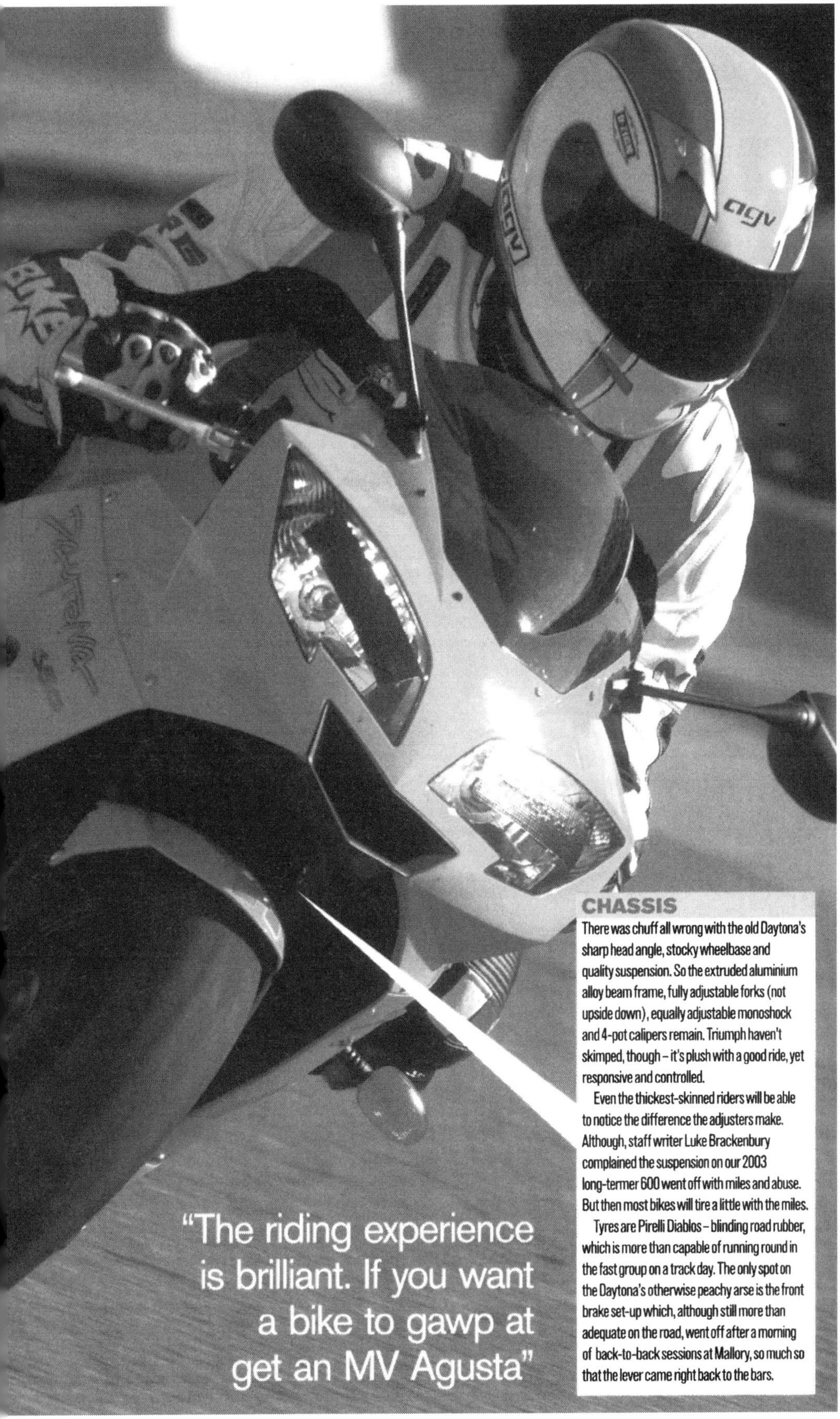

Functional but plasticky and on the dull side

Not an exhaust silencer in sight. Wonderful

Brakes faded after hard use on the track

CHASSIS

There was chuff all wrong with the old Daytona's sharp head angle, stocky wheelbase and quality suspension. So the extruded aluminium alloy beam frame, fully adjustable forks (not upside down), equally adjustable monoshock and 4-pot calipers remain. Triumph haven't skimped, though – it's plush with a good ride, yet responsive and controlled.

Even the thickest-skinned riders will be able to notice the difference the adjusters make. Although, staff writer Luke Brackenbury complained the suspension on our 2003 long-termer 600 went off with miles and abuse. But then most bikes will tire a little with the miles.

Tyres are Pirelli Diablos – blinding road rubber, which is more than capable of running round in the fast group on a track day. The only spot on the Daytona's otherwise peachy arse is the front brake set-up which, although still more than adequate on the road, went off after a morning of back-to-back sessions at Mallory, so much so that the lever came right back to the bars.

"The riding experience is brilliant. If you want a bike to gawp at get an MV Agusta"

SPEC

TRIUMPH DAYTONA 650

PRICE	£6499
COLOURS	red, yellow
WARRANTY	two years, unlimited mileage
AVAILABILITY	right about now
CONTACT	Triumph (01455 251700)

ENGINE

TYPE	liquid-cooled, 16v, dohc, inline four
BORE X STROKE	68 x 44.5mm
CAPACITY	646cc
COMPRESSION	12.85:1
FUEL SYSTEM	injection, 38mm throttle bodies
TRANSMISSION	6-speed, chain

CHASSIS

FRAME	aluminium alloy twin-spar
FRONT SUSPENSION	43mm forks, fully adj.
REAR SUSPENSION	monoshock, fully adj
FRONT BRAKE	2 x 308mm discs, 4-pot calipers
REAR BRAKE	220mm disc, 1-pot caliper
FRONT TYRE	120/70 ZR17
REAR TYRE	180/55 ZR17

DIMENSIONS

RAKE/TRAIL	24.6°/89.1mm
WHEELBASE	1390mm
SEAT HEIGHT	815mm
WET WEIGHT	165kg (claimed)
FUEL CAPACITY	18 litres

PERFORMANCE

POWER	101.33bhp @ 12,300rpm
TORQUE	46.33ft-lb @ 10,800rpm
TOP SPEED	152.94mph
S/S 1/4 MILE	11.55s @ 123.72mph
0-60MPH	3.54sec
40-90MPH TOP GEAR	9.43sec

Daytona 650 in its element #1 - a twisty backroad

Photo: Osborne

UPPING THE STAKES
TRIUMPH'S NEW DAYTONA 650

'Every so often a bike turns up and shakes the established order of things. Triumph's new 650cc Daytona is one of those bikes. The Ed explains why'

WORDS: Ed **PICS:** Osborne

NOBODY likes a smartarse but hey, I couldn't NOT start this story about Triumph's new 650cc Daytona without pointing out that we were right about the bike that spawned it — the TT600.

Much maligned it might have been but if it wasn't the best handling road-ready middleweight EVER produced....then I'm a Dutchman! It might have been one of the only things that ex-Ed Bentman and I agreed on but that aside the TT set a benchmark which few bikes — Yamaha's new YZF-R1 is one, the subject of this test, Triumph's new Daytona 650 is another — have since been able to match let alone better.

Never mind that the TT missed the boat in the looks department and had what history will record as a fundamentally flawed fuel injection system, the thing steered, turned and handled like a dream.....

Or, as it turns out, a Daytona 650!

But before I go on, let me give the new 'small'

Daytona a proper introduction. Born of a desire to 'break free' from the crowded middleweight 'race-rep' scene, Triumph followed Kawasaki's lead and produced a 'super' supersport via the simple expedient of increasing the engine's stroke by 3.1mm and the capacity by 47cc to 646cc.

The big difference in marketing strategies vis a vis the two companies is that Kawasaki continues to produce a Supersport-legal 600cc machine, while Triumph decided not to. Which came as a bit of a surprise to me particularly after our own Bruce Anstey won the company its first Isle of Man TT title in modern times in 2003 then Craig Jones won the final round of the British Supersport Championship (on a Daytona 600) last year.

But back to the bike.

Having taken a serious drubbing over the TT600 Triumph saw the error of its ways and made sure the Daytona 600 actually looked good as well.

The 650 continues the tradition with an 'even-better-in-the-flesh' combination of planes, angles, edges, and curves which has elements which truly

Daytona 650 in its element # 2 - stunting

turns heads.

CHARACTER

Dimensionally the new, 'small' Daytona still fits inside the TT's 'footprint,' though the new bike 'feels' somehow bigger and more substantial.

It's as if the feedback was that the TT was 'too small,' a 'ladies bike,' and 'not substantial enough,' so the factory built 'a bigger bike.' Now feel free to differ with me here because though it is longer and wider the Daytona is actually 5mm shorter in the wheelbase and 5kg lighter than the TT but the subjective 'feel' is that of a much bigger bike, one which a big tough Triumph-style 'hua like our own Big Dave would be quite happy being seen on.

So though dynamically it reminds me of the TT600 and subsequently the Speed Four derivative if you like the look of the Daytona but reckon you'd be better off with a 'bigger' bike don't discount it. In everyday riding situations it feels and indeed performs more like a smaller,

lighter litre-bike than a larger, more powerful middleweight — if you get what I mean.

ERGOS

One of the reasons is the size of the tank. Though at 18 litres it is no bigger or smaller than similar offerings from — for instance — Yamaha, it spreads your legs wider than is currently the trend in middleweight and even hi-po full-on litre bikes.

That said, the riding position itself has a nice neutral feel which sits your feet back aways but doesn't place too much torso weight on the clip-on style handlebars. It's sporty, but I wouldn't place it in the same league as that of more narrowly-focused sport middleweights, despite the seat squab being — marginally higher — than I would prefer.

POWER

With no dedicated press test bike I missed out on a ride on the original Daytona 600 so the 650 was all-new to me. Other testers were enthusiastic about the looks and — as always — the

Daytona 650 territory

51

Conventional front-end belies brilliant steering, stability and poise

dynamics of the 600 but did complain about the lack of mid-range and top-end power particularly compared with the competition from Honda, Suzuki, Yamaha etc.

The new engine — and indeed it is new, with a new crankcase and new head — addresses the issue head on (as it were) with a nice smooth, creamy flow of available oomph from around 3,000rpm to the 12,500rpm redline though at 114 PS (112 horsepower and bear in mind this is measured at the crank) the Daytona isn't going to win any Supersport dyno shootouts.

Having just jumped off Yamaha's razor-sharp '05 R6 I can state categorically that the Daytona 650 isn't in the same race as far as throttle-cracking snap at low to mid rpm let alone top end (where the Yamaha has a significant advantage) but

Triumph's decision to pullout of Supersport competition suggests that neither the factory nor its large potential pool of Daytona 650 buyers will care.

New too is the clutch, now fitted with a backlash eliminator gear, and the gear change system which now uses a linkage and molybdenum coating of the shift drum and forks). I immediately noticed an improvement over the TT600 in terms of selection action and it would be hard to find a better set of ratios to match the new, meatier power characteristics of the engine.

In real-world terms what the extra capacity has done is blur the peaks and troughs and flesh out what was already quite a nice, linear power delivery and with the new fuel-injection working like — dare I say it — the TT600's Sagem system SHOULD

HAVE you have got a recipe for some very satisfied owners.

There's still a definite digital 'snap' to the action of the throttle and in an ideal world I think the engine would feel a little sharper, a little more 'alive' particularly in the 'transition' area between 4,500 and 7,000rpm, but that is hardly a complaint.

You definitely notice the 'vibey' nature of the engine, but again, in its intensity (which eventually numbs your hands at constant motorway-type speeds) it is no better or worse than similar sporty middleweights.

HANDLING
Though in the white hot heat of competition conventional 43mm forks and non radially-mounted front brake calipers might work against you, on the road there are going to be few complaints

This is a bike which loves backroads as much as you do

2005 TRIUMPH DAYTONA 650

ENGINE
Type: . . . . .Liquid-cooled DOHC 4-valve transverse four cylinder four stroke
Displacement: 646cc
Compression Ratio: 12.8:1
Bore x stroke: . . . . .68 x 44.5mm
Fuel system: . . . . Twin-butterfly multipoint sequential fuel injection
Starting system: . . . . .Electric
Engine Management system: . . . . .Digital
Clutch: . . . . .Wet multi-plate
Transmission: 6-speed
Final drive: . . . . .Chain

FRAME
Type: . . . . .Beam-type aluminium
Swingarm: . . . . .Aluminium
Front suspension: . . . . .Conventional 43mm telescopic forks adjustable
for preload and compression & rebound damping
Rear suspension: . . . . . .Single coil-over shock and linkage system adjustable
for preload and rebound damping
Brakes: . . . . .Twin 308mm rotor floating discs w/four piston calipers
front/single 220mm rotor disc w/single piston caliper rear
Wheels: . . . . .Cast aluminium alloy 3-spoke 17 x 3.5 front & 17 x 5.5 rear
Tyres: . . . . .120/70ZR x 17 front/180/55ZR x 17 rear

DIMENSIONS
Wheelbase: 1390mm
Rake: . . . . .24.6 degrees
Trail: 89.1mm
LxWxH: . . . . .2112 712 x 1131mm
Seat height: 815mm
Dry Weight: 165kg
Fuel tank capacity: 18l
RRP: $16,595
Test bike: . . . . .Triumph NZ

about the Daytona 650's 'old skool' front end. In fact dynamically the Daytona is one of easiest and perhaps more importantly, most confidence-inspiring bikes I've ridden recently.

Not just confidence-inspiring in the 'good beginner's or nervous rider's' bike either. I mean confidence inspiring in what the English mags would describe as the 'Hooligan's' sense.

The Daytona 650 would be the easiest middleweight bike to wheelie and stoppie there is. Period. Like its TT600 predecessor it is also one of the best 'balanced' bikes on the market — period. There's a nice neutral feel to steering and turn in, being neither too light 'n flighty nor too heavy. And on its side the bike is simply sublime, providing enough feedback via the tyre and forks to let you make the tiniest of line corrections as if you had all the time in the world.

REALLY. You honestly have to

try it to really grasp how good the Daytona is.

WHAT ELSE?
It's hard not to sound enthusiastic about the Daytona 650, despite it not having quite the zing or the Whippet-like proportions of the current crop of Japanese middleweights.

It's funny too, in that, if someone had told me Triumph had built a special 750cc Daytona and I was riding it I would have believed them.....and I would have really liked it and I would have written it up as 'the next big thing' — a practical, sporty 750 which could double as a commuter and a track day bike. You know, like the sort of bike we all used to ride!

If that sounds like you, forget that the one you can currently buy is actually a '650' and a 'middleweight' and organise yourself a ride.

You owe it to yourself!

53

THREE-PEAT!

Triumph's all-new Daytona 675 is a breakthrough bike

BY DON CANET

IN THE HIGH-STAKES SPORTBIKE BIZ, THE sweetest triumph is often the result of persistence, trial and error and, ultimately, remaining true to your character. No one knows this better than the blokes at Hinckley, England-based Triumph Motorcycles Limited. Going toe-to-toe with the Japanese contingent in the hotly contested middleweight sport category has been a losing battle for Triumph.

Playing by the rules of convention, Triumph entered the arena with its TT600 in 2000, followed by the Daytona 600 three years later (see our Long-Term Wrap-Up, this issue). Both machines were inline-Fours sharing many similarities in engine and chassis design with their Japanese counterparts. Although the bikes gained praise for excellent handling, both lacked the engine performance and overall value of the competition. Last year's Daytona saw a mid-life model update that hinted of Triumph's new line of thinking. No longer constraining itself to the 600cc-displacement cap dictated by Supersport competition rules, Triumph focused on optimizing its middleweight machine for real-world street needs. With an increase in displacement and refined fuel-injection, the Daytona 650 proved a much better street package than its predecessor, but remained in the shadow of Kawasaki's ZX-636, a bike that most view as a superior example of a similar theme.

Triumph calls the all-new 2006 Daytona 675 "incomparable." While sounding like common marketing hype, it's hard to disagree, considering the new machine is powered by an inline three-cylinder engine that faithfully exudes the tactile sensation, sound and soul that *is* Triumph and Triumph alone. While undeniably trying to be different, the Daytona 675 also offers several tangible advantages over the middleweight status quo.

Foremost is the engine's broad spread of torque, extending much lower into the rev range than any middleweight Four. Being substantially narrower than an inline-Four, the 675cc, 12-valve, dohc Triple resides in an aluminum frame that is 20 percent lighter and narrower than that of the Daytona 650. The result is a very slim machine claimed to offer class-leading cornering clearance. At a claimed 365 pounds dry, the bike is a class featherweight as well.

Steering geometry is aggressive, with 23.5 degrees of rake and 87mm trail. A steering damper is tucked out of harm's way beneath the lower triple-clamp. The bike's 54.8-inch wheelbase is right in line with the best 600 supersports, as are its top-shelf Kayaba suspension and front brake system featuring Nissin radial-pump master cylinder and four-pot radial-mount calipers. The use of peculiar-sized 308mm-diameter front rotors underscores the attention to

detail that has gone into the machine, shaving unswept rotor area and unnecessary rotating weight.

Having covered the new 675 with a tech preview in the January issue, the stage was set for our first ride at the bike's world press launch held early this year in Kuala Lumpur, Malaysia. I spent 90 minutes lapping the spectacular Sepang Circuit and logged 100 miles on public roads. Not a lot of seat time, but enough to experience the breadth of the engine's versatility and the nimble, unflappably stable chassis over a wide range of speeds and pavement conditions.

I'm hungry for more! Triumph has nailed the recipe with the Daytona 675. This is not only the best sportbike to roll out of the Hinckley plant, but one the most enjoyable sporting machines I've ridden to date. I was surprised most by the fact I didn't find a single quirk when riding the bike on either the road or the track. Mechanically, everything works precisely and with smoothness. Throttle response is spot-on, power delivery seamless, clutch action fluid and driveline lash minimal.

If you're intent on digging for a complaint, okay, some may find a coarse band of engine vibration that creeps through the grips to be finger-tingling on longer rides. The engine features a gear-driven counterbalancer shaft located ahead of the crank that quells vibes to a subdued and characteristic Speed Triple-like growl. Didn't bother me much,

considering I frequently found myself revving the engine into five-figure rpm territory during the street ride without realizing it unless I glanced down at the tachometer.

Keeping pace with our swift ride guide as he sliced through the tropical landscape along traffic-clogged backroads and expressways was no jungle cruise. Lane-splitting hardly describes the way our point man displaced slower-moving motorists along the route, but I came away with no doubts as to the Daytona's ability to pull out and pass cars and trucks at a moment's notice. Several times, I didn't bother with toeing the shifter, simply leaving the bike in a taller gear and allowing its impressive roll-on acceleration to go to work. When we came upon the occasional red traffic light, I also noted the ability to roll away from stops with little more than idle revs.

Even though I wore jeans for the street ride, I felt no leg-roasting heat radiating from the upswept tailpipe–an issue with some bikes that feature underseat exhausts, including Triumph's own Sprint ST. The windscreen offered decent protection and caused only minimal buffeting, while the mirrors offered good rear coverage and remained relatively free of vibration. While I can't say I spent enough time in the saddle to rule on the bike's ergonomics for sport-touring duty, its firmly padded saddle and riding posture are certainly suited to track use.

In spite of the 675's track-inspired ergos and styling, Triumph has no intention to race the bike, and neither does it want the Daytona to be perceived as a Supersport contender. Still, while I arrived with somewhat limited expectations for the bike, I left truly inspired by its performance on the circuit. This could be the most grossly underrated track-day bike ever.

Although this was my first visit to Sepang, I got a primer

THREE-PEAT!

on the 15-turn layout prior to riding by playing a Formula One racing simulator on my laptop. Two things became immediately evident when I took to the track for real: The circuit was very accurately modeled in the game, and the Daytona 675 works so amazingly well that I was comfortably riding in full track-attack mode by my third lap! The bike felt light and compact beneath me, and its agile yet stable-handling chassis instilled great confidence and held the line with ease.

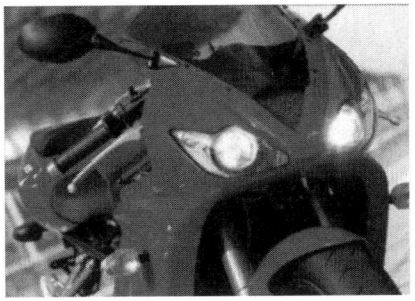

Feedback through the front was superb, and there were never any signs of tire patter or chatter. The stock-fitment Pirelli Dragon Supercorsa Pro radials provided plenty of grip, allowing ridiculous lean in corners with nothing more than the peg feelers ever touching down.

The brakes offered excellent power and feel without any grabbiness when initially applied and offered not a hint of fade throughout each session. Stability under hard braking was excellent as well, even over ripples left in the pavement by F-1 cars. I didn't experience any rear-wheel hop when braking hard and downshifting, even when going down through the gears from sixth to second at the end of the long main straight.

The meat of the engine's torque spans a broad plateau from 8500 to 13,000 rpm, making gear selection less critical than with other middleweights. Extracting the last ounce of power out of the Daytona calls for grabbing upshifts at 13,500, a full 700 rpm shy of the rev-limiter. This over-rev is a welcome departure from Triumphs I've ridden in the past that suddenly cut out right at the very peak of power output, easily baiting you into the rev limiter and costing time. No excuses accepted here as the 675's instrument cluster features a programmable shift indicator with a row of seven lights located adjacent to redline. As well as rpm of preference, the lights can be set to either illuminate sequentially or all at once.

Modern-era Triumphs have never held much visual appeal for me, often looking somewhat gangly and industrial, but there was instant attraction the moment I laid eyes on the 675. It appeals to my senses much like the Ducati 916 did when first introduced years ago. It's worth noting that the 675 is the work of an in-house stylist, a first for Triumph, having always outsourced that aspect of design in the past.

In many ways, the 675 is a breakout machine for Triumph. The Daytona offers proof that the company has come into its own and gelled in all aspects of motorcycle production. There's now a true and cohesive identity that spans the entire product line. Seems there is truth in the old saying, three's a charm. ◫

THREE-PEAT!

Special delivery

We had a sneak preview in October – we were blown away. And in the world's first track test, Triumph's new Daytona 675 more than lives up to the hype

Words by Steve Westlake Photography by Gold & Goose

Triumph is oozing confidence just now, and the stunning new Daytona 675 is the latest, greatest manifestation of it; a bike of such simple purpose and clear thinking that its existence seems utterly obvious. You look at it, you ride it, and you think, 'Of course Triumph had to build this bike, anyone could have told them that.'

Even before it goes on sale, success seems virtually assured. The company has already taken more than 900 deposits. With a production run of 1000 bikes for the UK, that means it's almost sold out before anyone has taken a test ride. The story's also very promising abroad.

Putting modesty to one side for a moment, some thanks for this must go *Bike*. Back in October we were given a world exclusive ride on a pre-production bike, and we were stunned. Riding it on roads near Triumph's Hinckley factory, we compared it against a Honda CBR600 and a Kawasaki ZX-6R, with amazing results. The bike felt quicker, more flexible and more intense >

THE BIG QUESTIONS

1. Is it as good as we said back in October?

Yes. The bikes feel just as agile, punchy and involving as the pre-production bike we rode exclusively last year.

2. Does it feel different from a normal Japanese sports 600?

Yes. The supersport class is very close in terms of purpose, performance and execution, and the Triumph is not hugely different. But the feel of the engine – the grunty midrange and power delivery – sets it apart from its rivals. Also in its favour is its slender look and timeless design.

3. Is it a comfortable all-rounder?

No. It's not that *uncomfortable* – the suspension manages to be sporty without being harsh and there's a decent level of protection from the fairing and screen. Even 6' 3" testers had no complaints. But this is an uncompromising sportsbike, so expect plenty of weight on wrists, a numb bum after a few hours and a cramped riding position.

Triumph's Daytona 675 in full *yeaharrr* attack mode at Sepang GP circuit, Malaysia. The 675 doesn't do subtle

than either of those ace Japanese bikes.

We knew the bike we'd ridden was special, but since then there's been a nagging little doubt that perhaps, just perhaps, the production bike wouldn't be as good. We were concerned that the machine unveiled in Malaysia would be a let down. We needn't have worried.

The bike is every bit as special as we first thought. On the track it feels like a 250 race bike with a 700cc engine. On the road it's easy to ride, reasonably comfortable and drives with bags of effortless torque. If you've been waiting for Triumph to build a sportsbike with performance and style to match its personality, the wait is over. The 675 has arrived.

There are three key ingredients that Triumph has got so right. Number one, it looks good. Arguably this is the critical victory. Triumph's previous entrants in this class, the TT600 and Daytona 600 and 650, were good bikes, but looked ordinary. Not everyone buys with their eyes, but very few people buy with them shut – which helped if you were shelling out for a TT600.

The Daytona 675 looks lithe, classy and aggressive, and Triumph arrived at its styling via an unusual route. Instead of using outside agencies to style it, they found someone within the company. He's an engineer called Chris Hennegan, and he approached the project team with a few sketches for how their new middleweight triple might look. They were so impressed they asked him to style the bike you see here.

Number two, it's different. By choosing to use a three-cylinder engine instead the in-line four of the TT600, the outgoing Daytona and every Japanese bike in the class, Triumph is playing to its strengths: character, tradition, offering an alternative. Instead of competing head on with the awesome array of bikes in the class (Honda CBR600, Yamaha R6, Suzuki GSX-R600, Kawasaki ZX-6R), all of which pack a highly-refined in-line four, Triumph gives us an engine that behaves and sounds differently.

This means that power figures and dyno curves become less critical in deciding the 675's place in the

pecking order, and feel and experience rise in the mix: areas where the Triumph triple scores highly. And the fact they've chosen a capacity of 675cc means that despite having one cylinder fewer, the 675 has a head start in the all-important grunt stakes. It also stays in insurance group 15, with the 600cc competition.

The triple configuration gives the 675 another advantage over its rivals. It only has to fit three cylinders across the frame, so the engine can be narrower. This makes the bike look extremely agile from the front, adds to its slender feel from the saddle, reduces its drag factor, and gives it a huge amount of ground clearance. In truth the other 600s don't suffer from ground clearance problems, so the advantage is one of feel and appearance.

In terms of technology, the 675 is not different at all. It's utterly conventional, breaking no new ground. The engine layout is nothing new, the chassis follows the same principles as every other sportsbike, and the suspension is standard. There's a valve in the exhaust to boost midrange and power (first seen on a Yamaha in 1988); the air intake duct goes through the headstock (Honda SP-1, 2000); and a flap in the air duct helps to control noise by closing at lower revs. The gear selection rod goes through the frame (Yamaha R1, 1998).

But even this conventionality is an advantage, because it means the bike can get on with what it's good at – the third killer ingredient. It works.

Waiting for me in the Sepang pit lane, the bike still looks as purposeful as I remember from that October test ride. It hunches low at the nose – the front wheel seemingly being sucked into the sharp bodywork – and is high and sloping at the back. The aggressive lines convey speed and purpose.

I ease into the saddle and that high rear, crouching front feeling remains, the suspension feeling firm and not compressing much under my weight. The engine settles into a familiar triple mechanical tickover. I blip the throttle >

TECHNICAL DEVELOPMENT

Engine
The inline triple revs to 14,000rpm and makes a claimed 123bhp at the crank. We estimate a rear figure of 110bhp. The stacked six-speed close ratio gearbox is designed with drive rather than top speed in mind.

Air Intake
Air enters the duct beneath the screen and travels through the headstock into the airbox. Up to 5000rpm, a flap is partly closed to limit noise at town speeds. Then it opens up to allow the engine to breathe and make a better noise.

Exhaust
The standard exhaust features a catalytic converter and a valve to optimise torque and power at all revs. Triumph has worked with Arrow to make an aftermarket titanium system that adds 5bhp.

Chassis
The frame is very slim and features open-back castings using Finite Element Analysis (FEA) to optimise strength and save weight. Chassis geometry is an aggressive combination of 23.5 degrees of rake, 86.8mm of trail and a 1392mm wheelbase.

Brakes
The brakes use a radial master cylinder, braided hoses and specially optimised Nissin radial calipers with differing diameter pistons - leading piston 30.2mm, trailing piston 33.9mm. They give huge bite and power and didn't fade on the track.

Tyres
Pirelli Dragon Supercorsa Pros, developed in the World Supersport Championship, are standard, and offer tons of grip and stability. The bike feels like it could be sensitive to tyre choice.

You look, it steers. Best not spend too long admiring the hedge, then...

Limited edition gunmetal paint is the preferred colour among designers and arty types. So, red it is...

and the engine responds instantly, purposefully. Clunk into first gear and we're off onto the circuit for the moment of truth.

The early laps reveal the bike's lightness and agility. The steering is so direct and immediate, it catches me out. Ease into a corner on a closed throttle and the bike turns really quickly, slicing to the apex and even beyond. In a momentary lapse of concentration I manage to run onto the inside kerb because I wasn't expecting the speed of turn.

While its nimbleness makes the 675 feel like a 250 on the track, the suspension set-up is not harsh. David Lopez, Triumph's Spanish test rider, has prepared the bike for the track with pretty soft settings, which means its attitude changes a lot: pitching forward on the brakes, squatting at back when hard on the throttle. It's a set-up that favours smooth riding and a light rider. With things firmed up a bit, the 675 becomes a real track tool. It reacts quickly to every rider input, turns sharply and eases to any lean angle you fancy, all the while giving plenty of positive feedback.

Despite Triumph's trademark aggressive geometry, stability is good even when hard on the throttle at high speed, over bumps while jiggling the bars. A steering damper obviously helps out here.

High speed direction changes take a decent bit of effort, which I couldn't quite square with the quick steering into corners – but this could

be explained by the geometry changing when hard on the power. The gearbox does a good job, but requires very positive inputs on clutchless upchanges. Occasionally I had to go for the next gear twice: it didn't want to shift with the engine under heavy, high-rev load.

But even on the track the midrange is very impressive. Sepang has long straights, and it would be easy for the midrange to be dwarfed. But the Triumph pulls well and gives you a choice of gears for most corners, all the time accompanied by the fruity triple tone as the airbox opens to give the full induction soundtrack.

Overall, the 675 makes you feel connected: in touch with the surface and exactly what the bike's doing. While the bike's very controllable, it's not neutral. It responds to every input, without filtering much out.

After such animated track performance I'm expecting it to feel a bit full-on on the road, but a couple of hours reveal a civilised bike capable of cruising at whatever speed you choose, from bimble to banzai. Of course it's no tourer – there's a fair amount of weight on your wrists, vibes through the bars induce numb palms after an hour. The digital speedo is another quibble: so low on the dash that it's hard to pick out, especially at a glance.

But this is a hugely impressive bike. Despite being cleverly labelled 'incomparable' by Triumph, it will inevitably be tested against the big-four Japanese Supersport 600s at

the first opportunity (see Bike May 2006). Ultimately it may not prove the quickest on the track or the most flexible all-rounder, but the Triumph will be many riders' favourite because it's a special bike to ride. It's a special bike full stop.

THE SPEC SHEET
Triumph Daytona 675

Price	£7199
Top Speed	155mph (est)
Power	110bhp @ 12,200rpm
Torque	50 lb.ft @ 11,750rpm
Engine	675cc, dohc, 12v, inline triple
Bore/Stroke	74.0 x 52.3mm
Compression ratio	12.65:1
Transmission	6-speed chain drive
Frame	aluminium beam twin spar
Front suspension	41mm usd forks
Front adjustment	preload, rebound, compression
Rear suspension	monoshock
Rear adjustment	preload, rebound, compression
Front brakes	2 x 308mm discs, 4-piston calipers
Rear brake	220mm disc, single-piston caliper
Tyres	Pirelli Dragon Supercorsa Pros
Tyres front; rear	120/70 ZR17; 180/50 ZR17
Weight	165kg (claimed dry)
Wheelbase	1392mm
Seat height	825mm
Rake/trail	23.5°/86.8mm
Fuel capacity	17.4 litres
Insurance group	NU15
Colours	yellow, red, metallic grey
Available from	Triumph, 01455 251700

Breathe easy.

Don't worry, this is one Triumph with perfect fuelling. Nothing revolutionary, but that's fine by us

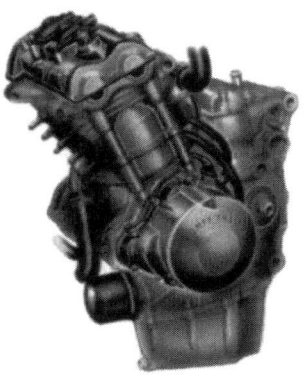

Thee only thing that's genuinely new about Triumph's 675cc triple is the combination of configuration and capacity. Individual components are simple, proven and to-the-point. Yet this 675cc triple undoubtedly represents Triumph's finest engineering hour. The complexity with which the engine management system (EMS) works is impressive and unprecedented. After being taken into Triumph's confidence and shown the gory details, it's hard not to be impressed by the way they've turned things around since the TT600 debacle.

We wouldn't want to give the game away to Japanese rivals, but Triumph's EMS makes decisions based on all kinds of logic. Is the engine warm? How long since it last ran? What speeds did it reach? Combined with high-resolution mapping in all sorts of dimensions, the fuel injection can honestly and genuinely be described as fault-free.

So now Keihin's simple 44mm throttle bodies are adequately controlled, just what do they give you? More midrange than any other middleweight, that's for damn sure. Open her up wide in second gear, on a first-gear hairpin and the first thing to notice is the rear Pirelli Supercorsa squirming for grip as you're propelled out of the radius with far more urgency than I remember a ZX-6R managing in the same gear.

Then there's the noise. The triple's unique sound is seemingly always on tap. From 4000rpm the deep-seated howl begins to rise, only muting as the EMS-controlled flap is moved across at particular EC-test points*.

Being experienced in the ways of Kawasaki, trust me when I say Triumph haven't just mastered induction roar, they've dressed it in a rubber gimp suit and forced it into the boot of their Ford Granada. They now own induction roar. Your move Kawasaki, if your want your crown back.

But it's not all about noise. The unique soundtrack is a bonus – a breath of fresh air in a crowded room. It's the first time I've really been properly 100 per cent impressed by a manufacturer. The fact that they happen to be British, I'm ashamed to say, amazes me.

* Pinch the vacuum hose off after the solenoid, but before the valve, right between the headlights, and you'll have a wide-open airbox all day long.

Throttle bodies
Keihin, 44mm. No secondary valves, no vacuum slides, no fly-by-wire, 'no gimmicks,' say Triumph.

Engine construction
Barrels are part of the the cases which mirrors the Japanese, apart from the new R6 which has separate barrels.

> WAVES, HARMONICS AND PULSE TUNING

On naturally aspirated engines, there's little in the way of help for gases entering or leaving the cylinder head. They're sucked in by low pressure and pushed out by the rising piston. Optimising performance is all about waves, harmonics and pulse tuning.

Consider the inlet tracts and exhaust pipes as canals full of water. Each separate explosion within the cylinder releases a large mass of water at speed up the canal. The waves are big and high. Wherever the canal changes shape the waves change shape and speed accordingly: where the canal narrows the waves are stronger and faster, sometimes with reflections heading back down the way they came.

Mistime these reflections and the wave trying to exit the cylinder head is slowed down by the wave trying to bounce back in. Time it right and the wave is sucked out forcibly into a low-point. See where this is going? In olden times, your exhaust and airbox would provide the best pulse effects at only certain points, dictated by the volume or length of both. You could tune for maximum efficiency, but again only at certain points.

Then Yamaha figured how to control these positive side-effects on one side by effectively lengthening or shortening the exhaust on demand. Hello Exup. The gains were percentages, but the smoothing effect on power delivery (and reduction of emissions) were big enough to warrant the now near-mandatory fitting of an Exup-style valve on nearly every major sports bike.

Since the late 90s we've also seen valves on the airbox – so-called flappers which control the effective volume according to what the ECU requires. In 99 per cent of cases, these don't produce any more power or torque, but are simply used to control both noise and emissions. The Triumph system is no different.

Here we can see the entire intake system. At the top right is the flap (blue), which is controlled by the EMS and moved by the vacuum actuator (black). The actuator is fed its vacuum from the intake manifold via a resevoir which can store enough vacuum for three full sweeps. Storing nothing, whatever next?

Leading or following?
As a balanced road/track package, we'd say it's leading

> ON THE TRACK
Triumph chassis have always been different. Where the CBR-RR and R6 feel plank-like and stiff, the TT and Daytona feel tall and cushioned. Maybe the language is inadequate, but what we're saying is that Triumph's have always been different – not worse.

With more suspension travel front and back, the Daytona 600/650 offered better cross-country suspension than any rival. But the ability to pitch the bike forwards or backwards so easily (the result of choppy throttle control, rough braking or a general lack of smoothness) could create more problems than could easily be solved.

The Daytona triple isn't slow. I'd bet my lunch money that it sails past the 100bhp mark with ease. And while Triumph reckon their design principles are the same, their latest chassis is an interesting mix of old and Japanese. There's significantly more suspension travel than there is on the R6 or CBR-RR. Like the new R6 (but unlike the Honda or Kawasaki), one click anywhere out of 20 and you start to change the bike.

But where the Daytona 650's chassis took some getting used to, the 675 feels quite Honda. Quite vanilla. A bit egg and chips. You know. Easy.

Put your feet on the well-placed pegs and grab the bars. Lines are held, changed and rescued with ease. Brake late, brake early. Your choice. The 675 doesn't criticise your style, it simply lets you get on with it. And with the optional taller screen fitted, I hardly bothered to tuck-in. That's amazing, because this bike really is small. A contradiction, I know, but the waistline is barely one-cylinder wide. And leant over, knee on the ground, bike at an easy 45 degrees, it's hard to imagine ever touching anything down. It's this mix of intuition and ability which will gain the new Daytona a serious following. I watched ex-GP riders taking advantage of the chassis to come up with serious lean angles and corner speeds, yet when I climbed on it felt safe, easy and compliant. And, above all, fun.

Evolution
Triumph quicks

> TT600 88BHP
The Hinckley Lemon, also known as 'that bike with the crappy injection'. Triumph's first attempt at a 600 was a disaster. It took months to develop a decent fuel map – shame that the development took place after the bikes were sold. Handled well though.

> DAYTONA 600 95BHP
The Daytona focused on fast, comfy riding that the CBR-RR and ZX-6R lacked. The chassis could win on track, too. Victories at the TT and short circuits were mainly thanks to tuning work by Valmoto but the standard motor was easily bested by the Japanese.

> DAYTONA 650 100BHP
The knee-jerk reaction to us fashion-concious Brits demanding the same power as the Japanese Joneses. More torque than any other 600 (well, it was a 650) and the same inspired chassis. But it just wasn't enough, not when both Honda and Yamaha sprouted usd forks, radial brakes and over 105bhp at the back wheel.

> ON THE ROAD
Consider the outskirts of Birmingham after Asian bird flu wipes out half the population and road repairs are swapped for leaky irrigation pumps and bigger potholes. That's what Malaysian roads are like. Twisty, bumpy stretches of patchy dry tarmac and concrete, overrun by dense traffic and loose animals. It's the sort of road where an Africa Twin could do with some help.

So can somebody explain why a sporty lightweight triple is making such light work of it all? Down the slope, easy upshifts through a painless gearbox, at a sensible 8000rpm. The suspension takes bumps in its stride, the steering doesn't wiggle (standard-fit steering damper) and we're accelerating up the other side. Overtakes don't always need a downshift, but it doesn't hurt either. The sharp turn-in on a GP track is your cake. But the road is where you eat it. While the Daytona will never compete with the twist 'n' zoom torque of a 1000cc machine, it does offer every other 600cc four a bloody nose and an ambulance home. And that makes it special.

UN No. **3166**

PROPER SHIPPING NAME

VEHICLE (FLAMMABLE LIQUID POWERED).

PACKING INST. **900** CLASS. **9**

NET CONTENTS — UN PKG. GROUP.

CONTAINER SPEC.

MAX AUTH.GROSS WT.

GROSS WT. DIMS

"INNER PACKAGES COMPLY WITH PRESCRIBED SPECIFICATIONS"

Triple treats

1 The 675's lean angle has been measured by Triumph at an incredible 57 degrees. Nearly there DL. The engine's included valve angle is just 23 degrees. What's English for Testastretta?

2 Computer-controlled valves in the exhaust and airbox control noise and emissions without restricting power as fixed baffles would.

3 Clocks log everything from 99 lap times to peak and average speeds, fuel used and the number of times you think about 'it'. 2:30.1, 22mpg and three times on a lap of Sepang.

4 Triumph's factory is 37 miles from the PB office and 7000 miles from Sepang.

Finally time to buy British?

When I heard Triumph were developing a triple, I thought it was a way to avoid confrontation. In truth, it was because someone at Hinckley simply had a good idea for an engine, and somebody higher up had the good sense to say, 'Do it'. Triumph have pulled it off.

The new 675 is not the fastest bike ever. It will (probably) be beaten by half the Japanese bikes on lap times – and for many that's the end of the story. But there's no doubt that on the road and in the corners it really does rock. Mix in a characterful engine and refined styling and the Trumpet starts to take on its own flavour. There's something for everyone in this bike and Triumph have spent most of their time making sure you're going to find it. Let's not get too giddy before it's been up and down the B1176 and round the PB TT, but it looks to me like this is the year the Brits have really built a performance bike. **DL**

Triumph Daytona 675

PRICE	£7499tbc
COLOURS	grey, red, yellow
WARRANTY	two years, unlimited mileage
AVAILABILITY	soon
CONTACT	www.triumph.co.uk
>Engine	
TYPE	liquid-cooled, 12v, dohc, four-stroke, inline three
BORE X STROKE	74x52.3mm
CAPACITY	674.8cc
COMP. RATIO	12.65:1
FUEL SYSTEM	EFI, 44mm throttle bodies
TRANSMISSION	6-speed, chain
>Chassis	
FRAME	aluminium twin-spar, adjustable swingarm pivot
FRONT SUSPENSION	41mm usd forks, fully adj.
REAR SUSPENSION	monoshock, fully adj.
FRONT BRAKE	2 x 308mm discs, 4-piston radial mounts
REAR BRAKE	1 x 220mm disc, single-piston caliper
FRONT TYRE	120/70 ZR17
REAR TYRE	180/55 ZR17
>Dimensions	
RAKE/TRAIL	23.5°/86.8mm
WHEELBASE	1392mm
SEAT HEIGHT	850mm
DRY WEIGHT	165kg (claimed)
FUEL CAPACITY	17.4 litres (including 4l reserve)
>Performance	
POWER	123bhp @ 12,500rpm (claimed)
TORQUE	53.3lb-ft @ 11,750rpm (claimed)

NOW YOU'RE TORQUE KING

Is the Triumph Daytona 675 the new class leader?

PRESS LAUNCHES of high performance bikes usually take place on race circuits. It makes sense as these are the only places it's possible to really push a modern sports bike and find out what it's like at the edge of its capabilities.

Many riders buy their bikes on the strength of how well they do in these reports. But what makes for a better track bike isn't always helpful on the road, in particular the very high revs needed to achieve big power figures in the supersport 600 class. It's also very difficult to guess how a bike might behave on the road after

thrashing it around a circuit, something which Triumph's recent presentation of its eagerly awaited new Daytona 675 triple at the Sepang MotoGP track in Malaysia underlined.

It's a compact, light-feeling machine which is narrow between your knees, giving it a wieldy, responsive feel before you've even fired up the motor. The engine bursts into life with a gravelly snarl and instantly feels different to its four-cylinder rivals. It doesn't respond to the twistgrip with the same electric sharpness as a four, but you can feel its extra mid-range

Triumph Daytona 675 £7199

Engine	I/c 16v, dohc,
	in-line four, 675cc
Power	123bhp @ 12,500rpm
Torque	53lb-ft @ 11,750rpm
Chassis	aluminium twin spar
Dry weight	165kg (363lb)
Seat height	825mm (32.5in)
NU insurance group	TBC
Top speed	160mph (est)
Fuel consumption	38mpg

urge even charging up the pitlane. Out on the track the rev limiter cuts in just beyond the 14,000rpm redline after a fanfare of blue upshift warning lights - the point at which these flash is adjustable.

The power really kicks in at 10,000rpm and the spread is plenty wide enough for the close ratio gearbox. At first you hit the rev limit too often, but get used to the deeper, meatier exhaust note and it stops being an issue.

The gearchange could be better as it has a slightly notchy feel and can take a deliberate effort - which is something you don't need when

Track testing new bikes doesn't tell you everything about how they'll perform on the road. Great fun though

pushing a bike hard.

The transmission also lacks a slipper clutch, available on some other high-performance middleweights, and although the bike is stable under braking, this would help and shave another half a second off your lap times. The suspension also needs firming up as the weight transfer from power on to hard braking unsettles the bike on stock settings. The adjusters are very sensitive, so it's one click at a time.

But with that sorted, the Daytona works a treat, combining exceptional stability with good agility and a very forgiving nature. Whether or not it's up there with the class-leading Yamaha R6 is hard to judge as the Triumph feels so different to a four.

I suspect that, like a Ducati, its more relaxed feel means it's going faster than you think. It's certainly in the same ballpark.

But how much does that really matter? Unusually, Triumph also let us out for a morning with the Daytona on the roads, which proved to be a very canny move. It's a fine track bike, no question, right on the pace, but on the road, where 95% of its owners will use

it 95% of the time, the Daytona is the new class leader.

That suspension, which feels slightly soft on the track, is beautifully firm yet compliant on the road. It soaks up bumps which would kick other 600s off-line while feeding back reams of info to the rider. The brakes are a perfect balance between power and usability. Even the back brake is useful – unusual for a sports bike on the road.

But what makes the really big difference is the low rev torque, which is astounding. The compliment for a 600 used to be that it pulled like a 750 from low revs – well, the Daytona pulls harder, grunting away like a rutting boar and making pretty much the same sound.

From 2000 to 5000rpm it's astonishing, although it goes a bit flat from 6000 to 8000. But then the high-end power starts to make its presence felt.

For overtaking, getting away from the lights, pulling out of bends and the other road-riding stuff, no other 600 will come close to the Daytona, and few will feel as good either.

The riding position is compact (and for taller riders the screen cuts off the top of the clocks) with a fair amount of weight on wrists, but it's not excessive. There's some buzzy vibration at a steady 8500rpm, which equates to around 90-100mph and could be a pain at high motorway speeds.

In the Malaysian warmth (30° or so) the seat started to feel hot from the exhaust underneath, and that also uses up all the storage space – you get none worth mentioning. The mirrors are set very close too, so even wearing a light jacket, the view is almost entirely of elbow.

But there's a good quality of finish and the dash displays a lot of information, including a 99-lap timer, current and average fuel consumption, and gear selected.

UNDER THE SKIN

Engine
Despite the extra capacity, the three-cylinder, liquid-cooled 675cc motor is the most compact in the 600 class. The motor's real advantage is its low and mid-range torque. And it sounds utterly awesome too.

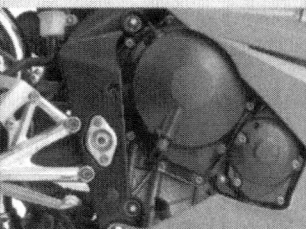

Transmission
The six-speed gearbox is the first 'stacked' design to be used by Triumph. This makes the engine/transmission unit shorter overall, allowing for a longer swingarm, which improves stability and drive out of corners.

Fuel injection
The system has three throttle bodies and three 12-point multi-spray injectors. The engine management is sent information from sensors measuring throttle and crank position, air pressure and coolant temperature.

Intake system
Air is drawn from the front of the fairing, through a hole in the headstock. There's an opening up at the front of the intake which helps with emission regulations and lets the bike snarl loudly the rest of the time.

Exhaust
The system is a conventional three-into-one finished off by an underseat exhaust, but it does have an EXUP-type valve, which improves torque and driveability as well as helping to keep noise levels down.

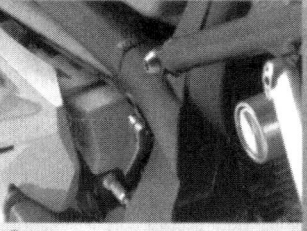

Frame
The frame comprises open-backed cast main spars that pass over the top of the engine, which makes the bike exceptionally narrow. The thickness varies according to where strength is needed.

Brakes, wheels and tyres
Radial four-piston calipers feature different diameter pistons, which results in an even pressure on the pad. The wheels are an ultra-lightweight five-spoke design. Tyres are Pirelli Diablo Super Corsas.

Then there's the bike's style, a class act available in three single colours - red, yellow and gunmetal grey - which is so much more sophisticated than the garish graphic-covered Japanese alternatives.

The 675 is up there with the best of its class on the track, but - where it matters for most of us, most of the time - on the road, the Daytona is the new king of the middleweights. **R**

Instruments and lights
As well as the usual basic information and analogue tachometer, the Daytona's dash displays instant and average fuel consumption, gear engaged, a 99-lap timer with average and maximum speed for each lap, and an array of gearchange warning lights which flash at an adjustable rpm level. The headlights are the projector beam type, one for dip and one for main. Rear is an LED.

TRIUMPH 675 *Daytona*
TRIPLE

Rejoice. The most innovative and eagerly anticipated sportsbike of 2006 is here, and it's British. Roland Brown caned it at Sepang in Malaysia for us

'm hunched over the Daytona 675's clip-ons, momentarily slowed by traffic on the crowded Malaysian coast road. The Triumph's three-cylinder engine gargles on part throttle as I follow a couple of cars and a three-up scooter. The young pillions, unused to anything bigger than a 'ped, grin broadly at the Triumph.

As a dusty truck rumbles past in the opposite direction I crack the throttle open, still in fourth gear, to send the Daytona leaping past the traffic. Seconds later I'm howling past the palm trees at 120mph, tropical air like a hairdryer in my helmet. As the tacho reaches 13,000rpm, change-up lights dancing on the dash, I flick up a gear and the 675 keeps accelerating at a blistering rate.

Then it all goes shit-shaped, as I round a curve to find the road blocked by jay-walking cattle, and have to haul on the brakes in a hurry. But it's no problem. The Triumph digs its front Supercorsa in the Tarmac, halting well before the bovine blockade. The controllable power of its four-pot Nissins is even more welcome now than it was yesterday, every time I sat up and squeezed the lever at the Sepang front straight's 200-metre marker during the track sessions.

Two very different situations, that the Daytona dealt with equally well. And the new Triumph wasn't only good under braking, either. On the racetrack it was fast, agile, and stable enough to suggest that it will be competitive with most, maybe all, of its middleweight rivals. As a road bike, it comes with an engine flexibility and character that make the 675 brilliant fun and seriously quick.

That three-cylinder character is a big step forwards from Triumph's previous four-cylinder middleweights. Nobody at Hinckley is admitting that it was a mistake to make a direct attack on the Japanese 600cc hegemony, but

Triumph has announced that it will only build twins and triples in future for unique selling points.

So much so, that when Triumph began planning its new middleweight in 2001, the key-word for the project was 'incomparable'. Having decided to create the class's first triple, a capacity of 675cc gave the potential to make competitive horsepower against 600cc fours and Ducati's 750cc V-twin, as well as to meet Supersport race regs.

An important early design decision was to make the new-generation Daytona as slim, compact, and light as possible. Following criticism of the TT600's dull styling, a modern, aggressive look was also vital. Having hired external stylists in the past, this time Triumph chose a design by one of the Hinckley firm's own team, an engineer named Chris Henneghan. That decision helped integrate styling and engineering, and speeded up the project.

It also produced a very sleek, distinctive motorbike. The lean, hunched-forward bodywork is easy on the eye and also contributes to the bike's small frontal area

Data Fact Sheet — Triumph Daytona 675

Engine

Type	Liquid-cooled, 12v, DOHC, inline triple
Capacity	675cc
Bore x Stroke	74 x 52.3mm
Compression	12.65:1
Fuelling	Digital fuel-injection
Claimed Power	123hp @ 12,500rpm
Claimed Torque	72Nm @ 11,750rpm

Chassis

Frame	Cast aluminium beam
Front Suspension	41mm Kayaba usd telescopic, fully adjustable
Rear Suspension	Kayaba monoshock, fully adjustable
Front Brakes	Four-piston Nissin radial calipers, 308mm discs
Rear Brakes	Single-piston caliper, 220mm disc

Dimensions

Wheelbase	1392mm
Seat Height	825mm
Dry Weight	165kg est
Fuel Capacity	17.4 litres

Price

Price	£7,199 otr
Importer	Triumph Motorcycles (01455 251700)

VERDICT 8/10

A new dawn for Triumph and a sure fire hit for character alone. The 675 offers performance that's right on the pace

 Character, speed, handling, brakes, looks, noise, details

 Gearbox, comfort, no slipper clutch, the 600s lead on paper

➤ **675CC INLINE TRIPLE**
➤ **KAYABA SUSPENSION**
➤ **UNDERSEAT EXHAUST**
➤ **ULTRA-SLIM PACKAGE**
➤ **165KG**
➤ **123BHP CLAIMED**

£7,199 otr

➤ **TECHNICAL HIGHLIGHTS**

ENGINE

The tiny width is thanks to the compact engine, that's notably smaller than the old Daytona 650 four-cylinder unit. Development centred on maximising combustion efficiency, using a narrow 23-degree included valve angle. Features include CNC-machined inlet ports, Nimonic (nickel-based) exhaust valves, low-friction DLC (Diamond Like Coating) of the top piston ring, and weight-saving nutless con-rods. The stacked gearbox helps too.

The Keihin fuel-injection system is fed by a duct running from the nose, via the steering head, to the airbox. There's a midrange-boosting EXUP-type valve on the three-into-one underseat exhaust system. Peak power is 123bhp at 12,500rpm, with maximum torque of 72Nm at 11,750rpm.

CHASSIS

The Daytona's slimness is also made possible by the way its aluminium frame rails run over rather then outside the motor. Triumph builds the frame at Hinckley using a combination of closed and open-walled frame spars, for optimum stiffness and weight.

The aluminium swingarm has an adjustable pivot point as well as a ride-height adjuster. The frame is 22 per cent lighter than the Daytona 650's, helping to keep total weight down to a competitive 165kg dry.

Suspension is from Kayaba, who also supply very similiar units for the Kawasaki ZX-6R. More so than any previous Triumph, you know that this chassis has pedigree to it.

The Pirelli SuperCorsa Pro tyres are the most track focused on any middleweight, hinting the 675 is too.

➤ **DON'T BE FOOLED BY...**
Triumph's previous form. This is a scorcher that promises to give the Japs a real fight for the title

and resultant low drag coefficient.

As I headed out onto the Sepang circuit I wasn't surprised that the 675 felt light and narrow. I was more taken with how comfortable all 6'4" of me felt on the bike despite its size.

Immediately I was grateful for the bike's manoeuvrability, especially the easy yet precise way in which it could flick through the tight and trickily cambered right-left combination at the end of the pit straight.

Even more useful when relearning the circuit in drying conditions was the engine's broad power spread by

showed 160mph on the comprehensive digital instrument console, which also records lap times and fuel consumption alongside the usual.

If there was an engine-related weakness at all, it was the six-speed gearbox which didn't shift with quite the effortless precision of most. I only failed to find the right gear once, when needing a second prod to find third while cranked over. The lever action was firm enough that some riders complained of sore toes at the end of the day.

There were very few moans about the

"...the handling combines quick and accurate flickability WITH REASSURING HIGH SPEED STABILITY..."

middleweight standards. There was no questioning its taste for revs, especially every time I hit a straight and the tacho needle ripped round the dial towards the 14,000rpm redline, accompanied by a gorgeously tuneful note from the optional race can fitted for the track.

Equally impressive was the way the Daytona pulled from lower down, such as exiting the final hairpin in second gear at 6,000rpm to avoid rear wheel chatter under braking in first. I've never been as much of an advocate of slipper clutches as some riders but the 675, which has more engine braking than most fours, would benefit from one at times, and there's no denying the showroom appeal.

When I wound on the power out of most bends the revs were up at 9,000rpm grand or higher, and the Triumph accelerated with a crispness and urgency that will surely put it near the front of the middleweight battles. On the main straight it

handling though, which combined quick and accurate flickability through slow sections with reassuring high-speed stability over bumps and surface changes that could set other bikes tankslapping. The wise addition of a steering damper limited the bars to no more than a wiggle to let you know the bike's alive.

The suspension excelled on track, especially after being firmed up with a touch more compression and rebound damping at both ends. On the standard settings the ride is appropriately firm, without being harsh. Through a fast, downhill left that I recall as very bumpy on the Kawasaki ZX-6R launch in 2003, the Daytona tracked through with total poise. The Kayaba suspension is the same brand as

Riding the hotted-up Daytona 675

Two Daytonas in the Sepang circuit pit-lane looked subtly different from the others, and sounded different too, thanks to the free-breathing titanium Arrow racing exhaust system ending in a free-breathing can beneath the seat. Developed by the Italian exhaust manufacturer in conjunction with Triumph, the system is a full-on racing three-into-one that adds 5bhp to top-end power and saves 7kg over the standard system.

The Arrow pipe also gives a gorgeously tuneful sound, as a few laps of Sepang confirmed. And the pleasant surprise was that the performance benefit is by no means limited to the top end. Removing both catalyser and exhaust valve has boosted midrange too, and the otherwise stock (apart from new ECU) 675 stormed forward from 6,000rpm onwards with a gorgeous howl and a kick not from that of a good 750cc sportster.

The Arrow system is expensive at £1,300, but at least there are plenty of cheaper accessories for the Daytona, including a stainless steel slip-on exhaust can. The list of carbon-fibre parts includes silencer cover, front and rear mudguards, cockpit inner panels, and various parts such as chain guards. Several of the launch bikes were also fitted with taller screens, pillion seat covers and paddock stand bobbins, all of which are accessories. Tank bags, panniers and gel seats are also available. Long-distance road riders might do well to investigate the latter.

Stuart Wood, Daytona 675 Chief Project Engineer

"We began thinking about a new middleweight project in 2001, but it wasn't until January 2003 that we'd put a development team together. The first styling sketches were done early that year, and the engine first ran in May '03. The motor was always going to be a triple, and 675cc was the obvious capacity. It's midway between 600 and 750cc, and right for racing homologation.

"Styling was obviously vital, and we had proposals from various places, external as well as internal. This is the first time that Triumph has done styling and engineering completely in-house. We tried to make the bike not just fashionable this year; we wanted to give it some longevity.

"Looking distinctive was very important too, but we were committed to using an aluminium frame, partly because casting gives the design freedom to make it very compact. The frame was designed to be just stiff enough, so we could keep it as light as possible. With the handling we were looking for speed of steering and precision, while also making the bike stable and confidence-inspiring as a roadster. We were always aiming for performance on the road as well as the track.

"This is obviously a hugely important bike for Triumph so we're delighted that the response so far has been so positive. We'll build about 4000 units in this model year [until June 2006], and we've already had cash deposits for almost all the UK market allocation before bikes have reached the showrooms. We'll only be building twins and triples with plenty of character from now on."

the Kawasaki's, but there's no doubt that it works better than that '03 model, suggesting it should be right on pace with the brilliant current ZX-6R.

Sepang's most entertaining section is a superb double-apex right, where the Triumph could be pitched hard and held cranked over as it carved out to the outside kerb and then back to the second apex in one flowing move. It was a huge buzz once I'd exploited the huge extent of the Daytona's clearance, and the vast grip of the Pirelli Supercorsa Pros.

The two long straights also gave the Daytona plenty of opportunity to show off the feel and fade-free power of its brakes, which combine 308mm discs and radial four-pot Nissin calipers with a radial master cylinder. The 675's light weight also helps, and I can't recall a production bike that stops harder.

"...the Triumph could be PITCHED HARD AND HELD CRANKED OVER..."

Those anchors earned their keep the next day on the road, especially during the aforementioned cow incident. The handling again impressed, and the suspension functioned as well on the bumpy surfaces as on the track.

However, on the streets of Malaysia it was the Triumph's engine that was its biggest asset. As is true of any sportsbike, it was great fun to unleash warp-speed acceleration and get the adjustable blue change-up lights flashing when the road was clear enough, yet the midrange stole the show.

The flexibility allows instant and effortless acceleration at the tweak of the throttle, with no need for the downshifting required or at least encouraged by most rivals. The 675 pulls from below 3,000rpm in top, and ripped forward with impressive enthusiasm from 6,000rpm. Better still,

it did so with a distinctive three-cylinder feel and a sexy exhaust note even with the standard silencer fitted.

Sadly, I can't be so complimentary about the thin seat, which combined with the

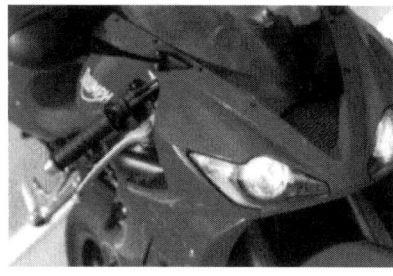

firm suspension and bumpy roads to make life slightly uncomfortable after little more than an hour. My wrists and legs were fine though, despite the low clip-ons and lofty footrests. Considered details such as the usefully wide-spaced mirrors and fair-sized 17.4-litre fuel tank were welcome too. The fully featured cockpit display adds showroom and ownership appeal in equal measure to everyday practicality.

Such is the performance focus of the middleweight supersports division that for some people the only thing that counts will be how the Daytona's lap times compare to those recorded by its four-cylinder Japanese rivals. It's impossible to answer that after riding the bike in isolation, but on paper the Triumph's 123bhp and 165kg stacks up very well even against the radical new R6's 127bhp and 161kg.

The key fact about the Daytona 675 though, is that this time the numbers are not the all-important factor, because the triple offers something else. Whether or not it's a few tenths quicker round a racetrack than all its rivals, the Triumph's style, flexibility, and unique three-cylinder character and sound make it a fantastic road bike. At £7,199 it's pretty well priced, too. Can't wait to see how it does in the group test...

Think Triumph
Think Jack Lilley
www.jacklilley.com
TRIUMPH
JL
Jack Lilley
Internationally renowned
Triumph Dealer
• Full range in stock • Stockists of Clothing
• Spares & Accessories • Free courtesy bikes
• MOT's • Performance parts • Bikes built to your spec!
Jack Lilley Ltd
Vitesse House, Ashford Rd,
Ashford, Middlesex
TW15 1XB
Tel: 01784 420421

The Triumph Daytona 675. With stunning looks and blistering performance, it's the best British sportsbike ever. Make one yours, today.
TRIUMPH
Flitwick Motorcycles
Station Road, Flitwick, MK45 1JR
Tel: 01525 712197
www.flitwickmotorcycles.co.uk
GO YOUR OWN WAY

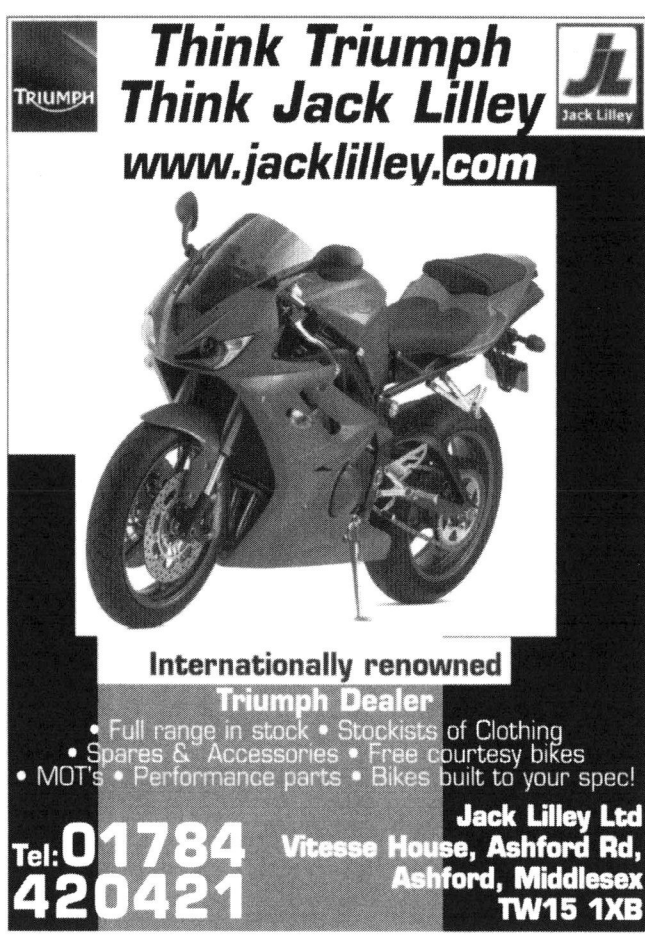

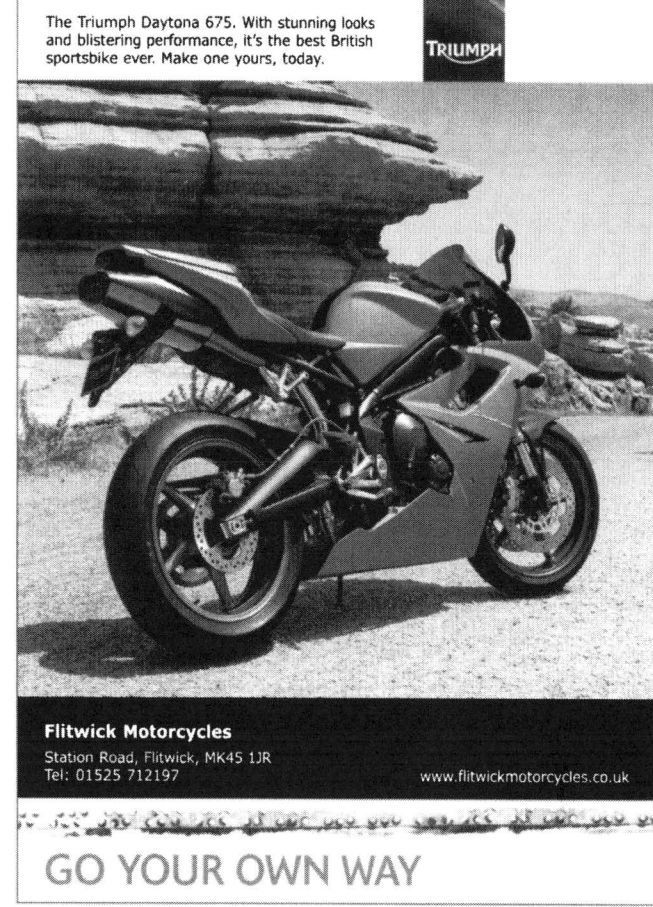

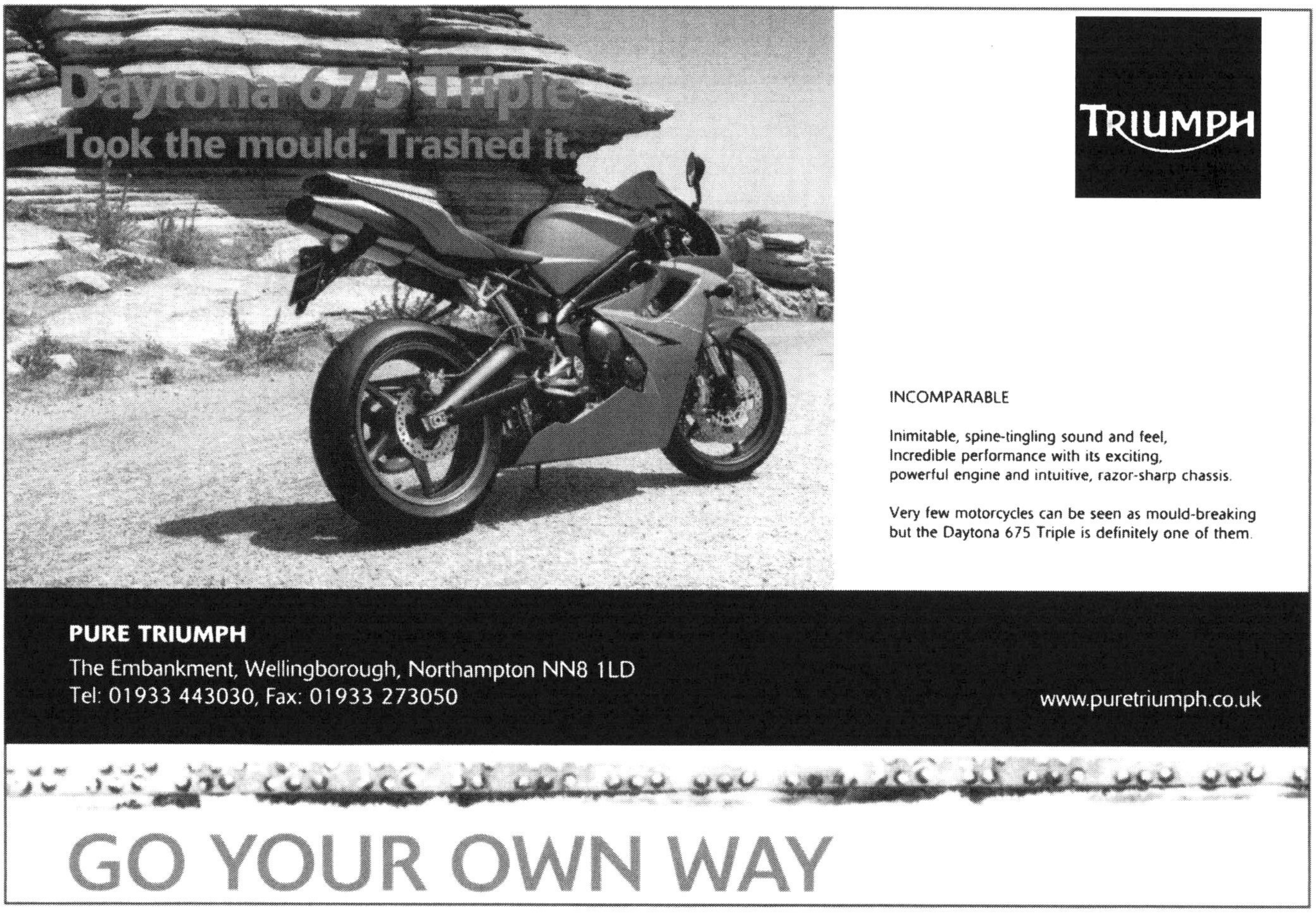
Daytona 675 Triple
Took the mould. Trashed it.
TRIUMPH
INCOMPARABLE
Inimitable, spine-tingling sound and feel,
Incredible performance with its exciting,
powerful engine and intuitive, razor-sharp chassis.
Very few motorcycles can be seen as mould-breaking
but the Daytona 675 Triple is definitely one of them.
PURE TRIUMPH
The Embankment, Wellingborough, Northampton NN8 1LD
Tel: 01933 443030, Fax: 01933 273050
www.puretriumph.co.uk
GO YOUR OWN WAY

WHILE WE OWE ULTRA-COMpetitive 600cc Supersport racing for propagating today's highly evolved middleweight sportbikes, working within race rules doesn't necessarily result in the best bike for the street rider. A year ago we rounded up the 2005 middleweight supersports and trained our focus on outright racetrack performance. The overall winner was closely wedded to lap times, dragstrip ETs, peak power and the *Wow!* factor. This year, we vowed to flesh out the best sportbike for real-world riders.

Last year's hardcore performance focus stemmed from spending two days at a race circuit, the first on track-day-spec tires at the tight and technical Streets of Willow Springs road course. Ultra-soft, high-grip race rubber and aftermarket performance exhaust systems were fitted for the following day's hot laps around the high-speed, 2.5-mile Willow Springs International Raceway. After we'd worn our knee sliders thin, multi-time drag-racing champion Rickey Gadson joined us

at Los Angeles County Raceway, where he scorched the strip at a record pace. (The Gadson Factor must be considered if comparing last year's times with the quarter-mile performance of the current machines–the bikes haven't slowed as the numbers might suggest.)

This time we set out to assess the class in a manner more suited to mere mortal sportbike enthusiasts. We limited our track activities to a single day at the Streets of Willow and a morning at the LACR quarter-mile, and spent more time riding highways, byways and backroads. Our goal: Name a winner based on most usable performance, competence and convenience.

While all the street miles were logged on stock tires, we mounted Pirelli Diablo Corsa radials on each bike for the road-course portion. Positioned as a track-day tire, the Diablo Corsa is available in both 120/70 and 120/65 front sizes, the latter of which allowed Kawasaki's ZX-6R to retain its standard tire size throughout the test. Before switching tires at the track, each bike was first lapped on its stock rubber so we could quickly identi-

Middleweight GREATS

Taking it to the road, racetrack and dragstrip

BY DON CANET

Middleweight GREATS

fy any handling-related issues that a tire swap can potentially induce. We need not have worried, as each and every bike took to the Diablos like hell on wheels, with excellent steering feel, stability and lasting grip.

Straws were drawn to determine the order in which the bikes were ridden during the comparative timed-lap sessions. MyChron Light TG lap timers fitted to each bike assured accurate times were recorded. Associate Editor Mark Cernicky led off, putting in five-lap stints aboard each bike before handing over to Executive Editor Mark Hoyer and then me in turn. After a few minor chassis adjustments, Cernicky ran through the rotation a second time, establishing each bike's quickest time in the process. Following the "official" timed sessions, our new Associate Editor Blake Conner and Brienne Thomson—the latter a competitive club roadracer borrowed from *CW*'s marketing department—were introduced into the mix for open testing throughout the afternoon.

I handled the riding chores at LACR, keeping the number of clutch-torturing launches to a minimum, while the entire group played musical chairs, swapping bikes repeatedly throughout the two-day street ride that followed. Now for our observations in the order the straws were drawn:

HONDA CBR600RR

Price	$8999
Dry weight	401 lb.
Wheelbase	54.6 in.
Seat height	32.2 in.
Fuel mileage	34.4 mpg
0-60 mph	3.0 sec.
1/4-mile	10.70 sec.
	@ 128.55 mph
Horsepower	101.53 bhp
	@ 13,640 rpm
Torque	43.10 ft.-lbs.
	@ 10,930 rpm
Top speed	156 mph

▲Ups
- ▲ Subtle and sinister in silver
- ▲ Superbly refined suspension
- ▲ Comfortable riding position
- ▲ Rheostat throttle response

▼Downs
- ▼ Give us some of that Formula Xtreme power…
- ▼ Softer saddle, please
- ▼ "Wow!" factor deficit

HONDA CBR600RR

As luck had it, Honda drew the shortest straw and was first in the rotation, the significance being that the CBR offers a "jump on and go," rider-friendly demeanor with solid and predictable handling that instills immediate confidence.

"Of the five bikes, the Honda tracked over bumps the best, and although it didn't have the top-end zing of the others, the torque available from 7000 rpm was a welcome friend on corner exits," remarked Hoyer. "Throttle response both rolling on and off the power upset the chassis least in the group (as in not at all), and the connection between the right grip and the rear contact patch felt the most direct, predictable and natural."

This was a common sentiment shared by others. "The CBR makes the most out of what it has," offered Conner. "It obviously has the least power of any bike in the test, but the engine is a flexible performer."

The Honda chassis drew praise for having a light-feeling front end–though Conner thought it was maybe bordering on being *too* light. "It can feel momentarily vague when you first flick it in," he said, "but it turns quick."

This fine balance of agility and stability lends a trustworthy feeling that translates very well to the street where you don't always know what's around the next bend. Relative comfort is also one of the CBR's strong suits, with a natural riding position and a shorter reach to the bars than the others. It was a good bike to find yourself aboard when covering the freeway stages between favorite backroads.

"If the Honda had a 636cc engine, it might be *the* choice," suggested Hoyer.

Suzuki GSX-R600

"Black and blue, with some white from years of experience in the racetrack fight," was our resident poet Sir'nicky's Suzuki surmise. With development ongoing since its introduction back in 1993, the 600 Gixxer has stocked its fair share of trophy cases over the years, and the new model continues that track-ready tradition. Which makes it all the more remarkable just how good this latest bike works on the street.

SUZUKI GSX-R600

Price	$8799	
Dry weight	410 lb.	
Wheelbase	55.1 in.	
Seat height	32.2 in.	
Fuel mileage	36.1 mpg	
0-60 mph	3.1 sec.	
1/4-mile	10.75 sec.	
	@ 129.41 mph	
Horsepower	106.09 bhp	
	@ 13,330 rpm	
Torque	43.61 ft.-lbs.	
	@ 11,140 rpm	
Top speed	157 mph	

▲**Ups**
▲ Adjustable footpegs
▲ Killer brakes
▲ Best-balanced "real" 600
▲ Some semblance of under-seat storage

▼**Downs**
▼ Brakes a little too killer?
▼ Packs the most pounds
▼ Hey, my muffler's missing!

Of the true 600s, Hoyer picked the GSX-R600 as his overall favorite, pointing out its torquey-feeling engine, excellent stability and killer brakes.

"Okay, it didn't have the top-end of the Yamaha or the bottom-end of the Honda, but rather combined the good qualities of both," was the Exec. Ed.'s declaration.

"As fine-tuned and specialized as these middleweights are, the GSX-R's blend of stability and smooth power delivery wins my vote for best all-rounder," read Brienne's ballot. "It's the best-looking too, a smooth contender on track and a

MiddleweightGREATS

Middleweight GREATS

confident canyon-carver off."

Despite the Gixxer being the bulkiest bike of the bunch when rolled onto the *CW* scale and the heaviest-handling too, working it into and out of turns was far from laborious. While it may require more effort at the bars than the others, that's a relative comparison. Raising rear ride height by inserting a 5mm shim into the shock's top mount helped quicken steering without adverse effects on the bike's super-solid stability. "The GSX-R turns-in nicely, certainly not as quick as the others, but good nonetheless," commented Conner. "What it lacks in quickness it makes up in bite, allowing the rider to trust the front when it gets chucked in on its side."

The Suzuki's brakes were very strong, offering the most power of any bike here, but could benefit from a more progressive feel. "They seem to give you everything they've got right away," stated Blake.

We all agreed the Suzuki felt reasonably comfortable on the street, had a good seating position and a fairly comfortable saddle, making it nearly but not quite as plush as the Kawi ZX-6R.

Kawasaki ZX-6R

Kawasaki's 636cc ZX-6R has been the over-bore poster-boy of modern middleweights, ignoring class boundaries as drawn by sanctioned racing, leaving the limited-edition 599cc ZX-6RR to mop up on the racetrack. Rules be damned, we're certainly not going to protest the results, as the ZX has proven a very practical performer and popular choice among non-racer sportbike enthusiasts.

Hoyer's comments hit the nail on the head: "That 636cc engine is great on the road, with all the torque you want and

KAWASAKI ZX-6R

Price	$8699
Dry weight	399 lb.
Wheelbase	54.9 in.
Seat height	32.2 in.
Fuel mileage	36.1 mpg
0-60 mph	3.0 sec.
1/4-mile	10.58 sec.
@	132.36 mph
Horsepower	109.43 bhp
@	13,210 rpm
Torque	46.46 ft.-lbs.
@	11,540 rpm
Top speed	160 mph

Ups
- ▲ Comfortable, roomy and plush
- ▲ Killer torque, great top-end power
- ▲ Drag racer's delight

Downs
- ▼ Scrapes soonest on-track
- ▼ Feels biggest there, too
- ▼ Buzzy Wuzzy are the pegs/bars
- ▼ Difficult-to-read LCD tachometer

plenty of top-end, too. The seat is comfortable, as are the overall ergonomics."

The ZX was the largest-feeling bike of the group, something you sense simply rolling it around the garage. It suits larger riders better than the other bikes, offering a more spacious seating position that makes it an easy choice for longer rides. There is one caveat to consider, however, as the Kawi's motor vibrates more than the rest, felt as buzziness in the bars and pegs.

"No learning the quirks here," said Thomson, who sided with Hoyer in choosing the Ninja as a top-two pick.

Cernicky's two cents regarding the bike's ease of use and high level of refinement lent further credence. "I thought Honda had the corner on that market, but the 636 is right there," he noted.

But he was referencing the Kawi's street showing more than its performance on the track, where it offered less cornering clearance than the others, grounding its shift and brake pedals when pushed hard. "During our days on the street, you couldn't beat the 6R's balance, all-around suspension, comfort and powerful brakes. A good package," was Cernicky's final assessment.

Triumph Daytona 675

Blending in like Prince Charles at a Tokyo train station, this British Triple brings a fresh dimension to the middleweight category. Judged purely by the 675 displayed on its flank, the Triumph appears to hold an unfair advantage in this test. Considering that it evenly straddles the gap between the 600cc Fours and 750cc Twins that have co-occupied the category for years, Triumph's entry offers logically legit engine performance parity.

There's no mistaking the Daytona for one of its classmates once you're under way. "The Triple powerplant has a neat growling sound that gives the impression of lower revs than it is actually spinning," noted Hoyer. "I hit the rev-limiter the first few laps because the aural cue was so different than with the Fours." Thanks to its easy-to-read tachometer and hard-to-miss shift light, this was not a frequent occurrence. Along with having the lowest redline, a "paltry" 13,250 rpm verified by the *CW* dyno (see "Tach Truths," page 51), the 675 also offers less over-rev than the rest. Still, the 750 rpm the Daytona does provide past its peak power output is a welcome departure from typical Triumph practice of setting the

TRIUMPH DAYTONA 675	
Price $8999	**Ups**
Dry weight . . . . 394 lb.	▲ Great engine note
Wheelbase . . . . 54.9 in.	▲ Dares to be different!
Seat height . . . . 33.4 in.	▲ Feature-rich dash
Fuel mileage . . . . 33.7 mpg	▲ Fun, Fun, Fun!
0-60 mph . . . . 3.2 sec.	
1/4-mile . . . . . . 10.76 sec.	**Downs**
@ 129.31 mph	▼ High seat
Horsepower . . . . 106.99 bhp	▼ Firm seat
@ 12,500 rpm	▼ No race team to cheer for
Torque . . . . . . 47.49 ft.-lbs.	
@ 9900 rpm	
Top speed . . . . 155 mph	

rev-limiter to cut in as power is still on the rise.

Super-slick shift action and a very low level of engine vibration are other elements that impressed us as we rode the Daytona on the street. We found the 675's on-throttle response a bit abrupt at first, but after removing excess cable slack and spending time in the saddle, we got used to its light throttle spring. Another aspect that stands out is the Daytona's taller saddle, measuring nearly an inch higher than any of the others here. The seat is narrow at the front, though, allowing firm footing at stops.

The tall saddle and slim overall nature of this Triple give an impression of limitless cornering clearance. "For me, the theme running through the 675 is *highfalutin*," observed

Middleweight GREATS

Middleweight GREATS

Cernicky. "High footrests, high seat height, high torque, high pipe and the highest amount of cornering clearance."

While each bike here has stellar front stoppers, the Triumph's Nissins were perhaps the best. "They have the same power as the Suzuki's, but offer a bit more feel," said Conner. "Not as progressive as the Yamaha brakes but impressive to say the least."

Quick steering geometry, reactive suspension and a feathery dry weight that only the Yamaha YZF-R6 could match made the Daytona chassis feel like a race platform–even if Triumph isn't marketing it as such. Add to this a broad torque spread that simply makes the bike hook up and go, and you have the Daytona setting fast time at the technical Streets of Willow circuit. Maybe Hinckley should reconsider its "no racing" policy?

"Overall this is by far the best engine for me," said Conner. "On the track it pulls out of corners with lots of torque and still has a decent top-end. The way it performs both on the track and on the street makes it the best overall compromise for a middleweight bike."

Perhaps the most telling testament is that unlike the race-focused R6, this bike has an engine that riders of any ability will be able to easily tap. "That big low-end torque advantage made it much easier to go fast for those of us who are less precise with our shift points," Hoyer confessed.

Yamaha YZF-R6

A Ten Best Bike winner with its 600 last year, Yamaha has unleashed a whole different animal with the 2006 YZF-R6. Why mess with success? Simply stated, Supersport titles are not won by those who stand still.

The engine powering this new R6 takes on a race-oriented focus that's a step beyond any other bike here, but as a result, lower-end performance was sacrificed for gains on top. The good news is the R6 has matched the peak horsepower of the larger-displacement Kawasaki 636. It's

YAMAHA YZF-R6	
Price............$9199	
Dry weight........394 lb.	
Wheelbase ....54.8 in.	
Seat height.......32.6 in.	
Fuel mileage ....33.4 mpg	
0-60 mph ....3.0 sec.	
1/4-mile ......10.67 sec.	
@ 130.79 mph	
Horsepower....109.40 bhp	
@ 14,420 rpm	
Torque......42.65 ft.-lbs.	
@ 11,800 rpm	
Top speed ....160 mph	

▲ Ups
- ▲ Finely focused track tool
- ▲ Fast and exciting
- ▲ Screams like a Banshee!

▼ Downs
- ▼ "Hello, is this thing on?" midrange
- ▼ Most expensive
- ▼ Least versatile
- ▼ Liar, liar, pants on fire!

a bold step for Yamaha, sure, but not a blind leap of faith–as last year's bike remains in the lineup for '06, offering buyers a more practical machine for everyday use.

If you're revved up on Red Bull you'll likely love this bike in any situation. "I had a lot of fun riding this R6," said a twitchy Cernicky. "Even though it has virtually no power down low, who cares? It's a 600 and you're supposed to wring its neck!"

That's exactly what's required to achieve a decent launch at the dragstrip. After a few bogged starts, a solid pass happened only after staging with revs held at 12,000 rpm and slipping the clutch throughout first gear with the tach needle hovering above 15,000 rpm. It sounded rather painful, not unlike a power saw slicing through a 2x4!

We found the R6 exhilarating to ride on the road course, although it was a bit more work than the others. "The racetrack-refugee engine is *sooooo* alive above 12,000 rpm, and the taut, controlled suspension means killer composure on the track," enthused Hoyer, adding this addendum following our street outing: "That engine is barely alive below 12,000 rpm. It runs fine and carburets cleanly below this rpm, but it just doesn't have the torque to make a street ride fun at less than nine-tenths. If I zinged the motor between 12,000 and 15,000 rpm, I could carry a great pace but felt like I was making a scene, and it was pretty frantic feeling."

Blessed with the most race-oriented chassis in the group, the YZF makes hitting your marks and holding or adjusting your line easy. "The R6 carves into turns with almost reckless abandon," was Blake's take. "It borders on the edge of being unstable without ever really getting there. Once the rider learns to trust the feel and feedback, this bike pays big dividends."

Conclusion

If you're a racer chasing after Yamaha contingency money at the track, then the new R6 is the cat's meow. But doggy delivery under 10K leaves the average street rider chasing his tail with

this one, or as Hoyer put it, "Livable as a streetbike, yes, but not that much fun."

If you bleed blue and white, the Suzuki could be the bike for you. Tractable power delivery, rock-solid stability and a high degree of streetable comfort and convenience make the GSX-R600 a bike that will complement any pit box or garage.

Honda hits the same mark it has for several seasons, and remains a familiar friend that can always be counted on. No slouch, either, as the CBR was the basis of Team Honda's Daytona 200 dominance this year (see "Special FX," page 54), take that, high-revving blue-bomber Yamahas.

Kawasaki nearly won this shootout last year, but the ZX-6R we tested had stability issues on the track, shaking its head and ours as well. No such symptoms surfaced this time out, a credit to the Pirelli Diablo tires, we think. A closer second place this year then for the 636.

But there's a new Britbike on the block, and pound for pound, Triumph's Daytona 675 offers the best all-around performance, versatility and visual flare in the middleweight sportbike class. See, you don't always need to race to win. ◘

MiddleweightGREATS

CAPACITIES COMPARED THREE '600s' TESTED ON ROAD AND TRACK

It's a question we get asked a lot these days. Which is the best Supersport 600? Answering it is hard, because – in the case of the three bikes featured in this compare – only one, the Yamaha, is a true 600.

WORDS: Ed **PICS:** Andrew Bright-Ultrapix

If you've ever wondered why you don't regularly see multi-bike comparos in Kiwi Rider blame the dynamics of the local market. Ex-Ed Bentman tried once - with a posse of Euro twins and things - and swore he'd never do it again. Even getting a second - similar- bike to do a meaningful comparison with is hard. There just aren't the test bikes available. There's also the simple fact of logistics. In preparing this report I checked out a number of overseas magazines to see how they approached comparison tests and I was gob-smacked.

At events like Masterbike in Spain (where magazines from all over the world pay a fee to join in a week-long comparison-fest of all the

new Superbike and Supersport machines) the manufacturers supply the bikes, a nominated tyre company supplies the tyres and there are technicians on hand to do all the tyre-changing, suspensioin fettling etc. Just, in fact, like a world press launch.

Even US magazine Roadracing World takes along a chief technician and nominates and sources a control tyre, not to mention approaches the data collecting with a zeal second only to that of a CIA operative.

Here we're lucky enough to get a handbook with the bikes we test, the rationale from the companies providing them that 'you guys always lose them!'

THE BIKES

And so, it was only a combination of luck and circumstance that saw us with more than one 600 Supersport-class bike in the Kiwi Rider Kompound at the same time. And when I discovered that there was a TT Track Day on at Taupo, the idea of pitting Yamaha's YZF-R6 against Kawasaki's ZX-6R (636) suddenly appeared not only possible but feasible.

It still seemed ridiculously hard to; 1) get the two bikes in Betty Blue (KR's Transit van) and 2) get away from the constantly ringing bloody phone, but BikeMart man Todd and I – eventually – freed ourselves of the shackles of magazine publishing and headed south. Which constituted part 1 of the comparison test.

Part 2 came about, again, pretty much by accident, when the lovely Leigh Beckhaus from Triumph NZ rang and asked if we wanted to (finally) test a Daytona 675? 'Of course we did,' came the answer, to which the reply was; 'we've got two here!!! Come and pick them up!' Which we did the day before – coincidence again – a nominated car and bike test day at Pukekohe's Pukekohe Park circuit.

KAWASAKI ZX-6R

All three bikes have had huge press this year so I'll assume you know the basic details. Starting alphabetically so as not to indicate any possible early favouritism, we have the Kawasaki, at $15,449

The key difference here is that its engine has a bore & stroke of 68 x 43.8 mm for a capacity of 636cc. You also need to know that though there is indeed a new 600cc-only model for the '07 model year the '06 636 was itself the result of a significant upgrade. The sporty, practical '06

had its genesis in 2003 when Kawasaki came out with a 636 for road and a limited edition 599cc RR for track work. The basic model/s continued in '04 with minor engine work then in '05 both bikes got a significant 'mid-term' upgrade based round a new frame, bigger petal-style brakes, a radial master cylinder to go with the radially-mounted front brake calipers and a slipper clutch.

TRIUMPH DAYTONA 675

If you read last month's Quick Spin you'll already know that Todd and I left Pukekohe Park very impressed with the new, small Trumpy. For the purposes of this comparo, again, the first thing you need to know is that its 74 x 52.3mm bore & stroke gives its unique (in this company anyway) in-line three cylinder engine a nominal capacity of 675cc, hence the name.

Bar the distinctive engine the wee Triumph is specced up just like the other 600s, with the accent on sharp looks, serious performance and a brake and suspension package with all the bells and whistles, including adjustable ride height and swingarm pivot. In fact bar the lack of a slipper clutch the 675 is just as well set up ex-factory for conversion to a racebike as the Yamaha and Kawasaki – it even comes standard with Pirelli's Track Day/Club Race-spec Supercorsa tyres.

The only other issue to contend with is the price, at $17,990 the 675 is the most expensive bike in the sample.

YAMAHA YZF-R6

No guesses which bike the Ed (me) thought would walk this comparo – Yamaha's new-for-'06 YZF-R6. The key thing you need to know

about the Yamaha is that it is not what it seems. Eyeball it and with its short, stubby wheelbase (10mm shorter than the other two bikes here), low-slung fairing and screen and stratospheric rev range (red line is set at what has turned out to be an optimistic 17,500rpm) it looks like it is going to be the wildest bull at the rodeo. In fact, it is the most stable, so stable and self-assured that it DOESN'T get a steering damper as standard!

Price-wise, at $17,495 it slips neatly between the Kawasaki and the Triumph but frankly you're not comparing apples with apples. All three are fuel-injected but the Yamaha is by far the most sophisticated from an engineering standpoint, coming standard with titanium valves, Yamaha's new YCC-T (Yamaha Chip Controlled Throttle) system and the first of the Buell-like under-engine muffler systems.

ERGONOMICS

Kawasaki ZX-6R: Though more and more riders are attending Track Days most buyers of 600 Supersport bikes are going to spend the vast majority of their riding time on the road, at or around 100-140 km/h. So ergonomics are important.

Starting with the Kawasaki. The ZX-R6 has the most 'old-fashioned' feel as far as riding position is concerned. Not necessarily a bad thing. You drop down 'into' the cockpit' with your arms stretching forward rather than down to the clip-on style handlebars, and there's plenty of room to push your bum back on the broad, comfortable seat slab. So, for everyday use, the Kawasaki scores highly from an ergonomic point of view. It's also quite a nice bike to ride at the track, with plenty of room for a tall-ish bloke like me to slip down and tuck his torso behind the fairing screen. The ZX-R also drops nicely into corners with very little inertia (a trait Kawasaki has also managed to achieve with the new ZX-10R) and you can slide on and off the seat with ease.

Triumph Daytona 675: Here's a turn-up for the books. First things first. Compared to the Kawasaki and the Yamaha, the Triumph feels quantifiably slimmer. It looks it too, taking a leaf out of the original Fireblade book with lots of 'holes' you can see through, cfm the Kawasaki with it's wrap-around fairing and the Yamaha with it's compact all-enveloping packaging. It feels so slim in fact, that after swapping from one to the other you could (almost) confuse the triple with something like a Ducati or Yamaha TRX850 twin. As delivered the 675 has a lot of rake (the rear is higher than the front) and when that is combined with the fact that the seat 'feels' taller than the brochure's 460mm, the riding position is not as immediately inviting or as user-friendly as that of the Kawasaki or even the stubby Yamaha. Factor in what – again – feel

like clip-ons set 5-6mm lower than those of the other two bikes and the position is one you're going to have to put up with on the road. It's also quite difficult, for one reason or another, to climb off the thing in the corners. Check out the pictures and you'll notice less knee-down action on the Triumph, something – I think – to do with the 'cut' of the seat squab. In its defence the differences are minor, but they're there.

Yamaha YZF-R6: That Yamaha is the future writ large, and if you don't believe me look at Honda's new 800cc MotoGP bike. Paint it white and stick Yamaha decals on it and it could be an R6. The interesting thing is, I found the R6 perfectly acceptable on the street, to the point where, when I had all three bikes in the garage it was my preferred commuter. You definitely do sit much more forward on the Yamaha than you do the old-skool Kawasaki or the half-way-house Triumph but the bars are as much as 20mm higher than those of other 600cc bikes so they don't carry as much torso weight as those of the Triumph, or for that matter the Kawasaki.

There appears to be less room between the seat and the footpegs than on other 600s but again, you don't ride along thinking 'hell my knees can't take much more of this.' Oddly then, it's a bit harder to climb on and off the Yamaha through the turns.

PERFORMANCE

Kawasaki ZX-6R: Here's where it gets interesting. For day to day use the ZX-6R is going to keep a good 70 to 80% of Supersport sector buyers as happy as Larry. Even those who test ride an R6 or the Triumph are going to think it is pretty damn fine. There's a nice revvy, light fly-wheel feel to the Kawasaki's power delivery and – if you hang on in their and keep it revving – an espresso jolt of a top end which if you don't mind me mixing my metaphors is the icing on the

Top: The Ed hard at it at Taupo on the R6. Above: Daytona didn't like Pukekohe's bumps...

cake. You have to keep the engine revving though because it'd be fair to say the mid-range is not in the same league.

While it's a tractable engine, and 'fuels' with a carburettor-like smoothness down low, allowing you to use second rather than first round Taupo, there simply is not the punch through the mid-range you get with the Triumph and – as long as you're in the right gear – the Yamaha. Strange because a quick look at the Masterbike dyno figures show the Kawasaki produces the most power (89 kW @ 14,010 rpm.) and Todd swore it felt like the quickest bike of the bunch.

The answer, methinks, lies in the relative torque figures, the Kawasaki producing 65NM at a relative high 11,500 rpm cfm the Triumph which produces 66 Nm at just 9800rpm. OK, the Yamaha is even worse off, producing just 61 Nm at 11,600rpm, but in its defence on the track at least you very rarely venture below 10,000rpm on the Yamaha.

Triumph Daytona 675: Woooohoooo! This thing lights up just off idle and hangs on in there until the redline, re-defining the way we (us journos) talk about the way a bike produces its power. Usually there's either a softish bottom end (any Ram Air Kawasaki) a dull, flat mid-range (the Yamaha in this case) and a searing top end (again, most Kawasakis).

The Triumph makes awesome, torque-infused power everywhere and if there is a bike with a set of gear ratios better matched to an engine I've yet to ride it. On the track this manifests itself as a small-bore like propensity to encourage its rider to simply hold the throttle open and keep shifting, slowing only to negotiate corners. You don't NEED to change gear as often as you do on the Yamaha, but the funny thing is, you end up doing it anyway, because that's what you do when you're riding fast!

Ultimately it doesn't have the top-end hit of either the Kawasaki or the Yamaha, but conversely it's the bike that has the potential – given the rider – to get off the line and into, then out of, corners quickest.

Yamaha YZF-R6: Todd calls the R6 the datum

– translated, the bike against which all others in the sector should be compared. And he's got a point. Much has already been written about the way the wee R6 produces its power, and it's fair to say that almost all of it is correct. What I personally like about it is that it is that from the minute you thumb the starter and the engine bursts into a lumpy 'take-me-seriously' idle, the R6 feels up-for-it.

Yes you have to rev the crap out of it and believe me you have to work at it to get it right but if and when you do you could bottle the feeling and sell it. Yes you might be in the rev stratosphere but the climb is worthwhile as there is a strong, broad seam of torquey power which hauls in the horizon as quickly as any litre-bike.

In a funny kind of way the R6 is also a deceptive little bugger, making light of the speeds you are travelling courtesy arguably the best chassis in the middleweight sports category – and definitely in our sample.

Even on the road I got to forgive it and chastise myself for any initial misgivings. Though you never need to rev it past 11,000 or sometimes 12,00rpm on the way to work, school or whatever, you tend to hold gears longer just to savour the rough-house exhaust note. Which is worth a sentence or too, courtesy Yamaha's move to an under-engine muffler and stubby MotoGP-style end pipe.

Because the pipe exits just behind your right shoe you hear and feel the exhaust note more than you do if your bike has an 'under-seat' muffler like the whisper quiet Kawasaki and the distinctive, raspberry-ish tone of the Triumph

HANDLING

Kawasaki ZX-6R: Now here it gets really interesting. The best bike for someone getting into the sport would be the Kawasaki. Simply put it is the roomiest, most genuinely comfortable, and – straight off the showroom floor – the easiest to set up and ride quickly on. Confidence-inspiring? That's an understatement. At Taupo I

Yamaha YZF-R6 scored top marks at the track

SOMETHING FOR EVERYONE

By Todd 'Gibernau' Sutherland

There's a bit of everything with these three.

The Yamaha is the datum. It's the hottest ticket in the sports-focused 600 sector and (on the track at least) it delivers. The other two are snubs at the convention of transverse in-line 600cc fours.

The Triumph 675 steals the Kawasaki 636's thunder by being so much more than a 'little different.' I've always been perplexed at the rational behind the Kawasaki. I mean, it's a four cylinder and despite its sporty pedigree it simply isn't able to compete in any production racing, and all

for 36cc more? What's the point of that?

However, having ridden the Kawasaki back to back with the R6 the mist did clear a little

ON THE TRACK

The 636 and 675 feel more 'old-skool 750' (i.e. GSX-R/FZR) after riding the diminutive R6. In a relative sense their power feels 'big-bore' too.

The R6 is brilliant but its engine demands a two-stroke-like throttling (what's wrong with that? Ed) to keep the party going on down there.

Like a small brush you can put the R6 right where you want it too, but you have to work fast and accurately to keep ahead of the other two. It feels great when you're 'on-it' but anything less

than hard-out the other two will be right there.

ON THE ROAD

On the road I was convinced the 636 would make the R6 seem like a duck out of water (track) but in the end my wrists suffered on both bikes. Perhaps because I only used the R6 to commute on, its lack of punch down low didn't seem obvious. Either that or the nice looks and that throaty exhaust note may have distracted me from any other road shortcomings.

And in case you're wondering, I can't really comment on the Trumpy because I didn't get to ride it on the road. 🛇

R6 is an acquired taste on the road

loved the way it dropped down into the apex and stayed 'on-arc' as you eased the power back on. Significantly too, neither Todd nor I ended up changing any of the clickers, front or rear. Yes it feels a more substantial 'older style' bike than either the Triumph or Yamaha but that's not necessarily a bad thing. Ride too is comfortable, the only Achilles heel the fact that it does shake its head under hard acceleration. Quite a bit actually and an odd characteristic considering how stable it is under brakes and how comfortable it feels on the edge of its tyres

Triumph Daytona 675: Hmmmm. If the Triumph has an Achilles heel it is in the area of ride. As delivered it was set up with more rake (nose down/tail up) than on pretty much any other road bike I've tested – ever! While both Todd and I were fairly happy with the handling, had we been able to keep the test bike another week it would have gone into the workshop for a major session. Ex-factory the front end felt a couple of clicks too soft, particularly in terms of the ride height (preload) and compression damping. Had the rear end not had so much rake (there no doubt to facilitate the required weight

over the front) and been a little bit more compliant in the spring we might have been happy to leave it alone. But even with my 86-or-so kgs the rear end kicked over bumps that the Kawasaki ploughed through and the Yamaha 'managed.'

That said, my lasting impressions of the little Trumpy is of how light the steering is, and how slim and nimble the chassis is. And, despite its feather-light feel the 675 is also commendably stable, making me wonder why Triumph bothered to fit a steering damper.

Yamaha YZF-R6: Oddly enough first impressions of the Yamaha at Taupo were a bit so/so. Having said that I better say straight up that I think the R6 is by far the best handler of the bunch, it's just that it took a bit to 'too-tooing' to 'dial it in' to my liking. At the world launch I commented on the lack of fore-aft weight transfer, and the taut yet compliant action of the suspension. What I noticed at Taupo was how much work I had to put in to get the thing to change direction, particularly at our slower corner entry speeds. Re-reading my notes from the press launch I find that Yamaha actually increased both rake and trail over the '05 model and after rid-

Everyone liked the spare, slimline look of the Triumph triple

ing the '06 I understand why. For such a stubby, just plain radical-looking bike the new R6 is amazingly stable, to the point where to make it 'feel' more responsive I'd like to ride it with Triumph Daytona 675-like rake. As it is the R6 is the member of the group which feels like it has the most potential, as if, as a mere mortal riding a bike straight off the showroom floor, you are just scratching the surface of its ability and potential

BRAKES

I'll cover this quickly because I'm running out of room. All three bikes have state-of-the-art radi-

ally-mounted front calipers yet the Yamaha has the best combination of feel and power, the Kawasaki lacks a little feel and ultimately power (in this company) and the Triumph has feel at the lever and perfectly acceptable power but is compromised by some chassis instability in extreme situations, something I'd attribute to all that rake and the rear end literally 'topping out.'

TO CONCLUDE

Pardon me for not including comprehensive graphs of possible fuel consumption while long distance touring on these three middleweights.

The simple fact of the matter is you want one or the other because it is the fastest/quickest/bestest looking bike you can afford. We've covered cost and we've covered the three in both the track and road environment. Distributors hate us doing this but Masterbike does, so we will too. The Yamaha's the best bike by a long-shot though the Kawasaki is an ever-so-slightly better 'all-rounder.'

And the Triumph?

While I can't quite understand how it beat the other two to the Masterbike title I can understand why it was always a contender. KR

SPECIFICATIONS

KAWASAKI ZX-6R

ENGINE
Type: Liquid-cooled DOHC 16-valve in-line 4 cylinder 4-stroke
Displacement: 636cc
Compression Ratio: 12.9:1
Bore x stroke: 68 x 43.8mm
Starting system: Electric
Engine Management system: Electronic
Fuel system: Electronic Keihin fuel injection w/ 4 x 38mm throttle bodies
Clutch: Slipper-type wet multiplate
Transmission: 6-speed
Final drive: Chain

FRAME
Type: Beam-type aluminium
Swingarm: Aluminium
Front suspension: 41mm ISD-type telescopic forks fully adjustable
Rear suspension: Bottom-link Uni-Trak w/gas-charged shock absorber fully adjustable
Brakes: Twin semi-floating 300mm discs w/radially-mounted 4-piston calipers front & single 220mm disc w/ single piston caliper rear
Wheels: Cast aluminium 3.5 x 17 front /5.5. x 17 rear
Tyres: Bridgestone Battlax BT014F 120/65ZR17 front & Battlax R180/55ZR17 rear

DIMENSIONS
Wheelbase: 1390mm
Rake: 25 degrees
Trail: 106mm
LxWxH: 2065 x 715 x 1110mm
Seat height: 820mm
Dry Weight: 164kg
Fuel tank capacity: 18 l
RRP: $15,449
Test bike: Kawasaki NZ Ltd

TRIUMPH DAYTONA 675

ENGINE
Type: Liquid-cooled DOHC 12-valve in-line 3-cylinder
Displacement: 675cc
Compression Ratio: 12.65:1
Bore x stroke: 74 x 52.3mm
Starting system: Electric
Engine Management system: Multipoint EFI
Fuel system: Multipoint sequential electronic fuel injection
Clutch: Wet multiplate
Transmission: 6-speed
Final drive: Chain

FRAME
Type: Perimeter-style aluminium
Swingarm: Aluminium
Front suspension: 41mm Kayaba USD-type forks, fully adjustable
Rear suspension: Kayaba monochock fully adjustable
Brakes: Twin 308mm discs w/ radially-mounted 4-piston calipers front & single 220mm disc w/ single-piston caliper rear
Wheels: Cast aluminium alloy 5-spoke 3.5 x 17 front & 5.5 x 17 rear
Tyres: Pirelli Supercorsa 120/70ZR17 front. 180/55ZR17 rear

DIMENSIONS
Wheelbase: 1392mm
Rake: 23.5 degrees
Trail: 86.8mm
LxWxH: 2010 x 673 x 1109mm
Seat height: 825mm
Dry Weight: 165kg
Fuel tank capacity: 17.4 l
RRP: $17,990
Test bike: Triumph NZ

YAMAHA YZF-R6

ENGINE
Type: Liquid-cooled DOHC 16-valve in-line 4-cylinder
Displacement: 59cc
Compression Ratio: 12.8:1
Bore x stroke: 67 x 42.5mm
Starting system: Electric
Engine Management system: Electronic
Fuel system: Electronic Mikuni fuel injection
Clutch: Slipper tyre wet multiplate
Transmission: 6-speed
Final drive: Chain

FRAME
Type: Beam-type aluminium
Swingarm: Aluminium
Front suspension: 41mm USD-type fully adjustable inc; high and low speed compression damping
Rear suspension: Yamaha Monocross
Brakes: Twin 310mm discs w/radially-mounted 4-piston calipers front/ single 220mm disc w/ single piston caliper rear
Wheels: Cast aluminium 5-spoke 3.5 x 17 front/5.5 x 17 rear
Tyres: Dunlop Sportmax Qualifier 120/70ZR17 front & 180/55ZR17 rear

DIMENSIONS
Wheelbase: 1380mm
Rake: 24 degrees
Trail: 97mm
LxWxH: 2040 x 701 x 1100mm
Seat height: 850mm
Dry Weight: 161kg
Fuel tank capacity: 17l
RRP: $17,495
Test bike: Yamaha Motor NZ

CLASS OF THEIR OWN

BY NICK IENATSCH

WE'RE THE LUCKY DOGS WHO RIDE EVERY BIKE, EVERYWHERE, EVERY year. Each sales season we pick the Ten Best, selecting a winner for categories such as Superbike, Cruiser, Sport-Tourer…you get the idea. Over the decades the categories have shifted with the market, but ingredients of the winning bikes remained constant: a magical combination of parts creating a motorcycle that drops us to ours knees to give thanks to the gods of internal combustion. In 2006 we had two surprise winners.

Suzuki's GSX-R750 has effectively eliminated its three-quarter-liter competition by excelling at everything a great sportbike should. Meanwhile, liter-bikes were getting lighter, 600s faster and the 750 death knell could be heard echoing off the walls of Kawasaki and Yamaha. But not Suzuki. So we stuck the 750 into our Best Superbike balloting and guess what? Balance won the day. The Best Superbike of 2006 award sat on the light-and-lithe GSX-R750. Last year, Superbike was spelled *Superb* bike.

Now let's meet our second Ten Bester of 2006, Triumph's Daytona 675. Some cried foul when this overbored Britbike took Best Middleweight honors, but consider two things: *We* define the categories around here, dang it, and secondly, this Triumph

2X2 Suzuki GSX-R750 vs.

Triumph Daytona 675

2×2 Suzuki GSX-R750 vs. Triumph Daytona 675

is magic. It had to win something! It runs hard through the revband, handles like a racebike, shrieks like heaven's own four-stroke and looks sensational from every angle. And like our Superb Bike winner, it possesses that magical balance of chassis and engine that makes every rider better.

Can you see where this is going? Here we have two Ten Best winners within 75cc of each other but neither *really* belongs in the category it won. What should we do with these two "Outclassts?" I know…let's lever on some Pirelli SuperCorsas for a day of hot lapping at Spring Mountain Motorsports Park with SoCal Trackdays (*www.socaltrack-days.com*) and create a new Best Track-Day Bike category!

Bikes unloaded and tire pressures checked, Mark Cernicky and I leathered up while both agreeing the GSX-R would leave the 675 in the dust to the tune of about 3 seconds a lap. "That Suzuki is just *so* good. I mean, I like the Triumph but it's up against one of the best track bikes I can think of," Mark said.

Thirty minutes later the helmets came off and we both confirmed the superiority of the Suzuki. Okay, its stock suspension settings permitted too much movement as the pace came up, but the GSX-R was just so incredibly rideable in every aspect of track lapping. Sure, we'd like more power, but one of the beauties of the 750's power delivery is the precise amount of acceleration the rider can dial-in from apex to exit. Several of Spring Mountain's corners have the rider playing with rear grip in long, sweeping exits, and it took a very good liter-bike rider to pull away from our hooked-up 750.

The GSX-R turned a bit too heavily in the quick transition before the start/finish straight and that problem goes hand-in-hand with the overly soft stock suspension settings that allowed us to drag things just a bit. We added two turns of rear spring, three turns in the front and cranked in more rebound and compression damping at both ends.

The initial laps on the Triumph went well, but it couldn't quite run the Suzuki's pace for several reasons, the most notable being instability during hard braking transitions. Getting into 5A quickly at Spring Mountain has the rider

SUZUKI GSX-R750

Price	$10,199
Dry weight	417 lb.
Wheelbase	55.1 in.
Seat height	31.5 in.
0-60 mph	2.9 sec.
1/4-mile	10.4 sec.
	@ 134.48 mph
Horsepower	121.3 hp
	@ 13,200 rpm
Torque	52.4 ft.-lb.
	@ 10,720 rpm
Top speed	167 mph

▲**Ups**
▲ Who needs 150 hp?
▲ Intuitive riding position
▲ Great brakes

▼**Downs**
▼ Footpegs could be a little higher
▼ Wish it revved a little faster

going from the left footpeg to the right as the bike brakes over a crest while snapping right into an uphill second-gear corner. Both Mark and I were forced to hold back the speed and aggressiveness because the 675 had to settle before turning.

Let's look at some numbers to help illustrate our first session impressions: The Triumph makes a maximum of 47.8 foot-pounds of torque at just over 10,000 rpm, while the Suzuki peaks at 52.4 ft.-lb. at 10,720 rpm, which sounds relatively close until you consider that the Suzuki makes 45 ft.-lb. or more from 7700 rpm to 13,900, while the Triumph climbs over 45 at 8200 rpm and drops below at 12,300 rpm. I apologize for all that number jargon lumped together in one sentence, but it explains one of the problems both Mark and I experienced during our lapping. With the nervous corner entrances and less torque to jump off the corner, making passes during a busy track day took significantly more planning and effort on the Triumph. While the 675 pilot was trying to figure a way around a cluster of liter-bike riders, the GSX-R could run a variety of entrance lines and still jet off the corner.

But don't run straight to the Suzuki showroom just yet. The Triumph needed a ride-height change, so we slipped the fork tubes down to put the caps flush in the top triple-clamp and went from five lines showing on the front preload

2×2 Suzuki GSX-R750 vs. Triumph Daytona 675

adjusters to 3.5. We both felt the 675 was transferring too much weight onto the front end under braking; our changes were aimed at calming that weight transfer and giving us more relaxed steering geometry.

Changes made, the pace went up and the grins widened. We added another half-turn to each of the Suzuki's damping adjusters and put in two more turns of front preload to further tighten the chassis. The bike remained absolutely wonderful to ride and we simply couldn't find much to fault. The recalibrated Triumph made Cernicky laugh out loud after 15 hard laps. The increased ride height and spring preload in front helped enormously and we both continued to experiment with the chassis, adding more and more corner speed and lean angle. We slowed the front compression damping two clicks and the rebound one click. Passing became significantly easier because the Triumph no longer required a moment to sort itself before getting zipped off into a corner and consequently carried significantly more rpm into and out of the turn, improving drive. Get the exit right and the Triumph hangs surprisingly close to the GSX-R.

We removed and rebalanced the Triumph's front wheel during lunch (thanks, Racer's Edge) and strapped on the laptimers. "Man, I don't know now," Cernicky remarked.

When the dust settled, we both went quicker on the GSX-R but the margin was *much* smaller than we initially estimated. Mark was 0.3-second quicker on the GSX-R and I was 0.9-second quicker. The GSX-R's horsepower advantage (121 at 13,200 versus 106 at 12,550) became more usable as we continued to firm up the chassis, getting away from streetbike comfy to racebike efficiency. Mark described the GSX-R750 as a 600 on steroids, entering corners with 600-like speed and confidence yet exiting with a verve no stock 600 can match.

TRIUMPH DAYTONA 675

Price	$8999
Dry weight	394 lb.
Wheelbase	54.9 in.
Seat height	33.1 in.
0-60 mph	2.9 sec.
1/4-mile	10.58 sec. @ 130.22 mph
Horsepower	106.5 hp @ 12,550 rpm
Torque	47.8 ft.-lb. @ 10,050 rpm
Top speed	156 mph

▲Ups
- ▲ Able to carry high corner speed
- ▲ Great exhaust note
- ▲ Unmistakable styling

▼Downs
- ▼ Borderline twitchy in quick transitions
- ▼ Required extra shifts per lap
- ▼ So good they're hard to get

Sure, the 750's acceleration will disappoint most liter-bike riders, but that loss is balanced against the time gained at corner entrance, the early throttle application and the less dramatic/scary/traumatic rear-tire traction dilemma. The majority of riders will reel off more fast laps on this 750 than on a 1000 during a track day, especially on worn tires. Mark's background combines roadracing and supermoto, so in this 2x2 he gravitated to the bigger hit packed by the Suzuki. The Triumph's abilities surprised him but the Suzuki fits his style perfectly.

I left Spring Mountain most impressed with the Triumph. Wow…what a fun bike, especially for an ex-250 GP pilot like myself. It's narrow, revvy, on the edge of being nervous and loves to rail off into a curve. Now factor in its $1200 less expensive MSRP–that'll pay for six track days, just about the most fun you can have on a streetbike.

Our smiles lasted through dinner and we honestly couldn't think of two bikes we would have enjoyed more. The Best Track-Day Bike of 2007? Triumph 675 for me, Suzuki GSX-R750 for Mark. ◘

WORDS BY: BENJAMIN 'BJ' KUBAS CRONIN **PICS BY:** FLOW IMAGES

TWISTED SISTER

The mad Street Triple is here. FB tests the transformation
of 675 from Daytona track hound to Street Triple nutter

The arrival of the Triumph Street Triple was as easy to predict as a kiss'n'tell on a Big Brother contestant. It's no slur on the bike, because from the first ride of the Daytona 675 it was obvious that its qualities would transfer into nakedness better than any rival. Triumph knew close to its donor bike in spec as any naked bike yet. We were gagging to see what it could do.

We arrived at this head-to-head test for two reasons. Firstly, the full group test, now at least six bikes, has to wait until the delayed Aprilia Shiver 750 tips out on these shores from its very slow

WE WERE GAGGING TO SEE WHAT THE STREET TRIPLE COULD DO

this was the case from the start, and always had both bikes in mind as the 675cc inline three-cylinder engine took shape on a computer screen (A fiver says there's a Tiger 675 on the way too).

That probably makes this the most thoroughly developed naked middleweight on the market, which may explain why the A-Force returned from the launch foaming at the mouth. It's also as

boat. Secondly, if these two triples share so much DNA, and the Daytona 675 is famously focused to the point of folly, then there's definitely a question to answer over which makes the best fast road and playtime bike. There's every chance that this latest British headbanger may well spring a surprise on its established sibling. We thrashed them good and proper to find out.

Lean it over, then some more. But settle that dodgy front end first

TRIUMPH DAYTONA 675

When Triumph announced in 2005 that they would no longer attempt to take on the Japanese directly in the fierce supersport 600 market, they had us fooled. The Daytona 600 and 650, hell, even the TT600, were all valiant efforts that punched above Triumph's weight. We'd never rated them highly from a Fast Bikes view, but we understood why they appealed to riders for whom the Union Jack decal meant more than the performance deficit at stuff-everything speeds.

How the Triumph staff kept a straight face, we'll never know. While we were expecting the Daytona 650 to grow old gracefully into a shrunken Sprint ST, they were polishing up the all-new Daytona 675. Then word leaked about the 675 and, with the first images of a lean and purposeful supersport bike, a glimmer of British hope. That became a bright new dawn when the performance really lived up to the looks and the promises.

The engine is its strongest asset. Flexible, forgiving, exciting, and peaky all at once, it does an incredible job of being all things to all riders. It can satisfy without ever taking the tacho into five figures, then rewards richly when you chase the redline like a fox hound. Only wonky fuelling and an average gearbox blot its copybook here.

> ❝ ASKING THE SUSPENSION TO TRACK BUMPS WHILE LEANED OVER IS LIKE ASKING MISS TEEN USA TO PAT HER HEAD AND RUB HER TITS ❞

TECHNICAL *TRIUMPH DAYTONA 675*

Power Graphs

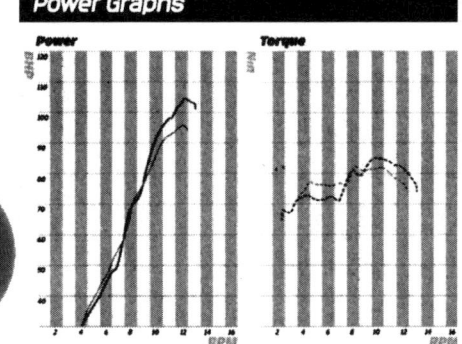

Specification

ENGINE	
TYPE	675cc, liquid-cooled, 12v inline triple
BORE X STROKE	74 x 52.3mm
COMPRESSION	12.65:1
FUELLING	Electronic fuel injection
TESTED POWER	106bhp @ 12,700rpm
TESTED TORQUE	65Nm @ 10,600rpm

CHASSIS	
FRAME	Twin spar aluminium
F SUSPENSION	41mm inverted fork, fully adjustable
R SUSPENSION	Monoshock, fully adjustable
FRONT BRAKES	Four-piston radial calipers, 308mm discs
REAR BRAKES	One-piston caliper, 220mm disc

DIMENSIONS	
WHEELBASE	1392mm
SEAT HEIGHT	825mm
DRY WEIGHT	165kg
FUEL CAPACITY	17.4 litres

PRICE	
PRICE	£7,199 otr
FROM	Triumph Motorcycles (01455 251700) Triumph.co.uk

Testing Times

0-60: 3.24s	0-100: 6.92s	0-120: 11.28s

Standing 1/4 Mile: 11.25s @ 127.85mph	Standing Mile: 29.71s @ 153.53mph

Statistics

Top Speed	155mph
Max Power	106bhp
Max Torque	65Nm

Highlights

- 🏍 **Unique triple layout**
- 🏍 **Huge ground clearance**
- 🏍 **Ultra-focused**
- 🏍 **Mega brakes**
- 🏍 **165kg**
- 🏍 **106bhp**

£7,199 (otr)

Engine

The tiny overall width is down to the very compact engine that's far smaller than the old 650cc four. Development centred on combustion efficiency, using a narrow 23° valve angle.
Features include CNC machined inlet ports, Nimonic (nickel-based) exhaust valves, DLC-treated piston rings, and lightweight nutless con-rods. A stacked gearbox keeps the motor short.
The exhaust has an EXUP-type valve.

Chassis

The slim profile is also helped by running the aluminium frame rails over the engine instead of around it. The frame uses a mix of open and closed walled sections for stiffness placement. There's an adjustable pivot point and a ride height adjuster, both for racers. The Kayaba suspension looks the same as other 600s, though specialists tell us the internals are lower quality, creating the difference in performance.

Verdict

Not complete brilliance, but bloody close to it. Could be top if Triumph upgrade sensibly.

➕ Flexible engine, wheelies, track speed, brakes, looks

➖ Fueling, suspension, build quality, no slipper clutch

Don't be fooled by:

Bras that give chicks perfect tits. By the time you're in bed it's too late. Not exactly sold as seen

TRACK **5** | FAST ROAD **4** | HOOLIGAN **4** | NEW RIDER **4** | DESIRABILITY **4**

Final Score

Score relates to other bikes in this test only

8/10

This is the Daytona's natural hunting ground: smooth, tight corners

The chassis is fickle, as it works well only when everything is right for it, hardly the mark of a good suspension set-up. It can feel totally different from one track to another. Even when it shines, like our '07 SBOTY test, it undoes all that good work once back on the road.

We like focused bikes, we really do, but this is perhaps more extreme than anyone needs on the road. It's so skinny and wrist-heavy that it reminds me of the 250 two-strokes that I, and many of you, learned to hoon on. It's the first real chink in its armour, opening a chance for the Street Triple to strike.

Our big complaint has always been that the suspension gets tied in knots too easily. Brake and steer? Track bumps while leant over? You may as well ask Miss Teen USA to pat her head, rub her tits, and tell you why the majority of Americans don't hold passports. The A-Force hit the nail on the head while out on this test when he said that it feels like the front tyre is soft. The forks are squishy and unpredictable.

In fact, the cheaper suspension of the Street Triple actually highlights that the Daytona's kit isn't all that. The sportsbike is compromised in one area where it should be pressing home an advantage. It's a key reason why the streetfighter can keep up way beyond any expectations you have.

Of course, on open A-roads, throttle bungeed to the stop, the Daytona is a faster bike. It has 10bhp extra, more revs, less weight, better tyres and brakes, and maintains a slight suspension advantage. With three digits on the LCD speedo, the fairing is useful and helps stability too.

The thing is, even amongst the UK's sportsbike riders, a minority spend much time over the ton. If that sounds like you, then you'd be amazed at how frequently the Daytona gets its toes trodden on and how rarely it has a trump card to play. Even the hooligans will be able to turn their back on the best wheelie machine in the supersport 600 class, as the Street has it covered and then some. This test has simply highlighted again that the Daytona 675, as much as we love some of it, is flawed as a fast road bike. ➤

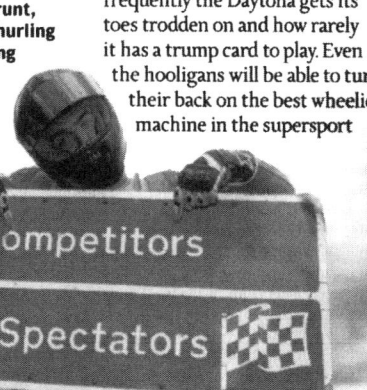

I could have been a contender

Competitors

← Spectators

TRIUMPH STREET TRIPLE

It's important to begin by saying that the Street Triple is absolutely everything Alastair said it would be, and more. In fact, I think he showed remarkable restraint in his launch copy because I'm struggling to think of any production bike I've enjoyed more this year, GSX-R1000 K7 included.

It's a pleasure simply to look at. There's family resemblance and a strong identity of its own too, thanks to funky Brit-pop style that mixes classic turns like the twin spots with modern ideas like the stubby tail.

The real beauty of the Street is in the riding, and the wealth of experiences it offers you. It's as skinny as a Daytona, though the wide bars sit you up into a comfortable and wholly natural position. You expect big fun.

It delivers too, on a scale we're still coming to terms with. That's largely thanks to the engine. The retuned motor makes 96 rear-wheel bhp, ten down on the Daytona, but crucially the torque in unchanged. This is nowhere near as detuned as most retunes.

Along with shorter gearing, it's so good that it's hard to tell the difference between the two bikes. In top gear 50mph roll-ons, the Street holds the Daytona at bay until the sportster eventually gets into its stride. In third, the Street leaps ahead briefly then holds the 675's shirttails all the way to the redline. It takes a big space to make the extra power count.

And then there are the wheelies. Oh my sweet Lord, the wheelies. It really doesn't get much better than this, big bruv Speed Triple included. It leaps up in the first two gears without the clutch, and it even lofts in third with some effort. At any speed up to 60mph, a finger of clutch is just enough to give you a wheelie treat. It floats along beautifully too because the fuelling actually feels better than that of the Daytona.

The Street can take the fight to the Daytona in the bends, handling in ways the Speed Triple can only dream of. You'd expect the budget bike to be severely compromised in the suspension department, but again Triumph bucks the trend, maybe as a result of the extended development time shared with the Daytona. The fork is non-adjustable, though, as we've always said, that doesn't matter if the stock setting is really good, and this is. The overall set-up is certainly the softer of the two, yet it feels more composed at most speeds. It only gets lively when flat out.

Time for your pills, little fella.

Timmay! Tiiiiiimmaayyy!

SHIVER ME TIMBERS

WHAT HOPE FOR THE APRILIA SHIVER AGAINST THE STREET?

Next - Aprilia Shiver 750
The most likely candidate to take on the Street Triple is Aprilia's new Shiver 750. At the launch it impressed us with its abundance of V-twin grunt and excellent handling traits. It looks more special too, and features trickery such as radial brakes and a Ride-By-Wire throttle. It will have an uphill struggle against the Triumph though. Aprilia only claim 95bhp, the same as the Street makes at the wheel. It's likely to be 7-10bhp down on a dyno. There's a hole in the midrange too, and that will be annoying compared to the perfectly linear triple. That's directly to blame for its relatively poor wheelie skills. The choice at for playtime is likely to be clear cut. The Shiver will also cost £400 more.

The frankly archaic front brake set-up lets the side down a bit. The two-piston sliding calipers don't live up to the standard set by the rest of the bike. They are surprisingly strong, but they lack finesse for hard retardation and when Al suddenly asked them to shift 167kg onto the bike's nose they became a bit grabby. It's hard to complain at this price point though, and usually the performance is terrific.

The Street Triple offers so much to so many riders. It's as at home on a Direct Access course as it is breezing a fat fourth gear mono. It can do economy, knee-down, chic café style; it's all there. The new Street Triple is every bit as good as you've heard and as you hoped and Triumph are going to sell thousands. ➤

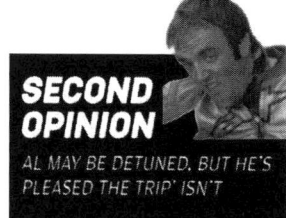

❝ IN ANY OF THE FIRST THREE GEARS, AND UP TO 60MPH, A FINGER OF CLUTCH IS JUST ENOUGH TO GIVE YOU A WHEELIE TREAT ❞

TECHNICAL TRIUMPH STREET TRIPLE

Power Graphs

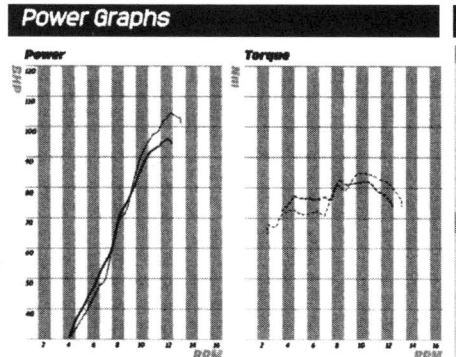

Specification

ENGINE	
TYPE	675cc, liquid-cooled, 12v inline triple
BORE X STROKE	74 x 52.3mm
COMPRESSION	12.65:1
FUELLING	Electronic fuel injection
TESTED POWER	96bhp@ 12,000rpm
TESTED TORQUE	62Nm @ 8,200rpm
CHASSIS	
FRAME	Twin spar aluminium
F SUSPENSION	41mm inverted fork, non-adjustable
R SUSPENSION	Monoshock, adjustable for preload only
FRONT BRAKES	Two-piston calipers, 308mm discs
REAR BRAKES	One-piston caliper, 220mm disc
DIMENSIONS	
WHEELBASE	1395mm
SEAT HEIGHT	800mm
DRY WEIGHT	167kg
FUEL CAPACITY	17.4L
PRICE	
PRICE	£5,395 otr
FROM	Triumph Motorcycles (01455 251700) Triumph.co.uk

Testing Times

3.38s	7.61s	11.38s
	11.56s @ 120.67mph	28.78s @ 143.16mph

Statistics

Top Speed	**144**mph
Max Power	**96**bhp
Max Torque	**62**Nm

Highlights

- ✈ Perfect donor motor
- ✈ Mega wheelie bike
- ✈ Top value
- ✈ Well equipped
- ✈ 167kg
- ✈ 96bhp

£5,395

Don't be fooled by:

The price. This isn't simply top fun for the cash, it's as entertaining as any bike at any cost

Engine

The retune, for once, doesn't ruin a good engine. The new cam profile adds more midrange bias to suit a naked bike. Peak revs are cut to 12,650rpm. There's a secondary air-injection system controlled by the ECU in order to meet emissions regs. Beyond that, this engine is refreshingly unfettled. The big 44mm throttle bodies and high 12.65:1 compression ratio are the same as used by the Daytona 675.

Chassis

The twin spar aluminium frame is basically the same as the 675's. Strip one down to see what we mean. Rake is nominally increased to provide more stability. The big bars keep the steering speed high.
The cheap two-piston sliding calipers are helped with standard steel hoses. The OE tyres are a smart choice. British-made Dunlop Qualifiers are miles better than the Japanese model on the R6.

Verdict

Utterly brilliant naked mad thing. You'll laugh and laugh as the insanity takes control

➕ Riding position, engine, chassis, brakes, fun

Vibrations, could sell out before you get to the shop

Final Score **9/10**
Score relates to other bikes in this test only

TRACK 3 | FAST ROAD 4 | HOOLIGAN 5 | NEW RIDER 5 | DESIRABILITY 4

SPEED TEST DATA *DRY, SLIGHT CROSSWIND*

Speed Test Notes

Very easy launch thanks to broad spread of grunt. Forgiving of errors. Not perfectly stable, even with damper. Peak power is late, so chase the redline for best drive

Also very easy to launch, but more wheelie prone due to shorter gearing and upright position. High-speed shimmy noticeable but not scary

Speed Test Results

Daytona 675			Top Speed	Power **106**
3.24s	6.92s	11.28s		
	11.25s @ 127.85mph			29.71s @ 153.53mph

Street Triple			Top Speed	Power **96**
3.38s	7.61s	11.38s		
	11.56s @ 120.67mph			28.78s @ 143.16mph

CONCLUSION

Now we can answer which bike is the best for fast road naughtiness, and we've also learned loads about how the Street Triple is likely to stack up against its class peers when the group test comes around.

As a toy, the Street Triple rules, and kicks the 675's sorry arse all the way back to Hinkley. It excites in all sorts of ways, and most of all by encouraging you to act the fool more than ever.

Beyond that, as a fast road bike the Street battles harder with its sports sibling than anything else from this class ever. What it lacks in outright Isle of Man crazy pace is offset by the Daytona's single-mindedness and lack of concessions to the 'real world'.

Neither is the perfect, do-it-all tool with the flexibility to monster the A-roads, race circuits, tour, and stunt like a GSX-R1000. What amazed us is that over a mix of quick road riding and dicking about, the Street Triple was always the bike we'd rather be riding.

Sure the Daytona is the faster of the two 675s, and it will pull away on an open enough road, but we were astonished to find that we'd always rather be chasing and having more fun on a Street Trip'.

Of course, all of this makes it the firm favourite when we get the naked middleweight class together. Against our launch experiences of the other bikes, we fully expect the Street Triple to be the sportiest and most entertaining too, with a great balance of practicality. I can't see anything getting near it in the class, it's too well-rounded. Perhaps best of all, Triumph are asking only £5,395, actually less than a Z750.

It'll make a brilliant first bike, teach you to wheelie, guide you through your first trackday, and entertain you endlessly. Words cannot do justice to how much fun we had on the test. We were gutted when the sun went down.

The Street Triple stands to become a cult hero, like the Hornet, Bandit, and RD350LC before it, all bargain nutters of their day.

Triumph already have 300 deposits, and that's bound to explode once word gets out. It's an XR3i on two wheels, soon to be seen outside a chip-shop near you, and that's no bad thing.

Beej uses his knees to catch the breeze and float wheelies

BJ is about to completely ignore that 'No Entry' sign

Keep looking. Bit further...

> **" THE STREET TRIPLE STANDS TO BECOME A CULT HERO, LIKE THE HORNET, BANDIT, AND RD350LC BEFORE IT, ALL BARGAIN NUTTERS "**

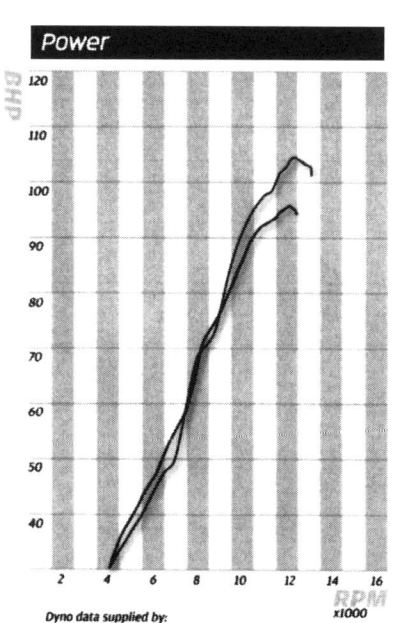

Power

Dyno data supplied by:

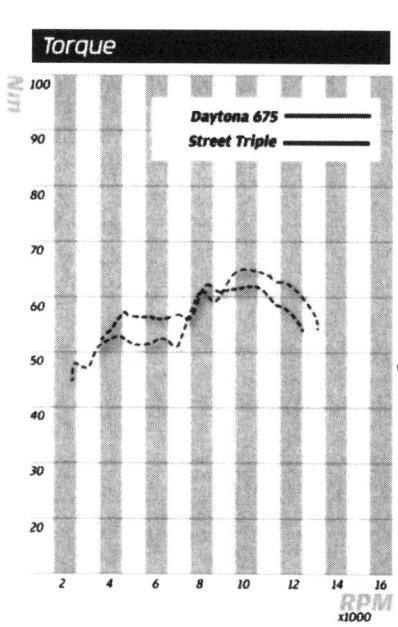

Torque

Daytona 675 ———
Street Triple ———

Location

BRUNTINGTHORPE TEST FACILITY

SOME CALL IT A TEST TRACK, OR 'TT' FOR SHORT. ACTUALLY IT'S JUST A SODDING GREAT RUNWAY.

2 MILE STRAIGHT   GRASS RUNWAY

It's a two-mile runway and a return road with a couple of modest bends. We use 'Brunters' to extensively performance test every bike we ride. It's a great place for speed testing, but it's not a long, ultra-twisty test course as some mags would have you believe...

TRIUMPH
TT600 & DAYTONA 600/650
From over-hyped under-achiever to seriously capable real-world road bike in three easy steps...

Words **Kev Raymond** Pictures **Mark Manning & RiDE Archive**

When we first heard Triumph were planning to take on the Japanese in the hardest-fought sector in motorcycling, we could hardly believe it. But in 2000 it happened, with the all-new TT600.

The first big disappointment was the styling – it looked like a mildy worked-over fusion of the first few years of the CBR600. Of more concern was the engine. It was 5bhp away from a CBR and 10bhp shy of challenging the class-leading GSX-R 600.

Worse, the power delivery was awful – no low-down drive, a gaping hole in the torque curve from about 7000rpm, an even bigger one between 9000 and 10,000 and inconsistent low-rev behaviour in town. It overheated too. Hurried remapping of the fuel injection at every service helped a bit, but not much. All of which was a shame because the chassis and brakes were absolutely superb.

It didn't sell well – 600 in its first year against 4000 R6s. The Italian importer started ripping the fairings off them and flogging it as a naked bike, and that evolved its way back to the factory in the form of the Speed Four. But the TT itself was doomed, even though by the time it was dropped in late 2002 a series of engine mods and FI re-maps had turned it into the bike it should have been in the first place.

Early 2003 saw the Daytona 600. Under the skin it had changed a bit, with engine mods giving more power and, more importantly, a better delivery. The chassis was pretty much identical to the TT but the bodywork gave it a whole new look. It was still down on power, but low gearing disguised that on the road and although it wasn't going to rival a GSX-R or ZX-6R at the extremes of performance, on the road it added CBR-style levels of comfort and stability to superbly composed suspension and great brakes.

2005's capacity hike, inspired by Kawasaki's similar move with the ZX-6R, finally gave us the mid-range we'd been craving and an extra few bhp at the top end as well. But despite winning road tests for the first time in its career, the 650 was just a holding move – the new triple Daytona 675 was waiting in the wings and the four's day was over.

The best thing about the bike is the chassis

FINISH
GENERALLY
GOOD

AVERAGES
40MPG

POWERFUL
BRAKES

THE HISTORY OF THE
TT600 & DAYTONA

2000 TT600
All-new. Alloy twin-spar frame, conventional forks, 68 x 41.3mm bore and stroke. Many unsold Y2K model TTs were heavily discounted the following year, so have '01 registrations. 599cc/108bhp (claimed)/170kg. Yellow/black, red/silver.

2001 TT600
New colours, a powder-coated silver frame and alleged engine mods (mostly just tweaks to the Sagem engine management system). 599cc/108bhp/170kg. Yellow, blue, black.

2002/2003 TT600
New colours, colour-coded air intakes. Triumph claimed engine mods, but again it was mainly ECU updates. 599cc/108bhp/170kg. Yellow, blue, silver, red, black.

2003/2004 DAYTONA 600
New name and completely new bodywork. Revised fork internals. Engine the same except for slightly different cams, some mild head mods and revised air intake. Main change is a new engine management system from Keihin, featuring twin-butterfly throttle bodies. 599cc/110bhp/165kg. Yellow, silver, plus red for 2004.

2005 DAYTONA 650
An extra 4.2mm on the bores gives a whole heap more midrange. Otherwise unchanged from 600 spec. 646cc/112bhp/165kg. Yellow, red.

Front suspension works perfectly on road and track

Engine

Despite Triumph's claims of major engine improvements during the four's model life, there's very little difference between a TT motor and a Daytona 600 – slightly different cam timing, a reshaped combustion chamber and that's about it. The biggest change was the move to Keihin fuel injection from the TT's Sagem, which was a big improvement, helped by a modified air intake. Otherwise you can fit a TT motor to a Daytona and vice versa. The really big difference is the 650's 4.2mm bigger bores - the good news is you can bore out a TT or 600 and fit 650 pistons. Otherwise the engine's boringly reliable, if prone to the odd annoying oil and coolant leak. The cam cover gasket's a prime cause for leaks post-service - it's easy to slightly pinch the gasket without realising, so that it holds for a while, then lets go and starts weeping, and the higher the revs, the bigger the leak.

They run hot in traffic (you really don't want to be waiting at the lights for long in hot weather), but paradoxically take a long while to warm up from cold. This means they're not great as city bikes or short-distance commuters - some owners bypass the temperature sender switch and fit a manual one, which helps on hot days as you can just have the fan running all the time.

Sandy at breakers and engine reconditioners Triumph-ant (08453 707666) has seen the inside of more TT and Daytona engines than most people. He's clear on the causes of major faults: "I've seen a few, but they're almost always traceable to the owners. All engines burn more oil when they're cold, and these are no exception. Almost all the engines I've had that've had major breakdowns have been city bikes, used for short journeys - they never get hot and owners don't check the oil between services. If it's only got a litre in the sump it'll ruin the crank bearings - that's not the engine's fault."

Engine mapping

Triumph delayed the TT's launch while they scrabbled around for a workable fuel map and for years the bike's fuelling was a work in progress. Virtually every service would see a new map downloaded to the ECU, making the TT one of the very few bikes where a main dealer service history really makes a difference. There's only one way to find out if your bike has the latest update, and that's to plug it into a proper diagnostic computer.

Economy

Owners report averages of around 40mpg, with highs of up to 55mpg and lows around 35mpg.

Clocks tend to break easily – our test one was playing up

Extra rest behind footpeg stops foot slipping back

Daytona shock is better than TT's for hard riding

Brakes have braided hoses as standard

Intricate styling even on gear lever

Standard silencers are tough as are downpipes

Front suspension

Boring old right-way-up forks were a bit passé even in 2000. But who cares, when they work this well? The damping and spring rates are perfect for spirited riding on real roads and will cope with a bit of track action too. The Daytona got lighter fork internals, as well as single rate springs (the TT had progressive springs). You probably wouldn't tell the difference unless you were a national level racer. If the forks feel a bit tired, don't panic - chances are they just need a change of oil.

Rear suspension

Like the forks, it's nicely balanced for road riding and better quality than some of the competition. Linkages can seize and need checking periodically. The Daytona's shock is reckoned to be a little better than the TT's for trackdays and hard riding - it fits the TT so it's worth looking for one in a breaker's.

Water in the plugs

Heavy rain and jet-washing can result in a small lake forming around the spark plug recesses. As well as causing corrosion, this can short out the HT current from the coil, leading to misfires. Go easy on the jetwash, and try to run the engine for a while after it gets really wet - it helps the water evaporate.

Corrosion/finish

The finish is generally pretty good. High mileage examples will start to look a bit scabby, with the brake disc and front fork legs coming in for criticism from owners. Mostly though it's no worse than any contemporary Japanese bike and better than most.

Throttle position sensor

There are quite a few reports of TPS failure, particularly on TTs, although that might just reflect the fact they've been around for longer. Symptoms include a sudden tendency to stall as you roll up to junctions. The part's not expensive and it's easy enough to fit.

Fuel pump connections

The TT originally had plastic connectors from tank to fuel pump hoses. These were very easy to damage while removing and refitting the tank and should have long since been replaced under warranty with metal ones. Even those are still a bit vulnerable though, so take care when removing the tank.

Exhausts

The downpipes are tough, as are the standard silencers, although the flange bolts can rust enough to allow the can to part company from the midpipe.

There are plenty of aftermarket cans available, but beware: on the TT in particular they can upset the already chaotic fuelling. Fine if you want to invest in a Power Commander and some dyno time to set it up, not so good if you're on a tight budget and just want to get on and ride. Some aftermarket cans are also reported as not fitting very well, with leaks at the midpipe join. Best bet is one of Triumph's own 'not for road use' cans, with dealer backup for the right revised fuel map.

Electrical

It's not unknown for alternators to give up, especially if the connectors have corroded, as this puts a strain on the windings. It's a two-part alternator and usually it's the stator (the fixed part) that fails, rather than the rotor. To check if you're getting a proper charge, use a voltmeter across the battery terminals. With the engine off it should read around 12 volts. With the engine running it should rise to mid 13s, with a max of 14.5 volts. Any higher than that and you'll start frying expensive electronics. Before suspecting the alternator itself, check all the connections for corrosion and tightness. New alternators are expensive and used ones hard to find. Fortunately pattern ones are available - try www.electrexworld.co.uk/

Vital statistics

£ Spares prices

Original-equipment new parts

Front brake lever	£33.72
Front disc	£174.99
Brake pads (pair)	£69.58
Indicator (front)	£36.30
Mirror	£50.70
Fairing top centre	£338.93
Fairing side	£156.66
Belly pan	£169.28
Handlebar	£64.23
Silencer	£290.96
Exhaust downpipes	£552.49
Oil filter	£7.50
Air filter element	£18.68
Chain/sprocket kit	£132.76
Full set clutch plates	£195.23

Prices are for a 2002 TT600 and include VAT
Source: Triumph

Aftermarket part prices

Oil filter (K+N)	£9.08
Air filter (K+N)	£33.01
Front brake pads (EBC HH, pair)	£25.85
Front brake pads (Brembo, pair)	£26.39
Front wheel bearing (pair)	£18.04
Rear shock (Nitron)	£346.62
Exhaust can (Remus)	£309
Exhaust can (Scorpion road legal)	£183.99
Screen (Skidmarx)	£39.99
Chain and sprocket kit (Afam)	£119.45
Spark plugs (Denso Iridium, each)	£15.98
Brake/clutch levers (Pazzo, each)	£65
Bars (Gilles clip-on)	£104.99
Clutch plates (EBC)	£37.88
Clutch springs	£8.64
Brake lines (Goodridge, front and rear)	£115

Prices are for a Daytona 600/650 and include VAT.
Source: www.demon-tweeks.co.uk or 01978 664474

Breakers

Brake calipers (recon, each)	£117.50
Front fairing side	from £59
Mirror	£23.50
Brake lever (front)	£7
Front wheel	from £117.50
Brake disc (pair)	from £95
Exhaust can	£117.50
Exhaust downpipes	£117.50
Handlebar	£23.50
Fairing top	from £59
ECU	£176.25
Alternator stator	£88
Alternator rotor	£88

All prices include VAT
Source: www.triumph-ant.co.uk or 08453 707666

↻ Recalls

The first batch of bikes were recalled for potentially loose sidestand bolts. Early Y2K bikes were also recalled for potential loose bolts holding the starter sprag clutch. All TTs up to June 2001 were recalled for a new clutch cable to be fitted.

TTs and Daytona 600s up to February 2003 were recalled to replace the plastic fuel pump unions with metal ones. In addition there were numerous updates to ECU mapping.

↻ Service schedule

A fairly simple schedule. Valve clearance checks are a bit close together, which bumps the cost up, but don't be tempted to ignore them – you could do serious damage if the clearance closes up.

500 miles

Oil and filter changed, engine and cooler checked for leaks, throttle cable adjusted, fuel system checked for leaks. ECU checked/updated, coolant checked for level and leaks, steering operation check, wheel and tyres inspected. Bake fluid level and leak check, brake calipers inspected for seized pistons, electrics checked, clutch cable adjusted, general fastener check service bulletin updates and road test.

6000 miles

As 500 miles, plus throttle bodies balanced, spark plugs checked/gapped, head bearings adjusted, drive chain rubbing strip check.

12,000 miles

As 6000 miles, plus valve clearance check, air filter and fuel filter replaced, secondary air injection system cleaned and reset, spark plugs replaced, head bearings greased, chain rubbing strip replaced.

18,000 miles

As 6000 miles.

24,000 miles

As 12,000 miles

Additionally

Brake fluid and coolant changed every two years.

○ Tyres

With standard supersport sizes there's loads of choice. Trackday fiends should opt for sports (S) tyres, while everyday riders will get better value from sports touring (ST) compounds.
Front: 120/70 ZR17 **Rear:** 180/55 ZR17

Make/type	F	R
Avon AV59/60 Viper Sport (S)	£79	£105
Avon AV55/56 Storm (ST)	£75	£96
Michelin Pilot Power	£81	£105
Michelin Pilot Road 2	£85	£112
Dunlop Qualifier (S)	£80	£105
Dunlop Roadsmart (ST)	£92	£118
Metzeler Sportec M3 (S)	£90	£119
Metzeler Roadtec Z6 (ST)	£86	£114
Continental Sport Attack (S)	£76	£95
Continental Road Attack (ST)	£72	£92
Pirelli Diablo T (S)	£76	£98
Pirelli Rosso (S)	£92	£120
Pirelli Diablo Strada (ST)	£74	£98
Bridgestone BT014 (S)	£78	£104
Bridgestone BT016 (S)	£88	£110
Bridgestone BT021 (ST)	£77	£99
Maxxis Supermaxx MA-PS (S)	£62	£85
Maxxis MR6029 F	£57	£81

Prices are mail order and include VAT. Add £6 per tyre or pair p+p. **Source:** SMD tyres (01942 604511)

£ Used prices

Price	New	Dealer	Private
2000	£6649	£2125	£1225
2001	£6649	£2475	£1525
2002	£6649	£2650	£1700
2003	£6649	£3095	£2125
2004	£5999	£3275	£2275
2005	£6149	£3450	£2550

£ Insurance

Norwich Union quote for a 2003 Daytona 600 worth £3000, garaged at home address and fitted with an approved alarm. Owner has five years' NCB and no

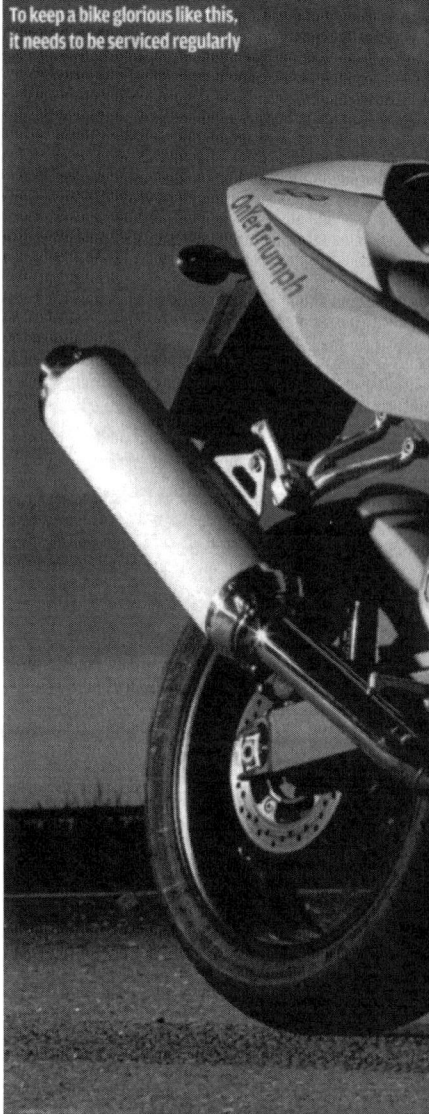

To keep a bike glorious like this, it needs to be serviced regularly

accidents/convictions, in a rural (NR13) or city centre (LS10) location. The Daytona is NU group 15.

TPFT	Rural	City
25-year-old	£308	£742
35-year-old	£131	£317
45-year-old	£97	£235

Comp	Rural	City
25-year-old	£466	£1123
35-year-old	£199	£480
45-year-old	£148	£235

I SELL THEM...

Russ Clay at D+K, Staffs (01782 861100)
"We've sold a good few - they're an alternative to an FX-era CBR600 and they're good for taller people. Earlier ones had some electrical issues but I think they're mostly pretty reliable. You have to watch out for the usual signs of misuse and neglect, but they're not highly strung or high maintenance. Really it's a cracking engine and you get a lot of bike for your money - you can get a good one for upwards of £2400."

SPECIFICATION
2004 TRIUMPH DAYTONA 600

Engine	Liquid cooled, chain driven DOHC, inline four, 599cc
Power (tested)	91bhp @ 12,600rpm
Torque (tested)	39ft-lb @ 11,100rpm
Chassis	Aluminium twin beam, 43mm RWU forks, rising rate monoshock rear, both fully adjustable
Dry weight	165Kg
Seat height	815mm
Fuel capacity	18litres (gal)
Tyre front	120/70 ZR17
Tyre rear	180/55 ZR17
NU insurance	15

CONSIDER THE ALTERNATIVES

2004 Honda CBR600F £2400-£3330

Engine: l/c dohc inline four, 599cc **Power (measured):** 95bhp @ 12,800rpm **Torque (measured):** 41ft-lb @ 10,300rpm **Dry weight:** 170Kg **Seat height:** 805mm **Fuel capacity:** 18litres **Economy:** 38mpg **NU insurance group:** 14 **Top speed:** 150mph

○ With the RR taking over supersport duties the F was free to keep going as a pure road bike. It's still the benchmark for real-world practicality, combining reliability, sound handling and a good riding position.
● They hold their value well, so they're less of a bargain than some of the competition. You need to keep an eye on the finish, and you have to make sure you're not getting a ringer - check frame and engine numbers tally.

2002 Yamaha YZF-R6 £1800-£2850

Engine: l/c dohc inline four, 599cc **Power (measured):** 99bhp @ 12,600rpm **Torque (measured):** 43.6ft-lb @ 10,600rpm **Dry weight:** 169Kg **Seat height:** 820mm **Fuel capacity:** 17litres **Economy:** 34mpg **NU insurance group:** 15 **Top speed:** 157mph

○ On the lairy side when new, nowadays the last of the carburetted R6 line looks roomy, flexible and practical. It's reliable and will put up with anything from daily commuting to trackday thrashing.
● The finish is a bit iffy, camchain tensioners can let go (listen for rattles), and some bikes suffer from carb icing in cold weather. Clutches can be grabby, and discs can warp if you upgrade the pads and use them hard.

2002 Kawasaki ZX-6R £1590-£2380

Engine: l/c dohc inline four, 636cc **Power (measured):** 96.6bhp @ 12,600rpm **Torque (measured):** 43.2ft-lb @ 10,300rpm **Dry weight:** 171Kg **Seat height:** 815mm **Fuel capacity:** 18litres **Economy:** 35mpg **NU insurance group:** 15 **Top speed:** 160mpg

○ The extra cubes give a decent midrange hike which is welcome on the road - far better drive out of corners. With a roomy riding position and stable handling, it makes a great all-rounder.
● It was already feeling its age when it got its big bore in 2002, and nowadays it feels tall, slow-steering and a bit cumbersome beside to current 600s. The rear shock's weak and the finish comes in for criticism.

Words **Tim Cummings** Pictures **Matt Howell**

BIG SIXES

Triumph Daytona 650 and Kawasaki ZX-6R A1P

Modern sports 600s are too small, revvy and uncomfortable for most people. Don't believe us? The manufacturers think so too – why else would they have started giving some of the very latest models a fraction more midrange and making the riding positions less radical?

Wind the clock back a few years and 600s were different beasts altogether. They were physically larger, more spacious, less revvy – and while they weren't quite a match on the track for the latest micro buzz bombs, they weren't far off. Plus they were massively superior all-round road machines.

We've picked two of the best of these past masters. Not only are they dynamically capable, they're also comfortable on road or track and they've a little something extra – oversize engines.

A few extra cc gives these bikes more midrange power and helps make them the best roadgoing 600s ever made. Their physical size gives them a presence too.

They weren't around for long before being replaced by tiny, more track-orientated models so they're quite rare. But we reckon they're a great choice as they do it all and do it very well.

Triumph's Daytona 650 is the newer bike of the pair. It has stand-out styling plus handling and performance to take on pretty much anything on the road. The A1P version of Kawasaki's ZX-6R is three years older. It's sporty but not quite as sharp as the Triumph. It is an incredibly versatile machine, though, combining the virtues of a sportsbike and a sports tourer in one reasonably priced package.

WHERE WE RIDE THEM
The RiDE TT is a 41-mile circuit of roads that we use for every test. We cover five laps on each bike, to create the most real-world used bike road tests in the business.

2005 Triumph Daytona 650 DK Motorcycles 0 1782 861100

Triumph came late to the 600 supersport class. The TT600 was a bold attempt to take on the Japanese on their home turf but it was always the class dunce. The Daytona 600 was a significant improvement but a slight lack of power and iffy fuelling meant it still couldn't catch the Japanese bikes on the road, track or showroom in this competitive class. Triumph added 50cc, got the fuelling right and, lo and behold, they had a bike that could mix it with the best in the class - and was arguably the pick of the bunch in many ways.

What exactly is so good about the Daytona 650? It manages to combine being track fast and road practical in one distinctive looking package. The engine's a stunner.

Triumph didn't take the easy option by boring it out to increase capacity; they lengthened the stroke, which focuses gains on midrange torque rather than top-end power. There's decent oomph right from idle. By 5000rpm there's quite strong drive. And the power grows all the way to the 14,000rpm redline, by which point you're into full-speed fast-forward mode. The gearbox, often criticised on the 600 Daytona, is improved too. It's positive rather than light and slick but it does the job well and doesn't get in the way.

The handling is excellent too. At 165kg it's as light as the latest sports 600s and will lap a race track just as quickly as any of the hard edged Japanese competitors of the

✳ Brakes

Excellent when in good condition. Some owners find the fluid goes off quickly and replacing it every year keeps things tip-top. The fastest track riders may find an aftermarket master cylinder gives even more power and sensitivity.

✳ Fluid leaks

Oil and coolant can escape. Check the main radiator hoses and look for flecks of dried coolant blowing back onto the bike. Oil can come out from a variety of places on the engine, generally in greater volume when the bike's warm.

✳ Comfort

Excellent for such a sporty bike. Some find the seat hard but there's an official gel option which is most easily identified by feel. Double bubble screens boost wind protection.

✳ Charging issue

Alternator failure isn't unheard of. Check the voltage across the battery with the engine running. It should be at least 13.5 volts and no more than 14.5 volts.

✳ Service history

All Triumphs benefit from the latest software maps. This was critical on the TT600 and Daytona 600. The 650 works best with the right downloads, available from Triumph dealers.

✳ Tyres

Common sizes take all the latest (and some older, outdated) rubber. We fitted new Bridgestone BT-016s and they worked superbly. They're the first tyres to have three different compounds – harder in the centre, with a grippier layer further out and an ultra soft, even grippier section right at the edge for big lean angles.

✳ Engine management light

Prone to staying on. Taking the bike through three heat cycles (running it until the fan cuts in, then turning it off) may sort it. If not bring the bike to a Triumph dealer to fix.

✳ Insurance

Norwich union group 15. That's the same as the Daytona 600 and the YZF-6R but it seems a bit unfair as the 1050cc Speed Triple and Sprint ST are one group lower. Get a quote before you buy.

✳ Loud exhaust cans

Official Triumph ones work well and dealers will be able to re-map the bike to suit cheaply. We've heard of other brands not fitting perfectly (so look/feel for leaks) and they may need a Power Commander to ensure the bike runs correctly.

same age. Like the most modern sportsbikes it's stable and turns fast. The suspension's supple enough to work on the road but firm enough for those fast lap times too. It proved extremely rapid everywhere on our road test circuit and while the really bumpy sections upset it slightly it still proved to be one of the fastest, most capable machines we've tested, putting it alongside more expensive bikes like Yamaha's R1 and Honda's VFR800 VTEC. The brakes are simple but superb.

The comfort is excellent for such a sporty bike. The riding position's not too radical and as it's a physically large machine there's space to move around. The screen is a little low and the seat a little hard but there are official Triumph options as well as other brand aftermarket kits to sort these. Our test bike had a Triumph double bubble screen and sitting at autobahn pace felt completely relaxing. Drop below 40mph and there's some weight on the rider's wrists but it's still incredibly comfy for something so sporty.

Details are decent too. The mirrors work pretty well (that puts them above 75 per cent of bikes), headlights are excellent and there's moderate underseat storage. Tank range is respectable, with 140-150 miles possible before the warning light comes on. The digital console with analogue tacho's fairly basic but functional. The bike's reliability's good, with few serious faults reported.

Tester's notes

* Tall seat height
* Stunning handling
* Pretty comfortable
* Excellent brakes
* Smooth, strong power delivery
* Big bike feel
* Excellent headlights

✷ Union Jack plastics

Some bikes have nose cones in Union Flag Valmoto Racing replica colours. Some people like them, others aren't so keen. A bike with regular, plain plastics will sell more easily.

I bought one

Rory Bridges
Model: 2005 Daytona 650
Miles on the clock: 6000
(my first one had 13,000 on the clock when I was knocked off it)
Miles by owner: 2000

Good points: I love the styling and the fact there aren't many about. Mainly I like the engine. It pulls much better at low rpm than my ZX-6R. The handling is also very good as it seems much more road focused, meaning the suspension absorbs a lot more impact, which in turn makes it much less likely to throw you off line half way round a bend.
Bad points: The paint scratches easily and I find the fuel injection snatchy.
Problems: The engine management light came on for a few hours and then went off again.
Mods: I fitted a K&N air filter but it seems to have made the bike run worse.
Anything else: I love the bike, it's comfy and I ride it to Spain every year. It's the best bike I've owned so far. People knock it for being British - some actually stand there and insult it while I'm sitting on it - but I think everyone should have a go on a modern Triumph.

✷ Specification

Engine	1/c, 16v, inline four, 647cc
Power	112bhp @ 12,500rpm
Torque	51ft-lb @ 11,500rpm
Chassis	aluminium beam
Dry weight	165kg
Seat height	815mm
Fuel capacity	18 litres (4 gal)
Tyres	120/70-17; 180/55-17
Fuel economy	42mpg
NU insurance	15
Top speed	160mph

✷ Rainwater

Can collect under the tank. It's not a huge problem but can upset electrics and cause corrosion. Ask the seller to lift it up so you can have a peek underneath.

Think less supersport 600, more a creditable but economical alterative to a top-flight all-rounder like the Honda VFR800. High praise indeed but this A1P version of Kawasaki's ZX-6R is a superb bike and it was only sold for one year.

The A1P on test here is light, stable and reasonably nimble on track and it's a superb road machine as well. The riding position's spacious, there's plenty of midrange power and it's not intimidating so anyone can exploit most or all of its ability. It can't quite match the combination of stability and agility of the latest sports 600s but it's not a million miles away.

The engine's a gem. Like Triumph with the Daytona 650 also on test, Kawasaki have 'cheated' by making it oversize, increasing the bore by 2mm to make the displacement 636cc. This boosts midrange to an extent and top-end power too, making the Kwak a flier in on the road. At very low revs it's quite flat and the clutch is a little grabby, so it's not the fastest machine off the line. But once you get it rolling the extra power's always noticeable. The midrange is strong for a 600cc-class four-cylinder bike and the power builds smoothly and progressively until it hits the banzai zone from 9000 to the 14,000rpm redline. A healthy induction roar from the airbox means it always feels alive and never sanitised like some ultra smooth Yamahas and Hondas.

✳ Frame damage
Lob a 6R up the road and they seem to suffer frame damage more than many machines. Check for filler and re-spray. If frame guards are fitted, peek underneath them.

✳ Carbs
Remember them? Great for kill switch backfires, cheaper than injection to adjust to suit a loud exhaust but they can ice up in winter. A fuel treatment like Silkolene PRO FST sorts it but adds a little to the running costs.

✳ Is it a 636?
The 599cc J models look similar. The 636cc A1P should have a 636 badge on the main fairing but the frame number's the best place to check. J models begin JKBZX600 while the genuine 636cc A1P will start JKAZ636.

✳ Camchain tensioner
We've heard of a few cases of premature failure. It's not a huge problem as it won't leave you at the roadside and replacement's not expensive. A rattle at tickover's the giveaway sign.

✳ Seized suspension adjuster
The damping adjuster screws on the lower fork leg get a pasting from the elements. If they're not cared for and turned every now and then they can seize. Check to see if they're free.

✳ Wheel paint
It flakes off – a common Kawasaki problem. It's not a disaster, and repainting or powder coating's not too costly. Paint condition gives an idea of how a machine's been cared for.

✳ Tyres
We fitted Bridgestone BT-016s as testing bikes on worn rubber is unfair. They gripped excellently in all conditions and the profiles worked well with the Kawasaki's handling. Standard front fitment is a 120/65-17 but lots of owners fit a 120/70 which works fine and makes the bike slightly more stable.

Generally handling's excellent. The bike's neutral, stable, reasonably quick to turn and doesn't misbehave. Suspension's a bit hard on standard settings for road use – the bumpy sections of the RiDE test course gave the rider's kidneys a good kicking plus had the bike skipping about so much that backing off the throttle was the only option. Reducing the spring preload and compression damping helped a bit but it's still a bike that prefers smooth surfaces. The brakes work well as long as they're in good condition. Many aren't on used machines so budget £100-£150 or so for new pads and cleaning out the calipers if they're lacking power. Braided steel lines will firm up the action if the lever comes back to the bar with fresh fluid in.

Performance wise it's a bike that'll run with most sports machines but, as we said, it also gives the level of comfort and luxury you'd expect from a sports touring bike. The screen provides extremely generous protection (particularly with a double-bubble replacement like on our test bike). Weight on wrists is minimal, the seat's better than many plus it's big enough to move around on and stay relatively comfy on long runs. There's plenty of leg room too. Pillions aren't so well catered for, unfortunately. But the headlights are excellent, mirrors acceptable, underseat storage OK and reliability's pretty good, with running costs fairly low. It's an excellent package and a great example of independent thinking.

Tester's notes
* Comfy riding position
* Excellent handling except over bad bumps
* Useable midrange, strong top-end power
* Good wind protection
* Frugal when ridden gently

✳ Colour
The A1P only came in green, grey, red and (very rarely) blue. They're all good sellers. If you're looking at the earlier J series bike they also came in yellow which can be a little slower to shift.

I bought one

Dave Lee
Model: 2002 registered ZX-6R J2 (599cc)
Miles on the clock: 21,000
Miles by owner: 5000

Good points: The best thing is definitely its performance, not just on the track but on the road as you can ride it fast and it doesn't seem to throw up any surprises along the way. Another good thing is the size of the bike, I'm 6ft 1in and 17 stone and at no point do I ever feel cramped on this bike.

Bad points: The pillion accommodation. This was the reason I changed the bike as my partner said the slippery, uncomfortable seat made her feel unsafe. We tried all sorts of things to rectify this but none of them worked. And as she would put more weight onto me, in turn my wrists would become extremely painful.

Problems: None.

Mods: I fitted a Carbon Can Co aftermarket end can (for looks and sound only). I also fitted some smaller indicators, again to make the front end look better.

Anything else: I'd buy another but not in yellow. You could wash the wheels and they'd look dirty again immediately.

✳ Specification

Engine	l/c, 16v, inline four, 636cc
Power	116bhp @ 12,500rpm
Torque	52ft-lb @ 11,000rpm
Chassis	aluminium twin beam
Dry weight	174kg
Seat height	820mm
Fuel capacity	18 litres (4 gal)
Tyres	120/65-17; 180/55-17
Fuel economy	43mpg
NU insurance	14
Top speed	160mph

✳ Head bearings
Original ones seem more prone to failing than on most bikes. Knackered ones will screw up handling, are an MoT failure and will cost about £150 to put right. Quality replacements fitted correctly with decent grease should last.

WANT ONE? KNOW THIS...

BUYING A TRIUMPH DAYTONA 650

Four things you must check

scratches on paint?

standard or gel seat?

pillion peg hanger corrosion?

charging system ok?

✳ The Daytona 650 was only sold in 2005 but there's the odd 2006 bike which was registered late. Prices are reasonable for such a capable bike: £3250 should get you a decent bike in a private sale. The best examples in dealers go for £4000 or even a fraction more. Don't pay OTT prices as a new ZX-6R can be had for £4999.

✳ Services are scheduled for every 6000 miles and cost about £200 at a main Triumph dealer. Every 12,000 miles the service required is much bigger, including valve clearance checks, and that can mean a £400-plus bill. Using an independent can drop prices by as much as 50 per cent.

✳ The Daytona 600's similar but not as good as it lacks the midrange and top-end poke, plus the fuel injection's less refined. They were sold in 2003 and 2004. They start around £3000 for a low-mileage bike while a minter from a dealer will be nearer £4000.

BUYING A KAWASAKI ZX-6R

Four things you must check

Colour can hit resale value

Frame damage?

Fork adjusters seized?

Is it a real A1P model?

✳ The ZX-6R A1P is excellent value as few people realise what a capable machine it is. They were only sold in 2002. A scruffy or high-mileage bike can be bought in a private sale for about £2250. Don't pay more than £3200, even for a minter from a trustworthy dealer.

✳ The service schedule's quite rigorous. An oil change and check over which includes taking the spark plugs out is due every 4000 miles (budget £100 to £200). A pretty major service including valve clearance checks is due every 7500 miles (reckon on £250 to £450).

✳ The A1P on test is quite a rare machine but the versions from the two previous model years are pretty similar and more common. Made in 2000 and 2001 with the suffixes J1 and J2, these have slightly inferior forks, a different front master cylinder and 599cc engines. They're still spacious, light, capable machines which work well in any role.

VIN should look like this

116

triumph 675 daytona

WORDS BY: BENJAMIN 'BJ' KUBAS CRONIN **PICS BY:** JASON CRITCHELL & PAUL BARSHON

The 675 was great. Triumph claim to have made it even better for 2009, so BJ went to Spain to find out if they've succeeded

As the Supersport category grows in popularity, manufacturers strive to keep their product ahead of the game. Or, at the very least, to keep their middleweight in the same ball park as the competition. You don't need a spanking new model every two years to keep up, sometimes a decent nip and tuck does the job.

That's what the 2009 Triumph 675 is; a streamlined version of the nutty triple we first tasted three years ago. It's rare manufacturers leave their bikes unmolested for three seasons, but Triumph don't have the resources of the Japanese, so things move a bit more slowly.

They don't even have a race department, which the Japanese rely on heavily for their development, so the fact the original 675 was so handy impresses even more.

We loved the 675, but there were a couple of issues on road and track that kept it from hitting top spot. Our main gripe was with the front suspension, and that the throttle could be more direct and precise, and Triumph have addressed both.

Some criticised Triumph because, at a glance, the bike looks identical to before. Get closer, look again, and the nose is actually quite different. But it wasn't the looks, or engine even, that we wanted sorted.

Triumph listened and have given us a re-worked Kayaba front end that now sports high and low-speed adjustment, allowing a greater level of accuracy when making changes.

The shock has also been given the same treatment; both units bolted to the unchanged yet capable aluminium chassis. The geometry is retained, and over 1kg of unsprung weight has been lost via the new rear wheel and sprocket carrier.

Slowing the show are all new and lighter Nissin monoblock calipers chomping on new discs, which Triumph claim have 15% more power and 5% extra bite over their predecessors. They look damn trick.

Stopping power is now pushed to the deck through brand new super-sticky Pirelli Diablo SuperCorsa SP tyres, which is something we're extremely happy about.

As for the engine, Triumph claim 3bhp more at peak, and there's an extra 400rpm to play with. Torque is up by a single Nm. The cylinder head, exhaust ports and the exhaust have all been reworked to give the gains. Con-rods are stronger to cope with the extra rpm, while the crank has also been tweaked, as has the EFI calibration ➤

A SLIP OF THE LIP

Wot, No Slipper Clutch?

The lack of a slipper clutch was a serious gripe we had with the Triumph previously. The Hinckley Massive rarely do what's de rigeur, so they worked with Keihin to modify the ECU. Now when you shut the throttle, the butterfly valves partially open, resulting in reduced engine braking, coercing the rear into not swapping ends. Turn one at Cartagena is a decked second gear high-rpm, fast and tight right-hander which leads immediately into turn two, an even tighter right. If there was anywhere the old bike would have shown up its slipper shortage, it's there. I tried hard to get the thing to misbehave, but couldn't. It easily stayed in line. Even banging down from fifth to second and dumping the clutch didn't faze it too much.

And a quick mention about the Pirelli tyres. They play a big role in the new found stability of the bike. They warm up quickly and offer ample grip with superb feedback, delivering oodles of confidence. God only knows what they're like in the wet, but we don't think Triumph reckon too many people would want to take their shiny new 675 out in the rain anyway. Spare wheels with wets, please.

software for a better throttle response. First gear is straight from the race-kit, and therefore longer. Overall, there are nearly 50 changes to the bike, but are they the right ones?

Our first day was on the twisty circuit of Cartagena, ideally suited to the triple's grunt. My first session was on a bike with a road-setup, which was pretty good for learning the circuit, though there were hints of our previous rebound gripes

during fast changes of direction.

But just hints; already it's clearly an improvement. In the next session and running on track settings, the 675 was cock-on. The 41mm fork compresses with finesse under heavy progressive braking power from the new Nissins, allowing for a fast and steady corner entry and apex.

Where the old bike could be unsettled at this point, the '09 machine scythes through a turn

with composure. Weight transfer is also far more controlled. The rear worked fantastically, damping out bumps and hard acceleration so well that I could concentrate on assessing and riding the updated front.

The tweaked

❝ OVERALL, THERE ARE NEARLY 50 CHANGES TO THE DAYTONA 675 FOR 2009, BUT ARE THEY THE RIGHT ONES? ❞

TRIUMPH DAYTONA 675

Highlights

- ❧ Clever slipper substitute
- ❧ Had a nose job
- ❧ Addictive engine
- ❧ High/low speed adj
- ❧ 162Kg
- ❧ 126bhp (Crank claimed)

£7,589 otr

Don't be fooled by:

The samey looks. This is one sportsbike that is going in the right direction. It surprised the hell out of us on the launch, actually.

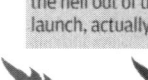

5 TRACK	5 FAST ROAD	5 HOOLIGAN	4 NEW RIDER	5 DESIRABILITY

Engine

The extra power comes from refining the cylinder head. New exhaust ports sport constant expansion profile and oval exits. The 25.5mm exhaust valve is tweaked, and lighter headers added. The 30.5mm inlet valves and buckets are new, as is the exhaust cam, and a new cam-chain tensioner increases smoothness. Beefier conrods withstand the extra 400rpm, while the crank and balance shafts have been modified, and the ECU tailored to suit.

Chassis

The 675's original chassis remains, geometry therefore stays 23.9° rake and 89.1mm trail. While fork internals aren't dissimilar from before, the way they now work makes the difference and they're fully adjustable, as is the rear shock. The rear wheel and sprocket carrier saves 1Kg of unsprung weight and reduces inertia. There's a 3Kg saving overall. More powerful monoblock Nissin calipers are present. The cockpit is also new, sort of.

Verdict

Superb update, which does cosseting just as well as carnage. Brilliant, fast or slow.

- ■ Handling, motor, comfort, barmy on demand
- ■ A few rattles, mirrors, erm...

Final Score 10/10
Score relates to other bikes in this test only

Specification

ENGINE	
TYPE	675cc, liquid-cooled, 12v, inline-triple
BORE X STROKE	74mm x 52.3mm
COMPRESSION	12.65:1
FUELLING	Electronic fuel injection
CLAIMED POWER	126bhp @ 12,600rpm
CLAIMED TORQUE	73Nm @ 11,750rpm

CHASSIS	
FRAME	Aluminium beam twin-spar
F SUSPENSION	41mm USD fork, fully adjustable
R SUSPENSION	Piggy-back monoshock, fully adjustable
FRONT BRAKES	Four-piston monoblock calipers, 308mm floating discs
REAR BRAKES	One-piston caliper, 220mm disc

DIMENSIONS	
WHEELBASE	1,395mm
SEAT HEIGHT	825mm
DRY WEIGHT	162Ig
FUEL CAPACITY	17.4L

PRICE	
PRICE	£7,589 otr
FROM	Triumph UK (01445 251700) Triumph.co.uk

Why do the Spanish get all the best roads? Stop hogging them!

motor also kicks on track. While the extra power and torque is mostly inconspicuous, the added 400rpm is a real asset, allowing you to hold a single gear for longer. The old bike was always banging itself off the limiter, but not now. Triumph also claim a 5mph increase in top-speed.

We could attack most of the circuit in third gear, allowing smooth yet urgent drive between turns with a satisfying howl from the new can.

For a faster lap time, you'd want to use second gear more often at Cartagena, for quicker exits via the highly improved throttle. And it is vastly better, because now you can open the taps gently when you're on the deck and it doesn't burp like Fagan after his 100th energy drink of the day. For me, this was the most impressive improvement, allowing the suspension to keep doing its job uninterrupted. It was precise enough for fast second-gear exits while on the edge of the power and grip.

It was also ideal for third-gear exits, where you could easily anticipate and twist the grip ahead of the engine's reassuring delivery, safe in the knowledge the power curve wouldn't suddenly overtake your right hand. And it's far more precise for wheelies. So far, so very good for the new Daytona.

But the road is where it can score serious points over its rivals, thanks to the deliciously usable motor.

I honestly don't think there's a better Supersport engine for road work, or one that impresses as much when the butterflies are opened wide. Even sporting a road setup, the improvement in stability was obvious as we thrashed through ➤

119

a local National Park. Smooth Tarmac, stringing together bend after bend, the front wheel rising at every opportunity, the 675 just lapped it up effortlessly.

The only slight niggle was that I could still feel a mote of instability at the headstock, but only when landing a wheelie or when the front lifted an inch on corner exit.

But it really is slight; the firmer suspension and steering damper quickly took control before any filthy slappers appeared. I also tend to ride with my bodyweight located far back too, which could easily have contributed to this.

On returning from the launch, I took a standard '08 675 home from work, and it became immediately obvious how much better the new machine is. The defining test will be on UK roads, granted, but it's looking good for the Brit.

Usually, picking faults these days is quite easy. Bikes are so good that any flaw tends to magnify itself, especially in comparison with rivals, but I'm struggling to find issues with the 2009 Daytona 675.

Apart from that speck of a potential slapper, and some typical British rattles, I'm almost

That silencer just says triple, doesn't it? The holy trinity at play

stumped! Sure, Racer Boy Fagan will be able to pick holes at a faster pace on track, but I reckon he'll be dead impressed when he chucks a stumpy leg over the seat.

Only two trivial things really bothered me; the mirrors and the bike's overall physical size on

could easily solve that!

I expected to be underwhelmed by the breathed upon Daytona, but I discovered that this superb new bike is truly more than a sum of its updated parts. Imagine your Doris has gone away and come back slimmer, hotter, five years younger, and far dirtier in the sack, and you'll be on the right track.

Model evolution has brought the 675 bang up-to-date without reinventing the wheel. Our first full Supersport test of '09 bikes is going to be mighty interesting, now that Triumph's shiny new tricorne hat is tossed in the ring.

Choosing the winner just got a whole lot harder. Cue the National Anthem, and Tally Ho, chaps!

❝ CUE THE NATIONAL ANTHEM AND IT'S TALLY HO, CHAPS! ❞

TRIUMPH ON TRACK

Daytona Race Bits

Despite not having a true race department, Triumph's racing exploits have nonetheless improved the breed. In line with the production bike, the comprehensive race kit has also been updated. Better yet, there are some cool bits and bobs you can chuck on your road bike. The most interesting is the plug-n-play quickshifter; just one plug-a-lug after fitment and you're away. We reckon that'll be most popular - make that one for our 'termer next year, por favor. The complete engine kit which weighs in at £4,968.62, offers virtually everything you'd need to build an incredible trackday bike, capable club racer, or decent Supersport contender. Game on!

Road

Quickshifter	£229.99
Arrow Slip-on	£449.99
Arrow Rearsets	£349.99

Race

Stage 2 Arrow System	£1,299.98
Race Kit Loom	£148.93
Race ECU	£273.56

track. No matter how I adjusted the mirrors, I only ever saw my elbows, but then, I am a gangly sod.

Due to its 250cc racer slimness, I occasionally had trouble hanging on. That may have been mostly when I wasn't going fast enough, I'll admit, but bracing my legs on the tank under braking kept me upright too long, compromising my corner entry. Considering that the missus is stronger than me, a bit of a workout

BJ finds a new use for the rock hard hotel breakfast butter - a slider!

When Triumph launched the Daytona 675 in 2006, it shook the applecart. We'd got used to the "old man's manufacturer" making steady-but-assured bikes. The odd half-successful foray into the sportsbike market always provided something different but never anything that seriously challenged the dominance of the Japanese bikes.

Then along came this good-looking, three-cylinder-engined oddity that not only took on the CBRs, GSX-Rs and YZFs of this world, but actually bettered them. The secret to its success was to match its rivals' sharp-handling chassis' and challenge their screaming four cylinders with an engine that not only performed on track but which literally trumped them on the road.

If I were asked what I'd improve about the old Daytona, I'd have said "Better suspension and a faster motor, please." Which is almost exactly what has happened, plus a slight detail change to the looks and the bonus of some better brakes. Job done, we can all go home.

What's not to like?

I'd like to balance this launch report with some negativity; by saying, for instance, that Triumph's changes haven't made a blind bit of difference, or some other grumble to disprove my glowing introduction. But I can't, because the alterations have made a difference – and there's not a lot to be negative about at all.

Like the subtly tweaked new nose and headlights, you might not notice the new engine character at first because the triple motor is always going to be a torquey one. But, after a while,

> ## "THE BIGGEST NOTICEABLE DIFFERENCE IS THE PROGRESSIVE POWER DELIVERY THROUGH THE WHOLE RANGE."

I began to twig something extra was firing me between corners. 3bhp and a piddly single foot-pound of torque in the middle doesn't look much on paper but, with bit of time, a slightly longer and stronger character emerges. The biggest noticeable difference is the progressive power delivery through the whole range, particularly the smoothed-out dip between 6,500 and 7,500rpm. The old model slumped slightly, but the new motor is more linear and gains a decent five (approx) bhp right in the 'thick' of the rev-range where it matters.

What this emphasises, even clearer than ever, is how much more usable the motor is than any 600cc sportsbike. In slow corners, where you might need first or second to drive out on a 600, the 675 is happier to pull second or third, which in turn keeps the bike more stable and allows you to work less hard for the same effect. On track, you're also helped by the power hanging on for longer up top, peaking later and remaining there longer before tailing off more gradually. 400 extra revs doesn't seem much but, as far as I can tell by looking at Triumph's own dyno chart for the Daytona, the old motor was tailing off roughly to the tune of 10bhp, 1,500rpm earlier.

As far as chassis changes go, the differences are harder to spot. We rode with chief test-rider David Lopez's Cartagena-specific settings on track and standard settings on the road, but without a back-to-back comparison I struggled to put my finger on exactly how it has improved. With high and low-speed damping adjustment front and rear, the new Kayaba suspension gives you more range for a start, so you can tailor the setting better to >

There are no complaints about the clear, well set-out dash, and you've less reason to keep an eye on the tacho now, as Triumph has erased the old motor's flat-spot

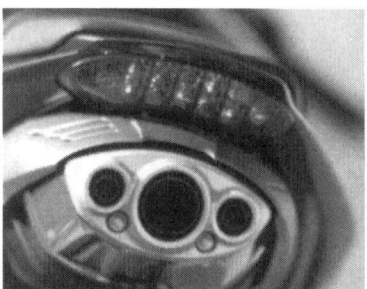

Triumph has stuck with an under-seat exhaust for the Daytona, which may not be the best position in terms of keeping weight low down, but you don't notice any negative effect

WHAT MAKES IT TICK?
TRIUMPH DAYTONA 675

❶ Engine
New exhaust port shape in cylinder head, lighter exhaust header castings, exhaust valve with re-profiled seat, each improve flow. Shorter intake trumpets increase power at high engine speeds up to a peak 126bhp and 53lb-ft of torque. New valves and buckets with narrower seats, new exhaust cam and hydraulic cam chain tensioner and track-developed shorter intake trumpets help raise the rev-limit by 400rpm.

❷ Bodywork
New bodywork is designed by the same engineer (rather than designer) who designed the original fairing. The new nose isn't just sharper but has slightly better proportions to deflect wind around the rider. Black powder-coated engine cases are classier and mark a difference between new and old 675.

❸ Suspension
Kayaba suspension features high and low-speed adjustment, giving better control in braking, accelerating and cornering (low-speed damping), without sacrificing compliance on the bumps (high-speed damping). Redesigned internals mean lower friction, reduced unsprung weight and wider adjustment range. Overall dry weight is down by 3kg.

❹ Brakes
New Nissin four-piston, radial-mounted monoblock calipers have a claimed 15-per-cent-better performance and five per cent more bite. New front discs improve heat dissipation.

❺ Wheels and tyres
The latest Pirelli Diablo Supercorsa SP tyres are standard on the Daytona, vastly 'out-speccing' Japanese 600s. New rear wheel and sprocket are 0.95kg lighter, producing a claimed 20 per cent less inertia.

❻ Race kit
The updated race kit shows Triumph's final and full acceptance that racing is good for the breed by giving racers better technology and more range or products. The list is too long for here but includes plenty of Arrow parts, a quick-shifter and race calibration software (TRACS) (allowing programmable ECU featuring selectable fuel mapping).

suit yourself and conditions. Internals are both lighter and have less friction too, making their action easier and smoother.

The whole bike is 3kg lighter (it's now 162kg), which inevitably makes a difference during corner entry. Where the outgoing model is looser and less controlled, the 2009 Daytona feels plusher and more certain. That good feeling is bolstered by stronger brakes and a general confidence in the chassis as you brake, allowing you to demand even more of the front tyre.

Changing down gears is interesting with Triumph's 'strategy to control engine braking'. The tweaked Keihin fuel injection system controls the butterfly valves more under deceleration, opening them up and allowing more air through, to reduce engine braking. According to Triumph, this means there's no need for a slipper clutch. I was a little sceptical about that on track, until someone pointed out that Glen Richards and Paul Young didn't use a slipper clutch on the Embassy Triumphs in 2008 (Glen won the British Supersport Championship). All of a sudden, I changed my mind.

Is there anything wrong with the new Daytona 675? Only if you're looking at it from very specific point of view and being particularly critical. The Daytona is still a tall bike with a high seat and a forward-biased riding position. For one vertically challenged member of the Japanese press on the launch, that was clearly a problem as he reached to put a foot down. At the end of the day of road testing, I knew I'd been resting on my wrists a bit too much as well.

You'll notice the height during turn-in, particularly on the road, where the Daytona is very quick to go from upright to knee-down; on a cold, damp road, that can be unsettling. In truth,

"THE MOTOR HAS MORE DRIVE AND A WEDGE OF EXTRA POWER TO HANG ON TO THOSE REVS FOR LONGER."

though, this doesn't make a blind bit of difference to how the bike grips in corners; it's only a feeling, but feelings can easily give confidence a knock. Personally, I don't think it's a problem, and I'd say it's a bit like getting a new car that has stronger power steering than your old one; it feels funny at first but you get used to it.

My other gripe is the gearbox, which remains a clunky one in comparison to the competition. The Daytona's gear lever needs a positive foot to lift it up a gear – too gentle and there's every chance it'll be a bit more stubborn than its supersport rivals.

Master of all trades
Triumph's Daytona 675 has quite a record at *SuperBike*; group test winner year-on-year, it also took the British Supersport Championship in 2008. It's skill has always been to buck convention in the supersport road bike class, being a blinder not only on track but also having the most usable motor. The 2009 model has only improved those skills with better handling and more power.

How well the new chassis works took a bit of thinking about, but I suddenly twigged, when I realised the great confidence I had in the Cartagena corners had nothing to do with going to bed early the night before and everything to do with trust and feel. The same agile chassis on more sophisticated suspension and better-feeling brakes challenge you to trust the tyres and carry more and more corner speed; it's an addictive track bike.

The motor has more drive where it matters, too, and a decent wedge of extra power to hang on to those revs for longer. You might notice it less if you're just popping down the shops, but if you're feeling like a more lively ride, especially on track, the 675 has more life force available. **SB**

Specification
Price: £7,589 O.T.R.
NU Ins Group: 15

Engine
Type: l/c 16v DOHC in-line three 675cc
Bore x Stroke: 74.0 x 52.3mm
Compression: 12.65:1
Carburation: Keihin EFI, 44mm throttle bodies
Gearbox: 6-speed chain
Max Power: 126bhp@12,600rpm
Max Torque: 54ft-lb@11,750rpm

Cycleparts
Chassis: Aluminum beam twin spar
Suspension: (F) 41mm USD Kayaba forks, fully adjustable (high/low speed comp) (R) fully adjustable (high/low speed comp) Kayaba monoshock **Brakes:** twin 308mm Nissin radial monobloc, 4-piston calipers (R) 220mm disc, Nissin single-piston caliper
Wheels/Tyres: (F) forged aluminium, 120/70-ZR17 Pirelli Diablo SuperCorsa SP (R) forged aluminium, 180/55-ZR17 Pirelli Diablo SuperCorsa SP
Rake/Trail: 23.9°/89.1mm
Wheelbase: 1,395mm
Fuel Capacity: 17.4 litres (3.8gals)
Dry Weight: 162kg (357lbs) claimed dry
Supplied: Triumph 01455 251700
www.triumph.co.uk

Not a lot wrong with the stoppers, then. New Nissin four-pot radial calipers offer improved power and more bite

DAYTONA
675

REVolution of the
British Supersport

BY MARK HOYER

_I_ T WAS PROBABLY ONLY A COINCIDENCE THAT TRIUMPH returned to the Cartagena circuit in southern Spain– where it introduced the first four-cylinder Daytona 600 in 2003–to show the world's press the updated-for-2009 Daytona 675. But coincidence or not, it underlined how far the company has come in a very short time.

I was the lucky fellow on scene for both of these events, and from a firsthand perspective can say that Triumph has made huge strides over the last six years. That '04 model was a solid effort with a particularly sweet-handling chassis, but the engine was still a bit behind on fueling refinement and outright power compared to its Japanese competition at the time. Riding the three-cylinder Daytona 675 again, and at the same track as the 600 Four, was a vivid reminder of what a fine bike Triumph produced in 2006 when the company decided to try something different in the supersport realm.

DAYTONA
675

Cool thing about the three-banger and its additional 76cc of displacement was that it discouraged direct comparison to the Japanese 600s...while also allowing them to be directly compared, except with extra beans in the engine room. In any case, the '06 version was lauded and loved by almost everybody, cleaned up in its category at the big MasterBike track test two years in a row (with a second place in '08) and brought lots of first-time (*i.e.* younger!) Triumph customers into the Union Jack fold.

It was, in other words, a huge success. Which is why this latest version, four model years later, is a thorough update rather than a complete redesign. Most obvious of the alterations is to styling, namely a sharpened upper fairing. "The original designer looked back at the first 675 and the only part he really wasn't fully satisfied with was the fairing nose, so he wanted to try to improve it," said Product Manager Simon Warburton.

Other changes are both more subtle and more significant. As ever, sportbike makers strive for more power and lighter weight. No surprise, then, that's what we have here.

Engineers nipped and tucked, reducing exhaust-system weight, cam-cover weight, lightening the rear wheel and sprocket, trimming suspension components, etc, dropping claimed dry weight 7 pounds to 356. But they also boosted

and massaged, usefully upping power and torque.

And at this point, it must be said that this is one of the sweetest engines ever to move a motorbike. It is soulful, snappy and high-revving without ever sounding frantic. The Triumph just sounds better and better as you spin it up, even if you don't need to rev its nuts off to get useful urge. Power is solid from 6000, but it is at 8K where the action starts, with healthy pull up to the 400-rpm-higher redline of 13,900. Zing!

The increased power and revs come from tuning primarily on the exhaust side. Valves feature a more flow-friendly shape, while ports are recontoured and machine-finished around the seat inserts for improved flow. The cam also has increased duration, but this comes from altered opening and closing ramps that were made more gradual to keep valve acceleration–and spring life–within acceptable limits given the higher rev ceiling (lighter buckets on inlets and exhausts also help here). Going along with the redone exhaust ports is a new header with cast spigots that accurately match the port shape. This was a change from the first-gen Daytona's regular ol' round pipes. The new exhaust system is also lighter, particularly where it counts–in the freer-flowing silencer–up high and at the rear of the bike.

In the airbox, shorter intake funnels ease high-rpm breath-

Reprogrammed ECU and pre-wired loom accept the plug-n-play accessory quickshifter that works with both street and race patterns. Faster processing is said to improve fueling while software also works to eliminate rear-wheel chatter during braking on this non-slipper-clutch engine.

ing. The ECU is reprogrammed to run about 15 percent faster for more accurate fuel delivery, and it is also trained to recognize the difference between aggressive throttle opening and easy street roll-on, smoothing response during the latter with retarded spark timing.

We'll let you know what the *Cycle World* dyno tells us as soon as we get a testbike in America, but for now Triumph says peak output is up to 126 crank horsepower (a 3 pony boost) with an attendant 1-foot-pound increase in torque for a 54 ft.-lb. peak. The factory dyno chart also shows a useful step up in midrange power, so it appears the peak gain didn't come at the expense of tractability.

It certainly didn't feel like anything had been given away, either on the 100-mile street ride or our day at the track. Cartagena is a fun, technical road course with a lot of leaned-over braking and unexpected cornering lines. Which is good, because I often take the unexpected cornering line... In fact, at the '03 launch I ran off into the gravel outside of Turn 1, luckily without tipping over. Glad to report no such off-roading on the 675.

Was it the new front brake discs with better heat dissipation and Nissin monoblock calipers? The fancy Showa high- and low-speed compression-damping-adjustable fork and shock with lighter internals and reduced friction? The

higher-spec Pirelli Diablo Supercorsa Pro SP tires? Perhaps the reduced dry weight? It was probably all of that and the fact that I wasn't trying to keep up with World Supersporter and Isle of Man TT regular Jim Moodie, on hand at the 600 launch in 2003!

Seriously, though, this bike is easy to ride at the track. The chassis is the picture of ease and composure. Triumph has for years been able to get away with pretty aggressive steering geometry on its sportbikes without compromising stability. The 675 transitioned quickly and easily from full left to right lean through Cartagena's chicane with no chassis windup or other untoward behavior. Engine torque is such that it is easy to unintentionally lift the front wheel when accelerating through such transitions or on corner exits, yet the bars (thanks in part to the steering damper) give only a quick shake upon front-wheel touchdown and the bike carries on doing what you told it to do.

Cornering clearance is over the top. If you are heroic enough to drag the peg feelers, don't take it much farther! Grip and chassis feel at extreme lean is phenomenal. As a testament to how well-sorted the 675 is, after about five laps at the track I hardly thought of the bike again, concentrating only on available traction, trying to find the best lines, braking later and throttling up earlier. About the only thing that gave pause was the occasional lazy-ish gear shift that didn't execute and stayed in the gear you were trying to change from. No false neutrals, but a deliberate toe up or down is best here. Overall, a good-shifting gearbox without being a great-shifting gearbox. On the plus side, first gear is now a usable track gear, which makes sense because the production bike has adopted the taller race-kit ratio.

Our street riding day was quite cold, so the jury will have to remain out on whether the new exhaust heat shield does a better job. Can it be warmer than a Ducati 1098? Probably not, and the Duc is livable. Even if this thing were cooking your thighs (or other bits of anatomy), the $9799 Daytona would remain a great way to rip through the Spanish countryside near the coast–or through less exotic locations much nearer your home–offering good suspension compliance, broad engine torque and easy steering.

So? The original Daytona 675 of 2006 was one of the best-balanced, most-fun-to-ride sportbikes on the track or street. The new one is the same, only more so. ◘

DEATH OF THE 600?

It's coming. And the new 675 triple is the reason why

WORDS PHIL READ
PICS RORY GAME

Triumph's new 675 rocks. At least, it does on a racetrack in the south of Spain (see PB, Feb 2009). PB gave the 2009 bike a big thumbs up in Cartagena. But I don't live in Spain. I live in the Midlands and ride to London all year round so I demand versatile performance. I need a bike to work here, on my terms.

While not wildly different to the first model there are enough improvements to consider this a worthy evolution of the original Hinckley fighter, particularly from an engineering and performance perspective. It wasn't even broke, just not perfect, and Triumph did enough to keep it interesting and ahead of the relentless race for faster, lighter, better. 3bhp is added and 3kg shaved in weight. Kayaba suspension adds quality with high- and low-speed adjustability. However, until I see it on a shock dyno I won't say what real level of adjustment you get.

The Triumph has that throaty, growling roar harking back to a glamorous age of hard living, fast dying and engineering bravery. It transports me back to the GP paddock of

'THE ENGINE IS THE ACE IN AN ALREADY IMPRESSIVE HAND'

Two years ago we blew a fast but flawed 675 triple to pieces. Since then it's become a very good bike with a great engine

my youth when I witnessed Agostini and Read (my dad) racing the all-conquering exotic MV Agusta 500s. If I didn't know the new 675 was designed and built 40 minutes from my door I would swear it came from Ferrari's Maranello factory.

IT'S A GOOD MOTOR THEN?

Triumph's decision to turn away from inline fours was a stroke of genius, returning them to their own, unique path. The engine is the ace in an already impressive hand. It delivers a tingling sensory payback to the rider.

But it's more than aural tricks. Pulling from as little as 4000rpm in a clean crisp wave the Triumph drives harder, with more panache than any 600. Without any fuelling hesitation or glitches you caress the bike through corners, allowing the motor to race up to its 14,000rpm redline, rolling off with a scrub of brake; the same gear has enough torque to balance the chassis mid-turn and drive out to the next.

CAN IT HANDLE OUR ROADS?

Light, composed and very responsive the performance from the chassis is remarkable as it allows instant line changes to avoid road kill and accumulations of gravel on our crumbling road network. All it takes is light input to make the line adjustment, no shakes or wobble, just an instant, flattering ➘ ➘ ➘

131

New 675 is still a
whole lotta fun,
even on cold,
damp British roads

change of path, as if it reads your mind.

In the absence of a slipper clutch, Triumph's cost-saving solution is to open the throttle bodies without fuel injection allowing the engine to breath, minimising rear wheel lock-up and chatter. It's crude but mostly effective in all but the most determined situation. Despite Nissin monobloc calipers that claim to deliver more power and feel over the original 675, I was disappointed with the brakes. They lack the outright anchoring I expect. The master cylinder or pads may be the cause. The lever needs a stiff squeeze to stop as hard as I like, when two fingers are usually enough.

The Triumph is slim by nature due to the narrow engine. The seat height gives enough room even for my legs. Tucking behind the small screen isn't as hard as it looks. The riding position is typical for a front-biased set up, yet not extreme, and the seat is flat and comfortable enough to prevent you sliding into the tank. Gripping with your knees and tightening your core helps protect from town wrist ache, but it still takes its toll on the old body after an hour of town riding.

FINISHING TOUCHES

Triumph made the decision to invest in areas that deliver performance rather than aesthetic benefits. Compromises had to be reached to deliver a list price a tickle over seven and a half grand and keep it in the ballpark of the mainstream 600s. Some of fastenings and brackets look basic and bodywork trim a little cheap. Triumph can't achieve the raw material savings or peripheral indulgences of the Japanese, but that doesn't mean the quality is sub standard – far from it.

Our group test in this issue has a two-year-old Street Triple with 21,000 miles on the clock. A blind survey in the office had people guessing it was only 7000 miles old, such was the feel and clean finish. The lesson, as with any motorcycle, is that if you look after them and honour the service schedule you will have trouble-free ownership.

SO, ARE 600S FINISHED?

From a performance and experience perspective, the Triumph beats any 600 with its versatility, power and ease of use in the real world. All 600s still deliver stunning performance, but you have to work a bloody sight harder for it. On a wet or cold surface the Triumph will offer more confidence and control. Despite winning the British Supersport championship, Triumph cannot claim MotoGP-developed technology is handed down to their road models. This is where Triumph's Japanese rivals steal a lead in the bullshit stakes. Some people will just want to feel closer to Valentino.

If you don't have £7589 burning a hole in your sky rocket and you're in the market for a secondhand 600 then you would be daft to overlook the original Daytona 675. A 2006 model with only 3500 miles can be found for £4400.

SHOULD I BUY ONE?

As the world is about to explode, banks collapse and Xbox points replace the pound, go and buy one now. If you want a performance motorcycle that makes your spine tingle, throw your earplugs away. This bike can deliver flexible performance and a soundtrack. Is there a strong case to trade up from a 600 and for disaffected big bike riders to trade down? Er, yes. **PR**

THREES AND ME

So is the new 675 the best Triumph triple ever? For me it's enough that it has three cylinders. Some folks get off on the angry grumble of a V-twin; others the urgent shriek of an inline four. Or perhaps the ringing and pinging of a two-stroke is your thing. They say that smell is the most evocative of the senses. They're wrong. It's sound that does it for those who develop a near obsessive attachment to a particular engine type. If I'd had a nanny as a kid I'd probably have developed a nurse fetish. As it was, a cousin's mate had a Triumph triple – an early 70s T150V Trident. They'd take this pesky kid along pillion and my invocations to go faster had less to do with speed than that plaintive wail of the three. I finally bought my own Trident in the early 90s and found first-hand the smooth turbine torque of a triple. And that sound. Always that sound. **AS**

Two high-profile domestic series wins and all of a sudden you can't keep the 675 away from the track

134

2009 TRIUMPH
DAYTONA 675

Triumph's iconic Daytona 675 receives its first major update.
Not a simple task when there's little wrong in the first place...

WORDS MIKE ARMITAGE PHOTOGRAPHY JASON CRITCHELL AND PAUL BARSHON

Improving on perfection isn't easy and some things are best left alone. Maybe Triumph's Daytona 675 isn't quite untouchable, but revising it to compete with the relentless development of rival machines is risky, if inevitable.

Triumph's hardcore triple has been a huge success, showing how a comparatively small player can compete with the Japanese in the toughest group and still be distinctive.

Fast, accurate, yet flexible and with character, the 675 has brought younger riders to the brand. Of 2008's buyers, 78% were new to Triumph (an increase) with an average age of just under 34 (a reduction). That's crucial for a company with no entry level machines in the range. Securing the British and German Supersport titles hasn't done any harm either.

Straying too far from the original blueprint for the 2009 model could be foolish. So Triumph hasn't. From day one, the Hinckley firm's biggest advantage over all its rivals has been a willingness to listen.

Triumph are never afraid to act on press and customer feedback to their machines. That the new 675 has changed so little shows how right the original was back in 2006.

This is gentle evolution: removing burrs revealed with the magic of hindsight, listening to feedback and carefully upgrading. The changes are small, but they're also numerous – over 50 – including new suspension, extra power and more of a track focus without losing the 675's advantage on the road. Too little, too much... or even closer to perfection?

2009 TRIUMPH DAYTONA 675: UNDER THE SKIN

❶ EXHAUST PORTS
and new exhaust headers give a longer distance for the transition from two side-by-side valves to a single round exhaust tube, increasing flow and hence power (the transition was previously all done in the port)

❷ INLET AND EXHAUST VALVES
have narrower seats to reduce shrouding, improving flow

❸ VALVE SPRING BUCKETS
are lighter, reducing loads on the springs at high revs

❹ EXHAUST CAMSHAFT
is open for longer to further reduce valve spring loading – they have more time to return valves – and allow higher revs

❺ MAGNESIUM COVERS
over the camshafts save 282g

❻ INLET TRUMPETS
are shorter to promote high rev power, but 'don't make much difference' to the midrange

❼ THROTTLE RESPONSE
is revised thanks to the ECU giving a softer power delivery at small openings by retarding the ignition (big, fast openings are unaffected)

❽ GUDGEON PINS
and conrods are stronger to cope with the additional 400rpm (13,900rpm limit).

❾ CAM CHAIN TENSIONER,
cam chain and tensioner blade are modified to reduce noise

❿ LIGHTER EXHAUST SYSTEM
uses thinner material (0.8mm instead of 1.2mm) to save 1.65kg. Different silencer internals give a higher flow rate and more power

⓫ INCREASED OIL LEVEL
and a baffled sump gasket cut down oil surge and avoid starvation in 'extreme riding'

⓬ TALLER FIRST GEAR
is the same ratio as the race kit. All the selector forks are molybdenum coated for wear resistance

⓭ NEW SUSPENSION
has separate high and low-speed compression damping adjustment. There's less friction for a plusher action and a wider adjustment range too. The steering damper also has reduced friction

⓮ NISSIN MONOBLOCK
calipers are made from one lump of material, flexing less for improved bite and power. Discs have reduced unswept area for better heat dissipation

⓯ LIGHTER REAR WHEEL
and rear sprocket save 1kg. Sprocket looks better too. Pirelli Diablo Supercorsa SP tyres are like cut slicks

⓰ BATTERY CAPACITY
goes from 6Ah to 8Ah, which should mean fewer bump starts

⓱ NEW HEAT SHIELD
keeps exhaust heat from the rider's legs

⓲ SIDESTAND BOLTS
are no longer cheap, hideous hex head jobs

675: THE CHANGES

When the 675 was launched it was designed as a road bike, Triumph's commercial director Tue Mantoni telling us 'you won't see a factory-backed race team'.

Then the Daytona proves a match for 600 fours on track and wins a couple of significant national championships. And all of a sudden track ability is paramount. Next year the Italian BE1 team are running an 'official world supersport entry', and the launch presentation dedicates as much time to the race kit and virtually slick Pirelli tyres as to what's changed on the bike.

The changes made are of the type we'd expect in the every-other-year updates to the Daytona's counterparts. More power. More revs. Revised gear ratios. Less weight. Stronger brakes. Extra suspension adjustment. There's even an optional quickshifter. As with a typical Japanese sportsbike, these amendments are measured in small units, rather than radical bounds: a couple of horsepower, a kilo or so off specific components.

Engine

Basically it's the same 74 x 52.3mm, 675cc, three-cylinder

Track ability is now paramount. The launch presentation dedicates as much time to the race kit as to what's changed on the bike

unit as before. Nothing wrong with that – despite the competition all using four cylinders with identical bore and stroke, there's no rule stipulating all sports middleweights must comply. Using a fatter triple gives class-leading flexibility and the haunting drone only three thrashing pistons can produce. A flat, wide torque curve gives an ease of use lacking in peakier (and admittedly smaller) 600cc fours, especially on the road, while there's still the high rev clout for outright performance.

However there's an abundance of changes. The cylinder head has different ports, valves and cams, plus there are intake mods, a revised crank, different conrods and a new exhaust. And it revs 400rpm higher. All for more power – a claimed 126bhp at the crank compared to 123bhp, produced 100rpm higher (last year's bike made 112bhp at the wheel, so expect about 115bhp).

This may seem small reward for large effort, but the motor was already highly developed. In order to find more revs and take output that smidge higher, work started in January 2007. Engineers were also acutely aware of the need to maintain low rev and midrange performance – concentrating the power high up would be a backwards step. The result is stronger everywhere, matching or exceeding the old version throughout the revs with a higher, longer crest – 3bhp more at peak, but beyond 13,000rpm there's up to 8bhp more.

Chassis

Fabricated from smaller cast sections, the twin-spar frame retains the same decidedly racy geometry (23.9° rake, 89.1mm trail and 1395mm wheelbase). The Kayaba forks and rear shock are updated, and now have separate high and low-speed compression damping adjustment.

Damping settings are a compromise. Set up a bike firmly for fast use or track riding and ride quality suffers, while a bike set up for comfort won't maintain composure if pushed. Giving separate control over the damping at different rates – speeds – of compression should give the best of both worlds, that is, the ability to absorb bumps and potholes (high speed) without spoiling the composure for cornering, acceleration and braking (low speed). Less internal friction is said to make the suspension plusher, with a wider range of adjustment.

Nissin monoblock calipers provide more braking power, while a revised back wheel and rear sprocket save over 1kg. Including the 1.65kg lost by using thinner material for the exhaust and a lighter cam cover, claimed dry weight drops by three bags of sugar to 162kg.

ENOUGH IS NEVER ENOUGH...

There used to be 18 parts in Triumph's expansive accessory range for the Daytona, from an alarm to tank bags and carbon fibre heel guards. There are now 11 further items in the range. Buried among the new dust cover (£45), taller screen (£70) and 10mm lower gel seat (£84) is some swanky kit: an Arrow slip-on, E-marked titanium silencer that saves another 1.5kg (and lightens your wallet by £450); Arrow adjustable rearset footpegs in road or race shift pattern (£350); and a quickshifter that bolts straight to the bike and plugs directly into the revised ECU that already has the required software. This allows you to keep the throttle to the stop, ignore the clutch and tap through the gears. A snip for budding racers at £230.

There are also plenty of new race kit parts. As well as tweaks to items like the slipper clutch, gaskets, cam sprockets, valve springs, intake funnels and other fripperies previously available, Triumph have added: full Arrow exhaust system; programmable ECU and race wiring loom; an oil pump gearing kit for improved supply; and

spare wheels. TRACS (Triumph Race Calibration Software) lets you set the rev limit and a pit lane speed limiter, fiddle with the cut times for the quickshifter, and adjust the fuelling map for each cylinder at 19 different throttle openings and in 500rpm steps throughout the revs. You can also mess with ignition maps for wet and dry settings, with different maps for different gears. The whole shebang downloads directly to the bike in 35 seconds while you slither into new Triumph-branded Alpinestars leathers, boots and gloves.

Red. Black. Road. Track. It doesn't really matter. It's good at it all really

675: THE FIRST RIDE

Nobody of sound mind would rattle on at length about improved performance, less weight, better handling, go-faster parts and the pancake-to-the-ceiling stickiness of their bike's new tyres, and then only to let the press loose on dirty, congested roads (and none of the Japanese would launch any sportsbike on the road these days). So it is that the line of 675s in this year's red and black colours burbles away in the pit lane of the compact, snaking Cartagena circuit in Spain – a regular Triumph test track. The road ride comes tomorrow.

I've always found the Daytona a little like a Ducati, requiring a period of acclimatisation not needed with the almost generic, fit-them-all ergonomics of a Japanese sportsbike. The seat feels high and comparatively short, with bars among the lowest of the low, the frame tall

and thin. There are hints of a 916. But head adjusted and settled in, the 675's as staggering as the spec list suggests. Steering has all Triumph's trademark rapidity and precision, the trim chassis rolling on to the fat contact patch of the new Pirellis with ease, balance and steadfast stability at full lean. And by buggery does it lean.

All of which was true of the previous bike. I'm sure the weight reduction, lower inertia and revised suspension make a difference with a fearless eight-stone racer at the controls, as do the stronger brakes. But I can't appreciate the difference – maybe I had too much at breakfast, cancelling out the weight saving. They were good sausages. Either way, the 675 was already fantastically light and sweet handling, and the new one is still far more capable than the vast majority of us.

Ability is presented at its

finest as test rider and local boy David Lopez has set up the bikes: one more click of rebound and four more clicks of low-speed compression at the front; two clicks of rebound and one click of low-speed compression at the rear. Cheating? Nah – it's what you'd do for Oulton Park on a summer's day.

I can appreciate the better throttle response. With a thick wedge of torque bang off tickover, all Triumph's three-cylinder engines can be guilty of suffering from a jolt in the fuelling. It's something you get used to, but picking up on small openings there'll be a noticeable step as the drive comes in. It's like trying to pour a small measure out of a bottle, only for someone to clip your elbow.

But changes to the ECU to calm the torque and give a smoother reaction have worked. Gathering up the engine mid-corner in Cartagena's multiple,

tight, second gear bends feels far more precise and controlled. And the addictive thrust of the 675 means there's no need for the taller new first gear, even in the severest turn. Lovely. Faster sections of track are also less taxing, as the revisions to the engine – more revs and a longer, stronger spread at the exciting end – mean it doesn't collide with the rev limiter as readily. There's more scope for hanging onto one gear through flowing sections of track. It's a small difference, but something the rivals had over the Triumph.

This smoother response and even greater flexibility are just as welcome on the road. Heading for the mountains on the second day and threading through villages, there's none of the clumsy take-up that could detract from the earlier model. The new one's better, simple as that. When we reach the cascading route and our guide

DETAILS

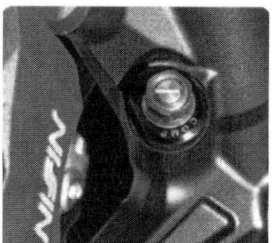

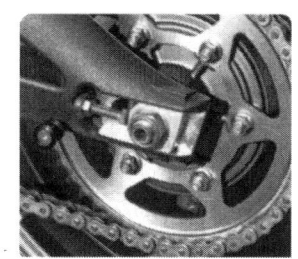

clears off, concentration can be focused on keeping the 675 between the battered Armco while the motor hauls a single gear with seamless, elastic momentum. Yamaha's peaky R6 would tie itself in knots in the same environment.

I'll have a tenner with anyone that the screamer with the tuning fork logos would be less kind to body parts as well. The Daytona has an extreme riding position, but the suspension has never been as firm as the more dedicated opposition. This year's changes make it better still – there's an extra degree of suppleness and compliancy, especially with high-speed compression backed off a turn or so at each end, with consideration to the modern scourge of speed bumps.

Whether the action is as good as Honda's floating, surreal CBR is hard to say. It's also tough to judge whether Triumph have

raised their product to the overall level of the standard-setting Honda. Certainly in our disposable, new-is-best world the subtle styling alterations (modified cockpit area, new lights and screen, pointy indicators, no more ugly bolts holding the sidestand on) don't scream 'latest thing'.

But then the Triumph doesn't compete on the same level. It races in the same class and is a natural sales competitor to the GSX-R, R6, CBR and ZX-6R, but there's something different about the 675. You can't get this cluster of sensations anywhere else and it wouldn't be a Daytona if the look or dynamic had been substantially changed. Triumph has it bang-on, stretching the performance and ensuring the package is bang up-to-date – responding to that feedback – but without detracting from the brilliance and charm of the original.

SPEC TRIUMPH DAYTONA 675

Price	£7589 otr (inc. 1st service and RAC cover)
Top speed	161mph (claimed)
Power (claimed)	126bhp @ 12,600rpm
Torque (claimed)	54lb.ft @ 11,750rpm
Engine	675cc, 12v, dohc inline triple
Bore x stroke	74 x 52.3mm
Compression	12.65:1
Fuel system	injection, 40mm Keihin throttle bodies
Transmission	6-speed, chain
Frame	aluminium alloy twin spar
Front suspension	41mm usd Kayaba forks
–adjustment	preload, rebound, high and low speed compression
Rear suspension	Kayaba monoshock
–adjustment	preload, rebound, high and low-speed compression
Brakes front; rear	308mm discs/4-piston radial calipers; 220mm disc/1-piston caliper
Tyres front; rear	120/70 ZR17; 180/55 ZR17
Weight (claimed)	162kg dry
Wheelbase	1395mm
Rake/trail	23.9°/89.1mm
Seat height	825mm
Fuel capacity	17.4 litres
Colours	red, black
Available from	www.triumph.co.uk

Brooklands British Motorcycle
'Road Test' Portfolios

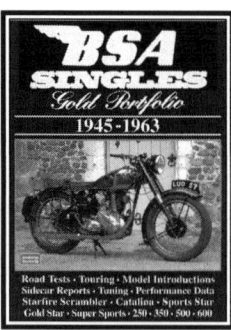

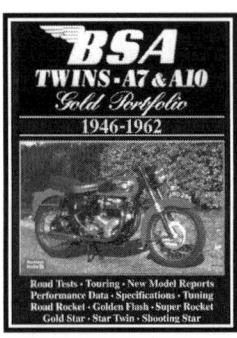

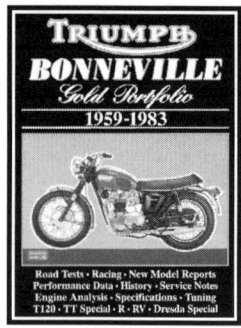

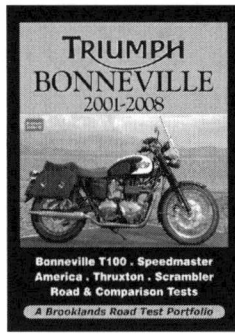

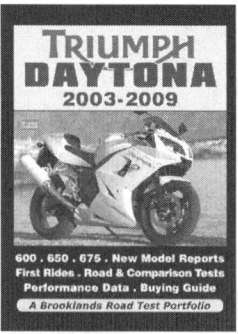

www.brooklands-books.com

From specialist booksellers or, in case of difficulty, direct from the distributors:

Brooklands Books Ltd., P.O. Box 146, Cobham, Surrey, KT11 1LG, England. Phone: 01932 865051
E-mail us at info@brooklands-books.com or visit our website www.brooklands-books.com
Brooklands Books Australia, 3/37-39 Green Street, Banksmeadow, NSW 2019, Australia. Phone: 2 9695 7055
CarTech, 39966 Grand Avenue, North Branch, MN 55056, USA. Phone: 800 551 4754 & 651 277 1200
Motorbooks International, P.O. Box 1, Osceola, Wisconsin 54020, USA. Phone: 800 826 6600 & 715 294 3345

36591259R00079

Printed in Great Britain
by Amazon